The Terry Lectures: The Court and the Castle

New Haven:

Yale University Press

1 9 5 7

Rebecca West:

The Court
and the Castle

Some treatments of

a recurrent theme

To my friends Margaret and Evelyn Hutchinson

Contents

PART ONE

The Court of Kings

1 *Was Hamlet without Will?*

During the rite of Coronation, as it is performed by the English, there is a moment which nicely presents the position of the arts in the framework of time. First the monarch is hailed by the assembled people as their ruler and takes the oath of just government, and then she is given the Bible, which is described as the most valuable thing that this world affords. Here is Wisdom, it is said, this is the royal Law, these are the lively Oracles of God. Then the epistle and the gospel are read, and the creed is repeated. But these are all preliminaries. The true rite begins with the anointing of the monarch with the sanctified oil which confers royalty; and there is then sung an anthem, based on two verses from the Book of Kings, which describe the anointing of King Solomon by Zadok the priest and Nathan the prophet. The Book of Kings is something like three thousand years old, and this text has been sung ever since the coronation of Edgar in 973. Here it is sung in a twelfth-century cathedral to music written in the eighteenth century by Handel. Yet there is no sense of anachronism. This is the temporal relationship between the arts as we are accustomed to it.

Literature has had a much longer life than the visual arts and music. This is not to ignore that there were temples and flute-players in Sumeria, but to remark that the literary scroll, of which our generation is holding one end, stretches far further back in an unbroken state than the scrolls the painters and the musicians have in their hands. All writers and all readers are affected by forces emanating from the Bible and classical literature. "Af-

3

fected" is perhaps too strong a word to apply to most cases, but it may be used here as it is used when it is stated that the world and all things on it are affected by the cosmic rays: the experience does not enter into consciousness yet nevertheless will be a determining influence. Hence literature takes its life from roots planted three thousand years ago, and it spread its branches widely, perhaps as widely as it ever will, quite a long time ago. It is fifteen hundred years since St. Augustine made what proved to be a rough inventory of what the literature that came after him was going to discuss; and the greatest writer of the West died three hundred and fifty years ago. But no architecture, no sculpture, no painting as old as the Bible has a determining influence on those who are not archaeologists, and though classical architecture and sculpture are part of our minds they reached us as the result of rediscovery from long oblivion, through the labors of Poussin or Claude, or the brothers Adam, of artists and scholars. It is the art of the Christian era and of the later Christian era which has worked continuously to make the lens through which we look at the visible world; the mere existence of what is important to us in art was not suspected when St. Augustine wrote. Music is still younger. It is only two hundred years since Mozart was born; it is not a hundred and thirty years since Beethoven died.

This long life-span which is the peculiar possession of literature gives it an advantage as the instructor of man. Bernard of Chartres found an apt image for its cumulative powers. "We are like dwarfs," he wrote,* "seated on the shoulders of giants; we see more things than the ancients and things more distant, but this is due neither to the sharpness of our own sight, nor to the greatness of

* Quoted in John of Salisbury's *Metalogicon*, III, 4.

our own stature, but because we are raised and borne aloft on that giant mass." Paradoxically, we can prove his case for him by pointing out that he wrote in the twelfth century and that we of the twentieth century have learned many things which show the advantage to be not so absolute as he thinks. It is possible that the dwarfs may in the course of time rebel against the giants, and kick and scream, and insist on getting down to the ground again, because the extended view they see from the giants' shoulders shows them things they would prefer to ignore, and that the greater the giants the greater will be the discomfiture felt by these dwarfs who cannot cope with too much knowledge of reality.

For any authentic work of art must start an argument between the artist and his audience. The artist creates that work of art by analyzing an experience and synthesizing the results of his analysis into a form which excites an appetite for further experience. If the experience which he has chosen as his subject is felt by his fellow men to be unimportant, the work of art is likely to be forgotten, even though his analysis may be intelligently conducted. A large number of modern novels fall into this category. If the experience be not important, and the analysis incomplete, but the synthesis be contrived in an enticing form, the work of art will be noted and will be subjected to a criticism of a purely superficial nature. This is the most popular form of art, and is rewarded by contemporary acceptance. But if the experience be one generally felt as important, the analysis scrupulous and searching, and the synthesis exciting, criticism will become a matter of either surrender or attack on the part of the reader. A major work of art must change the aspect of reality, for it is an experience of the order which breaks up the present as we know it,

5

transforming it into the past and giving us a new present, which we may like better or less than we liked the one just taken from us. It must have a bearing on the question which concerns us most deeply of all: whether the universe is good or bad. If a work of art should make a revelation which discredits what most human beings wish to believe, they will try to expose it as unsound. If they cannot do that, if the point the artist makes is incontrovertible, they may undertake the defense of their shattered universe in another way. They may pretend that he wrote something quite other than what he did. Then it is that the long life-span of literature is a source of danger, for though it gives the writer a many-branched and deep-rooted tradition to uphold him, it also gives time for his readers to repeat these defense tactics to the point of success. The repetition may be carried on so extensively through the centuries that in time a very large number of persons among those who have relations with literature, who move within the sphere of culture, may be under the impression that the content of a famous work of art is not that which the artist has carefully set down on his page.

This is surely what has happened to the play of *Hamlet,* and it is unfortunate that it should be so, for there has thus been obscured Shakespeare's development of a theme which runs through Western literature and has often provided genius with its material. This distortion was far from inevitable, for there is nothing obscure about the content of *Hamlet.* The action, though it follows an arbitrary time-scheme, is definite enough; and the language is as sharply explicit as it is in *Macbeth,* more so than it is in *Othello* or *King Lear.* But the practice of misreading the character of Hamlet, and hence the significance of the play, had been carried on by generation after

6

generation of persons interested in the play on widely different levels, all over the world; by many scholars, by people who are true readers—that is, who read all their lives —as well as by people who read only when they are at school or the university, by people who do not read at all but who have seen a version of the play acted in a theater or as a film or on television, or heard it on the radio, and by people who have no immediate knowledge of the play at all but have simply acquired a knowledge of it by repercussion from these other classes. A host of such people, vastly as they differ from one another intellectually and socially, misread the character of Hamlet in exactly the same way. They see him as a symbol of irresolution; and their unanimity is remarkable if it be considered that there is no justification for this view in the text.

Let me give two examples of this standardization in error which interested me when they came my way because of their historical and geographical background. Before the war I was in Yugoslavia, in the town of Zagreb. It is the capital city of Croatia, which, till its incorporation in Yugoslavia, was a province of the Austrian Empire, and held its face turned to the West, not only because of the Habsburg power, but because it was passionately Catholic and looked toward Rome. I was dining one night in a Zagreb hotel when I met an elderly gentleman who had translated many of the works of Shakespeare into Serbo-Croat. I told him that the next day I was going to Belgrade, and he said that he wished to go to Belgrade himself, as he had business there, so I invited him to come with me in my car. To this he replied, "Thank you very much, but I am like Hamlet, I want very much to go to Belgrade, but I cannot make up my mind to go, I hesitate and hesitate, and the journey

7

is never made." He spoke with a certain degree of coquetry. He was in intent saying to me, "I, like Hamlet, am a delicate, sensitive, melancholy creature, compact of thought and fancy, too fragile ever to find it easy to commit myself to the coarseness of action." This was surprising from a translator whose Slav intelligence should have made him quick to perceive that the text of the play does not in fact show Hamlet as revolted by the quality of action, particularly as the Slav genius has made more than one memorable study of irresolution. But after all this was a Slav who looked West, who had taken his degrees in Berlin and Vienna, and who had probably been still a boy when he first read Goethe's curious description of Hamlet as "a lovely, pure and most moral nature, without the strength of nerve which forms a hero" (*Wilhelm Meister*, IV, 13). That tide might have been expected to reach this spot.

I then went to Skoplje, a town in Macedonia, on the Greek border of Yugoslavia. There Western influence was weak indeed, and any cultural influence had a clean tablet on which to write. I was staying with two schoolteachers, a Serb who belonged to the Orthodox Church, and her husband, who was a Moslem. She was a graduate of Vienna University and he a graduate of the Sorbonne, but their faces were turned to the East. They spoke, as well as their native Serbo-Croat, French, German, and English, and some Italian; but they also spoke Hungarian, Greek, Russian, Turkish, and Arabic. Their pupils were either Slavs belonging to the Orthodox Church or Moslems; and the parents of these pupils were either doctors or lawyers or shopkeepers or farmers who had been born under the Turkish Empire, which had kept this country in darkness from the fourteenth century till the Balkan Wars liberated it in 1912. But liberation

8

had not meant the free enjoyment of the arts of peace, for the population was then caught into the first World War, and in this area the fighting was prolonged into the early twenties, and even after that the land was harried by the sporadic civil war conducted by a Macedonian Separatist Movement. The territory had thus been cut off from European culture about two hundred years before Shakespeare was born, and had not re-established its connection with it till three hundred years after his death; and there had been only about fifteen disturbed years in which the reunion with the West could be confirmed.

All the young students I met were familiar with *Hamlet*. All had read the play in translation, and a number of them had read it in English. They appreciated it, and did not merely eat it up because it was the food set before them by their teachers. They had indeed a quite individual way of looking at it. Among these South Serbs the most dynamic relationship in the family is the tie between brother and sister, and for them Laertes and Ophelia played quite a different part in the drama than we can conceive. The scene in which Laertes takes farewell of his sister before he goes to France was therefore charged with an intensity for these Macedonian students which we would find it hard to understand, and they all thought that one of the chief reasons why Ophelia went mad was that her brother was away when she was assailed by tragic events. But these students showed no idiosyncrasy at all in their views on Hamlet's character. Like the old translator on the other side of Yugoslavia, they wanted to go to Belgrade; and when they told me of this desire and their failure to gratify it, they, too, said that they were like Hamlet, that they could not make up their minds to go, they hesitated and hesitated, and the

9

journey was never made. Like the old translator, too, they wore an air of coquetry and presented themselves as too finely intellectual to regard the exercise of the will in the medium of solid fact as anything but a descent to a lower plane. But also they used Hamlet's name very often in their general conversation as a symbol of irresolution, often on quite a low plane, when they simply were indicating idleness, shiftlessness, life below the level of habit, as lived by people who cannot post letters or shave in the morning. I sometimes said to them, "But you are not speaking of Hamlet at all, you are talking of Oblomov, as he was drawn in the great Russian novel by Goncharov." But it was no use. The idea of Hamlet as an exquisite, whose exquisiteness is at once the cause and the result of his indecision, had been impressed on these young Macedonian students as soon as they had stepped out of their temporary entanglement with the East.

Surely this is a defensive falsification, contrived by readers who want to protect themselves from the duty of revising their opinions about the universe, which would be forced on them if they accepted the real significance of *Hamlet.* Let us turn to a view of Hamlet's character which was expressed by one who was defending his own essence when he let art have its say as the artist said it. Turgenev turned his poetic and sensitive and precise mind to Shakespearean criticism in an essay on the contrast between the contemporaneously conceived characters of Don Quixote and Hamlet, and in this he wrote:

> Hamlet is, beyond all things else, analysis and egoism, skepticism personified. He lives only to himself; for no man can have faith save in that which is outside self and above self. Nonetheless Hamlet clings tenaciously to this "I," this self in which he

has no faith. It is a center to which he constantly returns because he finds that in this world there is nothing to which he can cleave with all his soul. A skeptic, Hamlet is preoccupied with his own personality; but he ponders its strategical situation, not its duties. Hamlet, doubting all, has no pity for himself. His spirit is too developed a thing to be content with what it discovers within itself. Well aware of his own weakness, he delights in self-flagellation; ever burrowing in his own soul, he catalogues his frailties and feels contempt for them and himself; and all the while he lives on this contempt and draws nourishment from it. For all self-awareness is a force.

None of this touches on irresolution. Yet it is a just enough description of the character of Hamlet if the text and not the legend is considered: for though Hamlet certainly said, "I do not know Why yet I live to say this thing's to do," he said many other things as well. He would have been perfectly capable of going to Belgrade, provided that the journey was made for a self-regarding purpose. What would have kept him in Zagreb or in Skoplje, or wherever he happened to be, would have been the sense that he should have gone to Belgrade in order to serve the interests of another person. He would not have gone there to maintain any principle, save one, and that not the most obvious choice to our age: to preserve the state he would have engaged in any necessary work. There is no sign in the text that he was averse from any action, even of the most violent kind. It is true that he was sensitive and thoughtful and melancholy; but he was cruel as well as sensitive, impulsive as well as thoughtful, and though melancholy he was coarse as any barroom drunk. These less attractive attributes have been

11

traced through the play by Salvador de Madariaga, in an attempt to disprove the myth of Hamlet's irresolution, in a volume which has plainly been inspired by Turgenev's essay, though it does not name it. This volume is not entirely satisfactory, for it is marred by a punitive manner suggesting that it is based on the private papers of a District Attorney of Elsinore who had hoped to make an arrest, and would have made one had it not been for the holocaust in the last scene. But there is no use in quarreling with Madariaga's findings, which are not really much less favorable than the reluctant admissions of that wise and loving Shakespearean scholar, Wilson Knight. From the admissions of Hamlet's faults which these two very different critics are forced to make in common, we get some indication of the reason why the vast audience of Western readers has been shy about accepting Hamlet as Shakespeare drew him. Hamlet is universal. "We all," Turgenev says, "sympathize with Hamlet because there is not one of us but recognizes in the prince one or more of our own characteristics." That is in part, perhaps, a matter of technique. The verse which Hamlet speaks runs with the quick, ranging gait of thought, of the interior monologue, and as we listen to it we recognize that that is how we think. And thus identifying ourselves with Hamlet, we come to the conclusion that we, too, think well. "We have," Turgenev goes on, "a constant persuasion of his high value. No man but is flattered to learn he is Hamlet." So Hamlet is ourselves at our most attractive. Therefore we do not want to learn that he, who is us at our best, has some of the worst of human attributes.

Hamlet was so far from being incapable of action that he committed without remorse that extreme action, murder, and he committed it four times and killed one man in

12

self-defense. It is sometimes said that the violence of the times in which Shakespeare lived accounts for the many crimes in his plays. But there is surely a constant way of regarding murder, as we ourselves should know. Of all people who are elderly today it is true that when they studied Shakespeare at school they were looking back at an age more barbarous than their own, and that when they read him in later life they were looking back at an age more civilized than their own, for though the Tudors were bloodstained they were not stained with as much blood as the modern dictators. But at no time during the recent degeneration of history would an artist engaged on a pure work of art not involved in propaganda, or a person engaged in the disinterested study of a pure work of art, have considered murder as other than a horrible deed. There is built into our flesh a strong prejudice in favor of natural death. Moreover, Shakespeare was writing at the court of Elizabeth, which, despite certain outrageous deeds of royal vengeance, was a shrine of mercy compared to the slaughter-houses presided over by Henry the Eighth and Mary Tudor, and to him murder must have had all the horror of a recently escaped danger.

There is a passage in *Hamlet* which shows Shakespeare to have been very conscious of the efforts made by society to bridle its aggressive instincts. The middle ages had endeavored to check the European chronic condition of warfare by instituting formalized systems of combat; and in the first act we learn from Horatio that Hamlet's father, the older Hamlet, had fought and killed the older Fortinbras in a duel of this disciplined sort, arranged for the purpose of settling a territorial dispute between Denmark and Norway, on terms set forth "by a seal'd compact, Well ratified by law and heraldry" (I.1.86). There is no question but that Horatio approved

13

of the older Hamlet for having taken part in this combat; he speaks of "our valiant Hamlet, For so this side of our known world esteem'd him" (I.1.84). He also censures young Fortinbras for not abiding by the result of the combat and seeking to recover by warfare the territory thus lost. There is an acceptance of certain conventions here inconsistent with tolerance of common murder. Yet Hamlet committed both kinds of murder, premeditated and unpremeditated. On hot impulse he stabbed Polonius as he hid behind the arras; and he sent Rosenkrantz and Guildenstern off to England bearing their own death warrant in the forged letter to the King of England, requesting him to kill them.

Hamlet was, indeed, an exceptionally callous murderer. Not in the first heat of crime, but after he has had his long scene with his mother with Polonius' corpse lying on the floor, he says, "I'll lug the guts into the neighbor room" (III.4.212); "Where is Polonius?" King Claudius asks him, when Rosenkrantz and Guildenstern cannot find the body. "In heaven," answers Hamlet. "Send thither to see. If your messenger find him not there, seek him in th'other place yourself. But indeed, if you find him not within this month, you shall nose him as you go up the stairs into the lobby" (IV.3.32). His insensibility toward Rosenkrantz and Guildenstern is worse. When, after his return from the sea voyage to Denmark, he tells Horatio how he sent the pair to their deaths by forging the letter to the King of England requesting that "He should the bearers put to sudden death, Not shriving-time allow'd" (V.2.46), he is quite jaunty about it. The excuse he gives is, "Why, man, they did make love to this employment" (V.2.57)—that is, to their employment by Claudius to take him to his execution in England. But there is no indication that they were aware of the fate which Claudius

14

had contrived for Hamlet on his arrival. Hamlet himself says that the letter they carried from Claudius to the King of England was sealed till he stole it and opened it. They would believe that Claudius had sent him to England to hush up the trouble caused by what they thought to be his insane murder of Polonius, as they had no reason to suspect Claudius' good faith, since Hamlet had done nothing to inform them of his uncle's crimes. Yet of Rosenkrantz and Guildenstern Hamlet says, "They are not near my conscience" (V.2.58), so easy does he find it to commit murder.

He can kill only on his own behalf. When his father returns from the grave and bids his son avenge his death by killing Claudius, he cannot obey. It is true that he kills Polonius in the belief that he is Claudius, but this is so confused an action that it is almost a repudiation of the one desired. He could have sought out his stepfather at any hour he pleased and murdered him as they talked, but he chose to run a sword through an unidentified body on the off chance that it was his stepfather. It is true that he ultimately kills Claudius, but it is because Claudius, by inducing Laertes to fight with an envenomed sword, has committed the only offense which Hamlet recognizes an offense, that is, an offense against himself. He meets the ghost's command with an abstracted disobedience, and it is part of the oddity of *Hamlet* which so greatly distressed Thomas Rymer, and in our own day T. S. Eliot, that the reader knows this to be a sin, though the ghost is to us one of the most ridiculous preternatural beings ever invented. He talks fustian and he cannot establish his authority, even with the advantage of his supernatural state behind him; he is addressed by his son, whose blood he has sought to freeze, as old mole and truepenny. His requests are disregarded

15

even when he pays a special daylight visit to repeat them; and on this occasion he is seen in circumstances peculiarly unfavorable to the suspension of disbelief, for he is on the stage at the same time as the corpse of Polonius, who should, if the universe be consistent, also have a ghost. Yet Hamlet's father's ghost has authority over the reader, and over any audience, because he is the symbol of a reality. He represents tradition. His insistence that Hamlet should avenge his murder is an invocation of the Rule of Law, a warning that the existence of our kind depends on observance of the Commandments. When Hamlet fails to obey, he rejects the accumulated experience of his race; he has refused to aid society by transmitting a message; and he has taken as his government his individual impulses.

2 The Nature of Will

Yet Hamlet recognizes the value of tradition. That is made clear by the courage he shows in choosing to meet the ghost and in casting off the hands of his companions when it bids him follow it and they seek to hold him back. But he feels no real reverence for tradition. That is a very strange scene, when he swears his companions to secrecy on his sword, and the ghost raps upward on the earth they stand on, and Hamlet says, "You hear this fellow in the cellarage" (I.5.151). The root of this disrespect becomes explicable when we inquire into Hamlet's attitude to humanity. For tradition is the distillation of human experience, and it must be condemned if humanity is condemned; and Hamlet was disgusted by his own kind.

There are other crimes afoot in Elsinore, in the world, as well as murder. The ghost wishes Hamlet to avenge his murder and also to put an end to the unholy offense of the marriage between his widow and his murderer. But when Hamlet talks of these matters with his mother he loses all interest in that part of the command which relates to his father's murder, and in the course of over eighty lines addressed to her he devotes only three to a perfunctory mention of the fact that her present husband murdered her previous husband, and when she shows that she did not know that any such crime had been committed he does not take the opportunity of enlightening her. He simply tells her that she is behaving reprehensibly in living with her present husband, not because he had murdered her dead husband and his own brother, but because he was not so good looking as her dead husband. It is not surprising, though it is always comic, that

17

the ghost should then reappear in order to ask Hamlet to
stick to the point. "Do not forget: this visitation Is but
to whet thy almost blunted purpose" (III.4.110). But a
revelation is made in the course of the scene. The Queen
admits the charge of sensuality (III.4.88):

> Oh, Hamlet, speak no more,
> Thou turn'st mine eyes into my very soul,
> And there I see such black and grained spots
> As will not leave their tint.

Claudius is guilty, the Queen is guilty, and so as this
scene makes quite plain, is Hamlet. All that he says is
smeared with a slime which is the mark of sexual corruption. His curious emphasis on the physical difference between the dead King and the living Claudius hints at a
homosexual element in his nature, but that is irrelevant.
Hamlet could be neither a heterosexual nor a homosexual
lover. Such an egotist would be restricted to lust, for he
could not afford the outgoings of love.

That has been indicated earlier in the play by his
scenes with Ophelia. There is no more bizarre aspect of
the misreading of Hamlet's character than the assumption that his relations with Ophelia were innocent and
that Ophelia was a correct and timid virgin of exquisite
sensibilities. Probably the conception would not have
lasted so long in England had it not been for the popularity of the pre-Raphaelite picture by Sir John Millais
which represents her as she floated down the glassy
stream, the weeping brook; for his model was his friend
Rossetti's bride, the correct, timid, sensitive, virginal, and
tubercular Miss Siddal, and she was, poor thing, especially wan during the painting of the picture, for she
was immersed in a tin bath full of water kept warm by
a lamp placed underneath, like an old-fashioned hot-

18

water dish. We have certainly put Ophelia into the wrong category and into the wrong century. She was not a chaste young woman. That is shown by her tolerance of Hamlet's obscene conversations, which cannot be explained as consistent with the custom of the time. If that were the reason for it, all the men and women in Shakespeare's plays, Romeo and Juliet, Beatrice and Benedict, Miranda and Ferdinand, Antony and Cleopatra, would have talked obscenely together, which is not the case. "The marriage of true minds" would hardly, even in the most candid age, have expressed itself by this ugly chatter, which Wilson Knight has so justly described as governed by "infra-sexual neurosis." The truth is that Ophelia was a disreputable young woman: not scandalously so, but still disreputable. She was foredoomed to it by her father, whom it is a mistake to regard as a simple platitudinarian. Shakespeare, like all major writers, was never afraid of a good platitude, and he would certainly never have given time to deriding a character because his only attribute was a habit of stating the obvious. Polonius is interesting because he was a cunning old intriguer who, like an iceberg, only showed one-eighth of himself above the surface. The innocuous sort of worldly wisdom that rolled off his tongue in butter balls was a very small part of what he knew. It has been insufficiently noted that Shakespeare would never have held up the action in order that Polonius should give his son advice as to how to conduct himself abroad, unless the scene helped him to develop his theme. But "This above all—to thine own self be true; And it must follow, as the night the day, Thou canst not then be false to any man" (I.3.78), has considerable contrapuntal value when it is spoken by an old gentleman who is presently going to instruct a servant to spy on his son, and to profess great anxiety about

19

his daughter's morals, when plainly he needed to send her away into the country if he really wanted her to retain any.

There is no mistaking the disingenuousness of his dealings with his daughter. When Ophelia comes to him with her tale of how Hamlet had come to her as she was sewing in her chamber, "with his doublet all unbraced," and had looked madly on her, Polonius eagerly interprets this as "the very ecstasy of love," and asks her "What, have you given him any hard words of late?" Ophelia answers (II.1.106):

> No, my good Lord; but as you did command
> I did repel his letters, and denied
> His access to me.

At that Polonius purrs in satisfaction:

> That hath made him mad.
> I am sorry that with better heed and judgment
> I had not quoted him: I fear'd he did but trifle,
> And meant to wrack thee; but beshrew my jealousy!
> It seems it is as proper to our age
> To cast beyond ourselves in our opinions
> As it is common for the younger sort
> To lack discretion. Come, go we to the king.
> This must be known; which, being kept close, might move
> More grief to hide than hate to utter love.
> Come.

This is the Court Circular version of Pandarus. The girl is not to be kept out of harm's way. She is a card that can be played to take several sorts of tricks. She might be Hamlet's mistress; but she might be more honored for resistance. And if Hamlet was himself an enemy of the King, and an entanglement with him had ceased to be a means of winning favor, then she can give a spy's report on him to Claudius. Surely Ophelia is one of the few authentic portraits of that army of not virgin martyrs, the poor little girls who were sacrificed to family ambition in the days when a court was a cat's cradle of conspiracies. Man's persuasion that his honor depends on the chastity of his womenfolk has always been liable to waste away and perish within sight of a throne. Particularly where monarchy had grown from a yeasty mass of feudalism, few families found themselves able to resist the temptation to hawk any young beauty in their brood, if it seemed likely that she might catch the eye of the king or any man close to the king. Unfortunately the king's true favorite was usually not a woman but an ideology. If royal approval was withdrawn from the religious or political faith held by the family which had hawked the girl, she was as apt to suffer fatality as any of her kinsmen. The axe has never known chivalry. Shakespeare, writing this play only three reigns from Henry the Eighth, had heard of such outrages on half-grown girls from the lips of those who had seen the final blood-letting. He wrote elsewhere of Ann Boleyn; and he must have heard much of the worse case, which did not excite so much compassion because the edge of the tragedy had been taken off by repetition, the case of Katherine Howard. She, who had been beheaded half a century before, was one of the Catholic Howards, a poor relative of the Duke of Norfolk, and had grown up in the attics and passages and antichambers of a disordered country seat, where maturing beauty brought her several lovers, one of whom she loved. But she did not marry him, because she was presently procured for the King, whom she pleased so well that he made her Queen. Pleasure, however, was not the most important issue involved. The marriage was a token

21

of Henry's temporary softening toward Rome. But he hardened his heart again and turned again toward the innovators of Protestantism, and so the Howards fell out of favor, and Katherine's head was cut off when she was twenty years old.

Shakespeare had pondered on such massacres of the innocent, and he had thought it one of the worse offenses of the court (and he hated courts) that by the time the innocents were massacred, they were no longer innocent. The scene between Anne Boleyn and the bawdy old lady in the part-Shakespearean *Henry the Eighth* has an obvious pathos, because he knows and we know that the girl is doomed to die by the headsman's axe. But it is even more pathetic that she is deprived not only of her life, but of a noble death; for however bravely she bore herself when she laid her head on the block, she had nevertheless found her way there by a greedy intrigue which sought to snatch profit from the fall of an authentic queen. Like Anne Boleyn, Ophelia has lost her integrity. She fiddles with the truth when she speaks of Hamlet to her father, and she fiddles with the truth when she talks to Hamlet as her father and Claudius eavesdrop; and she contemplates without surprise or distaste Hamlet's obscenity, the scab on his spiritual sore.

Surely the picture of Ophelia shows that Shakespeare, who wrote more often of cruelty than any other great writer, was not a cruel man, and was great in pity, that rare emotion. He shows the poor little creature, whom the court had robbed of her honesty, receiving no compensation for the loss, but being driven to madness and done to death. For the myth which has been built round Hamlet is never more perverse than when it pretends that Ophelia went mad for love and killed herself. No line in the play suggests that she felt either passion or affection for Hamlet. She never mentions him in the mad scene, and Horatio says of her, "She speaks much of her father." Indeed she was in a situation which requires no sexual gloss. Her father had been murdered by a member of the royal house, and she found herself without protection, since her brother Laertes was in France, in the midst of a crisis such as might well send her out of her wits with fear. For the Danes hostile to the royal house made of her wrong a new pretext for their hostility, and the royal house, noting this, turned against her, helpless though she was. Claudius speaks of a general resentment (IV.5.78):

> . . . The people muddied,
> Thick and unwholesome in their thoughts and whispers,
> For good Polonius' death; and we have done but greenly
> In hugger-mugger to inter him . . .

When Ophelia wanders to the Castle and asks that the Queen should receive her, she is refused. The Queen says, "I will not speak with her." But Horatio tells her she is not wise (IV.5.5):

> She speaks much of her father; says she hears
> There's tricks i' th' world; and hems, and beats her heart;
> Spurns enviously at straws; speaks things in doubt,
> That carry but half sense; her speech is nothing.
> Yet the unshaped use of it doth move
> The hearers to collection; they aim at it,
> And botch the words up fit to their own thoughts;
> Which, as her winks and nods and gestures yield them,
> Indeed would make one think there might be thought,
> Though nothing sure, yet much unhappily.
> 'Twere good she were spoken with; for she may strew
> Dangerous conjectures in ill-breeding minds.

Courts thus threatened had their own ways of dealing with the threats, as all courtiers knew; and Shakespeare must have heard of women thus dealt with who had been frightened into madness. Lady Rochford, who had helped Katherine Howard to meet her cousin Culpepper after her marriage, was raving mad when she went to her execution.

But neither from fear nor from love did Ophelia kill herself. She did not kill herself at all. The Queen describes her drowning as an accident. "An envious sliver broke," she says, and there is no indication that she was lying. Many things are packed into the passage which begins "There is a willow grows aslant a brook," but insincerity is not among them. These lines achieve a dramatic value often not exploited in the theater. They are beautiful and expressive verse: their sound suggests heaviness submerging lightness, the soaked clothes dragging down the fragile body they encase, the inanimate flesh grown leaden round the spirit. But the lines are also in character. The Queen is one of the most poorly endowed human beings which Shakespeare ever drew. Very often he created fools, but there is a richness in their folly, whereas Gertrude is simply a stately defective. The whole play depends on her not noticing, and not understanding; and in this passage there are samples of her stupidity. The botanical digression about the long purples is ill-timed, and the epithet "mermaid-like" is not applicable to someone saved from drowning by an amplitude of skirts or to the skirts themselves. But the fusion of perception and obtuseness in these lines, and the contrast between their distinction and the empty rotundity of all the Queen's other speeches, convince us that just once this dull woman was so moved that her tongue became alive. It is not credible that at that moment she

24

would have taken thought to deceive Laertes about the object of her emotion; nor indeed does Shakespeare suggest that she practiced any such deception.

For that Ophelia drowned herself is stated definitely only by two people: the clowns in the graveyard, typical examples of the idiot groundlings gorged on false rumor who appear so often in Shakespeare's plays. Whether we like it or not, we must admit that there is very little in the works of Shakespeare which could be used as propaganda for adult suffrage. For the rest, the priest declares that "her death was doubtful" (V.1.228), and that the doubt was enough to make it necessary that she should be buried with "maimed rites" (V.1.220). But surely we are not intended to believe him, for he is drawn as a bigot, who finds it possible to answer her brother coldly when he asks, "What ceremony else?" (V.1.224), and it is to be presumed that such lack of charity would invent a doubt. Shakespeare will not allow anyone in the graveyard scene, even to the priest, to be without sin. Each of them has helped to dig the girl's grave. Hamlet was the most guilty, for he had been her spurious lover and a tyrant prince, giving her no protection as a mistress or as one of his people; but it was the whole court that had destroyed her. She was a victim of society, which abandons principle for statecraft, for politics, for intrigue, because of its too urgent sense that it must survive at all costs, and in its panic loses cognizance of all the essentials by which it lives. Even her brother Laertes was not fully aware of his sister's tragedy, for he was tainted with the vice which Shakespeare feared most as a distraction: he was subject to lust.

This is indicated clearly enough in the early scene when Laertes warns Ophelia against the nature of Hamlet's courtships and she mocks him (I.3.46):

25

> But, good my brother,
> Do not as some ungracious pastors do,
> Show me the steep and thorny way to heaven,
> Whilst like a puft and reckless libertine,
> Himself the primrose path of dalliance treads,
> And recks not his own rede.

To this Laertes replies:

> Oh, fear me not.
> I stay too long. But here my father comes.

If Ophelia offers a *tu quoque* defense which we do not usually offer unless we are guilty, Laertes does not trouble to put up a defense at all. These two are no better than they should be; and Polonius, when he instructs his servant Reynaldo to spy on his son in Paris, speaks of drabbing and visiting "a house of sale, Videlicet, a brothel" (II.1.60), as if these were fairly certain to be among his son's activities. When Laertes leaps into his sister's grave, he cries (V.1.252):

> Now pile your dust upon the quick and the dead
> Till of this flat a mountain you have made
> To' o'ertop old Pelion or the skyish head
> Of blue Olympus.

For Shakespeare there was a connection between this outburst and the primrose path, the drabs, and the house of sale, Videlicet, a brothel. In his analysis of love that is not love, the hundred and twenty-ninth sonnet, he uses the word "extreme."

> The expense of spirit in a waste of shame
> Is lust in action; and till action, lust
> Is perjured, murd'rous, bloody, full of blame,
> Savage, extreme, rude, cruel, not to trust.

26

Laertes' expressions of grief are extreme. His mind rushes away from the dead girl on too long a journey, all the way to blue Olympus, and forgets its true grief in the excitement of travel. The essence of Ophelia has again been ignored, and the waste of a human being not appropriately resented.

It is Shakespeare's contention that the whole of the court is corrupt: society is corrupt. There is a flaw running horizontally through humanity wherever it is gathered together in space. It would seem natural therefore that Hamlet should obey the ghost and punish Claudius, who controls the court, who is an emblem of society. But the flaw runs vertically also; it runs through time, into the past. For Hamlet's father, the ghost, is in purgatory, doing penance for his sins, which were of the same gross kind as those he desires his son to punish. Shakespeare tells us this, stating the fact, and again using bombast to suggest immoderation (I.5.9):

> I am thy father's spirit,
> Doom'd for a certain term to walk the night,
> And for the day confined to fast in fires,
> Till the foul crimes done in my days of nature
> Are burnt and purged away. But that I am forbid
> To tell the secrets of my prison-house,
> I could a tale unfold, whose lightest word
> Would harrow up thy soul; freeze thy young blood;
> Make thy two eyes, like stars, start from their spheres,
> Thy knotted and combined locks to part,
> And each particular hair to stand an end,
> Like quills upon the fretful porpentine.

The ghost was indeed a sinner; the voice of tradition speaks from a tainted source. The evil in the world is not the product of the specially corrupt present generation,

27

it has its roots in the generations that went before and also were corrupt; it has its roots in the race. There is no use pretending that we can frustrate our sinful dispositions by calling on tradition, because that also is the work of sinful man. This is the situation of our kind as it is shown to us in *Hamlet*, which is as pessimistic as any great work of literature ever written. The theme of the play could never appear to any reader who kept his eye on the text as the irresolution of Hamlet, his lack of the nerve which forms a hero (as Goethe put it), his failure to achieve a virtue which would consist simply of capacity for action. For what excites Shakespeare in this play is the impossibility of conceiving an action which could justly be termed virtuous, in view of the bias of original sin.

What does Shakespeare see written on the other side of the ledger? Nothing but beauty. This is the play which more than any of the others reminds us of the extraordinary advantages which he enjoyed. For it was his luck to see the human race at one of the moments, in one of the places, when it blossomed into a state of exceptional glory; and he moved among men and women who were beautiful, intelligent, learned, and fearless beyond the habit of our kind, and whose way of life, with its palaces and its pageants, was a proper setting for the jewels that they were. Here we ourselves enjoy an extraordinary advantage. Literature cannot always do its business of rendering an account of life. An age of genius not of the literary sort must go inadequately described unless there should happen to exist at the same time a literary genius of the same degree, who works in circumstances enabling him to accumulate the necessary information about his non-literary contemporaries. It happened that the Renaissance man was observed by Shakespeare. "What a piece of work is man! How noble in reason! How infinite in faculty! In form and moving how express and admirable! In action how like an angel! in apprehension how like a god! The beauty of the world! The paragon of animals!" (II.2.305). Here is a coincidence. Shakespeare was himself "the paragon of animals," therefore he could describe to us the man who was "the beauty of the world." He could write this description and make the whole character of Hamlet as shown from scene to scene bear out what he said about man.

All through the play Hamlet speaks with a quick, springing harmony recognizable as the voice of physical and mental splendor; his mind travels like lightning yet strikes below the surface, and is impulsive not in surrender to folly but in search of wisdom. How superior, to use Turgenev's words, he is in mind and temperament, how daring, how proud. In fact, Shakespeare has given us a picture of the Renaissance man, without the lacuna which makes the other attempts to portray him, which were made by the Elizabethan and Jacobean dramatists, notably Ford and Webster. They tried to depict the new man created by the new wealth of Europe, the new community and continuity of culture, the new opening of windows on far parts of the globe and on the minutiae of matter. But they fall into the trap of showing the Renaissance man at his experiments without explaining why he felt free to experiment, without bringing forward the good reasons he had for thinking that he might tamper with the existing moral world. Even Marlowe took the Faust legend for his great work, and accounted for his Renaissance man by devil-dealing; but Shakespeare in Hamlet makes the Renaissance man his own Mephistopheles, and depicts a being so gifted that he needs no supernatural being to raise him above the common lot.

But Shakespeare, the supreme artist observing this supreme man, immediately adds, "And yet to me what is the quintessence of dust?" And his genius has been asking that question throughout the play. Scene after scene has demonstrated the paragon of animals to be an animal, the world to be so diseased that even its beauty is infected. This speech of homage to man is indeed an example of teasing ambiguity; it can be read without irony or with irony; each reading is equally faithful to the text.

Shakespeare hopes for little from the dust. It is quite certain that he wished to present Hamlet as a bad man, because he twice makes him rejoice at the thought of murdering men who had not made their peace with God. He might have killed Claudius when he came on him at prayer. But he decided this might mean that Claudius would go straight to heaven (III.3.88):

> Up, sword; and know thou a more horrid hent;
> When he is drunk, asleep, or in his rage;
> Or in th'incestuous pleasure of his bed;
> At gaming, swearing or about some act
> That has no relish of salvation in't;
> Then trip him, that his heels may kick at heaven;
> And that his soul may be as damn'd and black
> As hell, whereto it goes.

Later on, when he tells Horatio of his peculiarly cold-blooded murder of Rosenkrantz and Guildenstern, his description of the letter he forged to the King of England shows traces of a like perverse determination to kill the soul as well as the body (V.2.38):

> An earnest conjuration from the king,—
> As England was his faithful tributary;

As love between them like the palm might flourish;
As peace should still her wheaten garland wear,
And stand a comma b'tween their amities;
And many such-like As-es of great charge,—
That, on the view and knowing of these contents,
Without debatement further, more or less,
He should the bearers put to sudden death,
Not shriving-time allow'd.

There would be no question at all in the minds of an Elizabethan audience that a murderer who could cheat his victims of their chance of salvation was a very bad man indeed; and indeed most of us would think with repulsion of such an action, if, through the hazards of war or dictatorship, it came within our experience.

But to this bad man Shakespeare ascribes one virtuous action; and the nature of that action is determined by his most lasting preoccupation. It is a political action. Hamlet gives his dying breath to thought for the future of his people; his last words choose a ruler for them (V.2.343):

> O, I die, Horatio;
> The potent poison quite o'ercrows my spirit;
> I cannot live to hear the news from England;
> But I do prophesy th' election lights
> On Fortinbras: he has my dying voice.
> So tell him, with the occurents, more and less,
> Which have solicited—the rest is silenced.

Hamlet was never more the Renaissance man—who was a statesman, a true Macchiavellian, a prince careful for the safety of his subjects. Even if one be disillusioned with the race, and suspect paragons and the beauty of the world, this is still admirable. These fragile creatures, so little changed from dust that they constantly revert to it, show bravery in their intention that their species shall survive as if it were marble. Yet, all the same, how horrid is the sphere in which they show their excellence. The court was saved by its political conscience; yet it was damned by it too.

3 *The Will of Kings*

Shakespeare feared sex as a force which he knew to be constructive but believed to be destructive; and he feared power hardly less and almost in the same way. To it he might have applied the terms that he had used of the more primal peril (Sonnet 129):

> The expense of spirit in a waste of shame
> Is lust in action, and till action, lust
> Is perjur'd, murd'rous, bloody, full of blame,
> Savage, extreme, rude, cruel, not to trust.

Power was as dangerous. For "till action, lust," read "ambition" and the epithets would fit. By that sin fell the angels, and the Macbeths had not even time to fall, they were damned where they stood.

One of the plays into which Shakespeare packs the largest amount of material regarding his obsessional preoccupation, power, is *Richard the Second*. There are others which would seem to deal with its problems more directly; but the fault of Coriolanus would have been a millstone round his neck even had he been a slave; and Julius Caesar and Brutus and Mark Antony might have been knit in the same relationship had they been partners in an industrial or commercial concern. But *Richard the Second* is a highly political play; even if it had not had sequels, it would make it astonishing that George Bernard Shaw accused Shakespeare of having no interest in general ideas. For it is very hard to gather anything about the middle ages from reading *Saint Joan* except the actual existence of certain historical personages and the legal and penal practices at that time; and even in the Inquisitor's speech there is no hint of the conflict of forces which produced the prosecution—there is no indication that the shepherdess of Domremy might have been allowed to listen to her voices, had they not, in a roundabout way, supported the case of Dante's *De Monarchia,* and that the Papacy's claim to international temporal power forbade the Church to tolerate independent nationalist heroines. But a reader could derive a rough idea of the main political debates of the middle ages simply by turning to *Richard the Second.* He would learn that England had to work out for itself a theory of monarchy which demanded other decisions, a choice between a king who was "under God and the law, for it is the law which makes the king," and a king who rules by divine right and therefore should act as an absolute monarch.

The play begins with the brawl between Bolingbroke and Norfolk, which explains that the institution of the monarchy was of supreme importance, since such disorders might destroy the unity of the state if sovereignty were subdivided among the nobles and there were no supreme authority to compel them into amity. It is then demonstrated how the exercise of royal power works on Richard the Second. He becomes violent and ambitious and nourishes a delusion that his appointment by God to his high office is a good luck charm. He begins to believe that he cannot fail, and this makes him reject all counsel and claim absolute power. When wise old John of Gaunt on his deathbed begs Richard to be merciful and move within the confines of prudence, he insults the dying man. By his arbitrary acts he forces his nobles to rebellion, and marches to defeat at a pace which, both when the play is read and when it is seen, is unconvincing in its speed. Shakespeare is so determined to cram into the play all he knows about monarchy that it has to run too

34

fast. He puts into Richard's mouth a superb example of
the vanity which is the autocrat's occupational disease
(*Richard II*, III.2.61):

> God for his Richard hath in heavenly pay
> A glorious angel: then, if angels fight,
> Weak men must fall; for heaven still guards the
> > right.

But it is really rather too much to have in the same scene
(only a hundred or so lines on) that cry of final despair
(III.2.156):

> For God's sake, let us sit upon the ground,
> And tell sad stories of the death of kings.

But then think how much Shakespeare does in this single
play; for he shows us the reverse of the medal. He
hastens to some purpose.

When Richard the Second is deposed, he is revealed
as a piteous human being of normal affections, and the
just men who rose against the oppressor become unjust
as he was. There had been a particular brutality, smell-
ing of the court, in the insults Richard had thrown at
John of Gaunt as he was borne away on his litter to
die. The old man said in farewell (II.1.137):

> Convey me to my bed, then to my grave;
> Love they to live that love and honour have,

and Richard rejoined,

> And let them die that age and sullens have;
> For both hast thou, and both become the grave.

But when the tide turns and Richard himself appears
before the usurping Bolingbroke, he breaks down and
cries (IV.1.261):

O that I were a mockery-king of snow,
Standing before the sun of Bolingbroke,
To melt myself away in water-drops!
Good king—great king—and yet not greatly good—
An if my word be sterling yet in England,
Let it command a mirror hither straight,
That it may show me what a face I have,
Since it is bankrupt of his majesty,

and Bolingbroke says,

Go, some of you, and fetch a looking-glass.

At the beginning of the play old John of Gaunt had lamented with the widow of his brother, the Duke of Gloucester, because their nephew Richard has had her husband murdered; and at the end of the play there is the same inhuman disruption of family relations to Richard's disadvantage, for another uncle of his, the Duke of York, tries to deliver his own son over to Bolingbroke, newly crowned Henry the Fourth, for death as a traitor. The switch is complete. Bolingbroke himself becomes worse than Richard, because he has a finer mind and therefore sins more subtly. His murder of Richard is worse than the murder of Gloucester, because it is one stage more remote and is more confusing to morality. One of his courtiers, corruptly anxious, as courtiers are, to please his monarch, divines that Bolingbroke would be glad if the former king were dead and seeks Richard out in his prison cell and first tries to poison him and then stabs him. But Bolingbroke's crime is not merely the encouragement he had given, by the historical situation he had produced and perhaps by his demeanor to the assassin. It was something worse (V.6.31):

36

(Enter Sir Pierce of Exton, with a coffin)

EXTON

Great king, within this coffin I present
Thy buried fear; herein all breathless lies
The mightiest of thy greatest enemies,
Richard of Bourdeaux, by me hither brought.

HENRY BOLINGBROKE

Exton, I thank thee not; for thou hast wrought
A deed of slander, with thy fatal hand,
Upon my head and all this famous land.

SIR PIERCE OF EXTON

From your own mouth, my lord, did I this deed.

HENRY BOLINGBROKE

They love not poison that do poison need,
Nor do I thee; though I did wish him dead.
I hate the murderer, love him murdered.
The guilt of conscience take thou for thy labour,
But neither my good word nor princely favour:
With Cain go wander through the shades of night,
And never show thy head by day nor light.—
Lords, I protest, my soul is full of woe,
That blood should sprinkle me to make me grow:
Come, mourn with me for that I do lament,
And put on sullen black incontinent:
I'll make a voyage to the Holy Land,
To wash this blood off from my guilty hand:—
Mark sadly after: grace my mournings here,
In weeping after this untimely bier. (*Exeunt*)

Bolingbroke is so much repelled by Exton's deed that he
feels he must cleanse himself of his responsibility for it

by a pilgrimage to the Holy Land. Yet this same deed preserves the people of England from the horrors of civil war, since Richard living would necessarily be a constant inspiration to revolt. So it seems that Bolingbroke, being a king and dedicated to the service of the people, must approve this deed, of which as a private person he disapproves. This scene, though dealing with the solemnity of death and the pomp of history, is written in verse so simple as to come close to doggerel; and this befits a revelation that great men cannot conduct their business without falling into inconsistencies which make nonsense of the moral world, as surely as idiots who never rise to the conception of consistency.

In play after play Shakespeare was to record his sense that monarchy is at once a necessary and a dangerous institution. On the other side of the ledger is the picture of Henry the Fifth, which begins with a glorious vigor in its evocation of the monarch who guards his manhood unspoiled, who has the charm of the light-minded, yet knows it his duty to bend his neck to the yoke of responsibility, and a nature so sweet that it can correct the sourness of the court. It goes on to the great scene when young Prince Henry watches by the deathbed of his father, Henry the Fourth, that Bolingbroke who usurped the throne of Richard who lies asleep, his crown on a pillow beside him. The prince's eye is drawn to it (*Henry IV*, Pt. II, IV. 4. 151):

> Why doth the crown lie there upon his pillow,
> Being so troublesome a bedfellow?
> Oh, polisht perturbation, golden care!

Pondering on it as the symbol of the responsibility which has digested his father's life and now will eat his own, he takes it into another room. While he is gone the King awakes, and filled with royal suspicion, cries out for his attendants (IV.4.188):

> KING HENRY
> Where is the crown? Who took it from my pillow?

> WARWICK
> When we withdrew, my liege, we left it here.

> KING HENRY
> The prince hath ta'en it hence: go, seek him out.
> Is he so hasty, that he doth suppose
> My sleep my death?
> Find him, my lord of Warwick: chide him hither.
> This part of his conjoins with my disease
> And helps to end me.

When the prince returns, he rages at him with that mean immoderation, at once large and picayune, which Shakespeare regarded as the royal mode (IV.4.237):

> Thou hidest a thousand daggers in thy thought.
> Which thou hast whetted on thy stony heart,
> To stab at half an hour of my life.
> What! Can thou not forbear me half an hour?
> Then, get thee gone, and dig my grave thyself,
> And bid the merry bells ring to thine ear,
> That thou art crowned, not that I am dead.

Yet his son answers with such grace and gentleness and honesty that the venom is dissolved, the malevolence of the crown converted (IV.4.307):

> O my son,
> God put it in thy mind to take it hence,
> That thou might'st win the more thy father's love,
> Pleading so wisely in excuse of it!

39

This young king, when he inherited that crown, could work a miracle on himself. He could lead armies to war when the safety of his country demanded it, yet never lose his sense that his soldiers were men like himself, and like himself hated pain and death (*Henry V*, IV, Prologue, line 22):

The poor condemned English
Like sacrifices, by their watchful fires
Sit patiently, and only ruminate
The morning's danger; and their gesture sad
Investing lank-lean cheeks and war-worn coats,
Presenteth them unto the gazing moon
So many horrid ghosts. O, now, who will behold
The royal captain of this ruin'd band
Walking from watch to watch, from tent to tent,
Let him cry, "Praise and glory on his head!"
For forth he goes and visits all his host;
Bids them good morrow with a modest smile,
And calls them brothers, friends, and countrymen.
Upon his royal face there is no note
How dread an army hath enrounded him.
Nor doth he dedicate one jot of colour
Unto the weary and all-watched night;
But freshly looks, and over-bears attaint
With cheerful semblance and sweet majesty,
That every wretch, pining and pale before,
Beholding him, plucks comfort from his looks:
A largess universal, like the sun,
His liberal eye doth give to every one,
Thawing cold fear. Then, mean and gentle all,
Behold, as may unworthiness define,
A little touch of Harry in the night.

No, no, this is too much. By now, something has gone wrong. Shakespeare comes very near to telling us that His Royal Highness looked bronzed and fit. For all that the not epicene type of actor loves to play Henry the Fifth, the character is in its later phases not a character at all, but the platonic idea of a patriot king, which degenerates into a Prince Charming because Shakespeare's intellect will not stay with him on this enterprise. It is unfortunate that we cannot really tell how he would have developed the story of the English monarchy, because he wrote the last part of the story first. *Henry the Sixth* and *Richard the Third* were among his earliest plays, and in them he set down impetuously his first obvious thoughts about power. He writes of the sorrows of a good weak king, of the disgusting brawls of the barons, of the hideousness of civil war, where father kills son and son kills father, of the coarseness and cruelty that come naturally to the great. But the subtlety of the later historical plays is not here, though there already is present one of the ideas about which Shakespeare was to write most subtly. That is a masterpiece of scorn, the scene at St. Alban's where the Queen and her nobles bait the old man, Saunder Simpcox, who has claimed to be cured of blindness at the saint's shrine, and prove him a fraud. Richard Crookback, Duke of Gloucester, calls for a beadle to whip the old man; the Queen says (*Henry VI*, Pt. II, II.1), "It made me laugh to see the villain run," and Henry, the anointed king who has no power to rule, says, "O God, seest Thou this, and bearest so long?" But Richard Crookback says, "Follow the knave, and take this drab away," and while the drab, Simpcox's old wife, quavers, "Alas, sir, we did it for pure need," he answers, "Let them be whipped through every market-town till

41

they come to Berwick, from whence they came." For Crookback was the usurper, who, no matter how well he could rule, was a bad man, and haunted Shakespeare's mind throughout his life as the figure that could not be fitted into the moral pattern. For the usurper fulfilled a purpose, since the legitimate king so often could not rule, yet in that fulfilling seemed to prove that there was no benign purpose in the universe.

4 *The Will of Usurpers*

It recurs again and again in the works of Shakespeare, this notion that a king was a man put in a position where it was very difficult and sometimes impossible for anybody to stop him from doing as he liked, and where it was certain that at some time or another he would like to do terrible things, and that if he did not, it was apt to be a proof that he was not able to do anything at all, and was therefore a bad king. The theme of *King Lear* is that paradox by which all men were created with a desire to be loved but not with the faculty to love, but Lear's monarchy affects the development of the theme. Lear's strangeness does not begin with his excessive reaction against Cordelia's temperance; it appears earlier, when he disposes of his kingdom and its population according to the compliments paid him by his three daughters in conditions which preclude sincerity. There is a reason why he strikes out wildly at Cordelia for this repudiation of a silly business: he has for a long time been raised by his royal state so far above humanity that he has lost touch with reality. When the play unfolds its action he is isolated and not to be companioned. The only man who wants to travel with him as a friend is obliged to disguise himself as a lunatic before he can do the old man that kindness.

Shakespeare was so deeply committed to this line of thought that it governs *The Winter's Tale*, which is a late play, and a fairy tale. This means that it was his ripe opinion, expressed when he was working calmly and not under the compulsion of a great tragic theme, that royal caprice lunges as madly to earth as a thunderbolt. But no idea was stronger in his mind than that men must take on themselves the guilt of royalty if the people were not to perish. He knew that man is a political animal and must not abdicate if he wants to keep his high place among animals, and he wrote constantly of the man who fails morally by being unable to assume the dangerous role of governor: the good man born to be king, who cannot rule because of his virtues, which disincline him to perform the harsh task but who is for that reason a bad man— since as soon as he ceases to govern, a man inferior to himself becomes king in his stead. And he wrote constantly of the worse man, the usurper: of Henry Bolingbroke, who was a good man apart from this taint; of Richard Crookback, who was no better than that taint, who was that taint itself. There seemed to Shakespeare something inherent in the usurper's position which was against virtue. This is demonstrated very oddly in *Measure for Measure;* here we see the Duke Vincentio going into a monastery and explaining to a friar (I.3.7):

> My holy sir, none better knows than you,
> How I have ever loved the life removed;
> And held in idle price to haunt assemblies,
> Where youth, and cost, and witless bravery keeps.
> I have deliver'd to Lord Angelo—
> A man of stricture and firm abstinence—
> My absolute power and place here in Vienna,
> And he supposes me travell'd to Poland;
> For so I have strew'd it in the common ear,
> And so it is received. Now, pious sir,
> You will demand of me why I do this?

FRIAR THOMAS
Gladly, my lord.

44

DUKE

We have strict statutes and most biting laws—
The needful bits and curbs to headstrong wills,—
Which for this fourteen years we have let slip;
Even like an o'ergrown lion in a cave,
That goes not out to prey. Now, as fond fathers,
Having bound up the threat'ning twigs of birch
Only to stick it in their children's sight
For terror, not to use, in time the rod
Becomes more mock'd than fear'd; so our decrees,
Dead to infliction, to themselves are dead:
And liberty plucks justice by the nose;
The baby beats the nurse, and quite athwart
Goes all decorum.

FRIAR THOMAS

       It rested in your grace
To unloose this tied-up justice when you pleased;
And it in you more dreadful would have seem'd
Than in Lord Angelo.

DUKE

       I do fear, too dreadful:
Sith 'twas my fault to give the people scope,
'Twould be my tyranny to strike and gall them
For what I bid them do; for we bid this be done,
Where evil deeds have their permissive pass,
And not the punishment. Therefore, indeed, my
               father,
I have on Angelo imposed the office,
Who may, in th'ambush of my name, strike home.
And yet my nature never in the fight
To do it slander.

But there is an odd inconsistency in the Duke's decision (I.3.49):

> More reasons for this action
> At our more leisure shall I render you;
> Only, this one:—Lord Angelo is precise;
> Stands at a guard with envy; scarce confesses
> That his blood flows, or that his appetite
> Is more to bread than stone: hence shall we see,
> If power change purpose, what our seemers be.

The ambiguity of this remark becomes more sinister when we come to the scene in which the Duke Vincentio eavesdrops on Isabella's conversation with her brother and learns that Angelo has attempted to blackmail her into buying her brother's life with her chasity. He shows a curious lack of surprise at this revelation, and is immediately able to come forward with an assurance to Isabella that Angelo was merely testing her virtue and had no intention of ravishing her: an assurance which is manifestly insincere. For he goes on to suggest that she grant Angelo a rendezvous at night in which she is to be impersonated by Mariana of the moated grange; a substitution which would be pointless unless Angelo was going to take full use of his opportunities. Moreover he selects Mariana because he knows who she is; and she is the affianced wife of Angelo, repudiated only because her dowry was lost at sea, although Angelo puts up a blackguardly pretense that he has discovered her to be of bad character. He knows Angelo to be a wicked man.

This incident should surely have prevented one of the greatest Shakespearean critics from seeing in *Measure for Measure* a new gospel, which put in Tudor dress the story of God sending a deputy to do his work on earth. It is really a very ugly invention. Nothing can excuse Mariana for consenting to carry through this imposture with a man who abandoned her for mercenary reasons and betrayed her again by the excuse he made for it;

and it tarnishes the Duke that he procures her for this act of abjection. Surely we have here the intellectual, in the person of the Duke, coldly considering that only a morally inferior being can undertake the coarse business of action, and growing humorous and cruel at the expense of this creature, Angelo, who is not a dancing bear, but a governing bear.

It is to be remarked that the Duke is carefully represented to the audience as a good man. When, disguised as a friar, he visits the condemned prisoners, he shows the fastidiousness that Hamlet proclaimed he had not in the cases of the praying Claudius and of Rosenkrantz and Guildenstern: he will not let the drunken Barnardine go to the hangman (IV.3.66):

> A creature unprepared, unmeet for death;
> And to transport him in the mind he is
> Were damnable.

But as he mocks the wielder of the power he has abdicated, as he reassumes power in order to correct the misdeeds of his deputy, he becomes a governing bear himself. This play devours itself as it goes along: it begins as if it were going to deal seriously and candidly with its theme, and in the scene between Isabella and Claudio it rises to the heights of tragic solemnity, but it ends with the heartlessness of light comedy. At the public tribunal which closes the play the Duke torments Angelo like a cat playing with a mouse, and he is hardly more merciful to Isabella, whom he keeps in suspense longer than is necessary, and he ends by decreeing two of the most unsuitable marriages in all literature.

It is really shocking that he himself should marry Isabella. She is first shown to us when entering a convent to take up her novitiate, and her speeches throughout the play convince us that she was born to be a nun. They are, indeed, offensive if it be not granted that that was her character (III.1.36):

> O, fie, fie, fie!
> Thy sin's not accidental, but a trade.
> Mercy to thee would prove itself a bawd,
> 'Tis best that thou diest quickly.

It is just possible to take this address to a condemned man from a bride of Christ, but not from a future Duchess. The sudden affiance which deflects her to the less impressive state is given the tawdry confusion of a fancy dress ball by the circumstance that until that time she has known her bridegroom only in the disguise of a monk. But the marriage between Angelo and Mariana is even worse. Of course Shakespeare had treated the same subject a short time before in *All's Well that Ends Well,* and had presented as a potentially happy event the entrapment into marriage of a man by a gross sexual fraud which, had it been practiced on a woman, would be called rape; and many a writer had used the situation before him. It was a smoking-room story long before tobacco was discovered. It is odd to find Shakespeare's delicacy concerning itself twice with this coarseness; but in *All's Well that Ends Well* the persons involved were a couple of extroverts who would forget the whole thing in no time, and his irony may have enjoyed suggesting that especially for extroverts are all cats grey at night. There is, however, no way of regarding the marriage of the inglorious humbug Angelo and the cringing Mariana as other than purely repulsive, and it tarnishes the Duke that he should have a hand in such an ugly business and think it congruous with the restoration of justice and his own nuptials. But it must have been difficult to bring *Measure for Measure* to an end; for it is a play inspired by a preoccupation with the problem of power

48

which has by some accident been written round a sexual plot. The bride of Christ has been made to talk about virginity instead of the coronation oath, which would have been more to the point.

The story of the good man who was a bad king and therefore a bad man is told in yet another guise in *The Tempest*. Prospero explains to Miranda (I.2.66):

My brother and thy uncle, called Antonio,
I pray thee mark me—that a brother should
Be so perfidious! He whom, next thyself,
Of all the world I loved, and to him put
The manage of my state; as, at that time,
Through all the signories it was the first,
And Prospero the prime duke, being so reputed
In dignity, and for the liberal arts
Without a parallel: those being all my study,
The government I cast upon my brother,
And to my state grew stranger, being transported
And rapt in secret studies. Thy false uncle . . .
Being once perfected how to grant suits,
How to deny them who t'advance, and who
To trash for over-topping, new created
The creatures that were mine, I say, or changed 'em,
Or else new-form'd 'em; having both the key
Of officer and office, set all heart i' the state
To what tune pleased his ear; that now he was
The ivy which had hid my princely trunk,
And suck'd my verdure out on't . . .
I, thus neglecting wordly ends, all dedicate
To closeness, and the bettering of my mind
With that which, but by being so retired,
O'erprized all popular rate, in my false brother
Awaked an evil nature; and my trust,
Like a good parent, did beget of him

A falsehood, in its contrary as great
As my trust was; which had indeed no limit,
A confidence sans bound. He being thus lorded
Not only with what my revenue yielded,
But what my power might else exact, like one
Who having into truth, by telling of it,
Made such a sinner of his memory,
To credit his own lie, he did believe
He was indeed the duke; out o' the substitution,
And executing the outward face of royalty,
With all progative: hence his ambition growing . . .
To have no screen between this part he play'd
And him he play'd it for, he needs will be
Absolute Milan. Me, poor man, my library
Was dukedom large enough . . .

This passage is of some interest to us because it reminds us from what source Browning derived his narrative style; but Shakespeare is at some pains to tell us that it did not greatly interest Miranda, who was in any case distracted by the violence of the storm her father had conjured up. "Dost thou attend?" he asks, and she assures him, "Sir, most heedfully," but a little later he says flatly, "Thou attend'st not," to which she answers, "Oh, good sir, I do." Still later he asks quite testily, "Dost thou hear?" and it is with the very voice of boredom that she replies, "Your tale, sir, would cure deafness." There was perhaps a like fatigue in the reply given by Friar Thomas in *Measure for Measure* when the Duke asked him, "Now pious sir, you will demand of me why I do this?" "Gladly, my lord," he says. The Duke is not deterred; but, brief as the friar's assurance is, it manages to be definitely not that which any of us would hope to receive were we confiding the story of a major perturbation to a friend.

Perhaps Shakespeare sought to show that these dispossessed kings, speaking of their dispossession, even to sympathetic listeners must fail to evoke a true response, since sorrows reserved for the highest cannot be understood by those of lower estate; or perhaps he used such tales of visible public misfortune as symbols of the invisible and private tragedies of the inner life which cannot be fully confessed between man and man.

In *The Tempest* the dispossession of the rightful king is peculiarly brutal in character. Antonio is the worst of the usurpers. He is inferior to Angelo because he does not even pay virtue the homage of hypocrisy. Into his mouth there is put as succinct a statement of the bad man's position as has ever been made. When he is shipwrecked on the island with the King of Naples and his brother Sebastian, and he is urging Sebastian to kill his brother and seize Naples from its rightful heir, explaining that he himself has usurped his brother's dukedom and has found the enterprize most satisfactory, Sebastian reminds him of his conscience, and he replies, "But I feel not this deity in my bosom" (II.1.275). His motive is what Shakespeare would regard as unkingly. There is no thought of the state and the people in this interference with the international hierarchy; for his motive is to help Sebastian to the throne in return for exemption from his existing obligation to pay tribute to Naples. Again we are shown the bad man who can find it in his heart to murder the unshriven; he and the seduced Sebastian are about to kill Alonso and Gonzalo in their sleep when Ariel stops them. Yet Prospero cannot scorn him, for against himself also there is a case. Indeed he could be tried on a double indictment. He is guilty of letting Antonio into the palace by his neglect of his duties, as the Duke Vincentio let Angelo into Vienna;

51

and he is guilty of a further sin, more subtle in its nature.

As a duke he let power over man fall out of his hands while he pored over his books; but from them he learned the magic art which gave him power over spirits, which he exercised on the island. To Shakespeare not even this rarefied and fantastic variant on government is immune from the taint of tyranny. When Prospero found Ariel enduring painful imprisonment in the cleft of a tree, so just a man should have released the delicate spirit as an act of charity and asked no price, but he exacted in exchange that Ariel should serve him as a slave, on tasks that injured the creature's ethereality. Though he delights in the exquisite and courageous quality of Ariel (who surely personifies imagination), he deals with him unjustly in a sphere where the noble should be most careful to behave nobly. He cheats him on the terms of their master and man relationship (I.2.242):

ARIEL
Is there more toil? Since thou dost give me pains,
Let me remember thee what thou hast promised,
Which is not yet perform'd me.

PROSPERO
                    How now? Moody?
What is't thou canst demand?

ARIEL
                    My liberty.

PROSPERO
Before the time be out? No more!

ARIEL
                    I prithee,
Remember I have done thee worthy service,

52

Told thee no lies, made thee no mistakings, served
Without or grudge or grumblings; thou didst promise
To bate me a full year.

Prospero does not deny that he made this promise, but
turns for the moment into a preincarnation of Mr.
Brocklehurst in *Jane Eyre,* fearing lest the pupils of Lo-
wood, given bread and cheese instead of burned porridge,
might so feed their vile bodies but starve their immortal
souls. For Prospero reminds Ariel of the ill-treatment he
had suffered at the hands of Sycorax, the mother of Caliban (I.2.264):

PROSPERO
This damn'd witch Sycorax
For mischiefs manifold and sorceries terrible
To enter human hearing, from Argier,
Thou know'st, was banish'd; for one thing she did
They would not take her life. Is not this true?

ARIEL
Ay, sir.

PROSPERO
This blue-eyed hag was hither brought with child,
And here was left by the sailors. Thou, my slave,
As thou report'st thyself, was then her servant;
And, for thou wast a spirit too delicate
To act her earthy and abhorr'd commands
Refusing her grand hests, she did confine thee,
By help of her more potent ministers,
And in her most unmitigable rage,
Into a cloven pine, within which rift
Imprison'd, thou didst painfully remain
A dozen years, within which space she died,
And left thee there, where thou didst vent thy groans
As fast as mill-wheels strike. . . .

53

                                    Thou best know'st
What torment I did find thee in; thy groans
Did make wolves howl and penetrate the breasts
Of ever-angry bears; it was a torment
To lay upon the damn'd, which Sycorax
Could not again undo; it was mine art,
When I arrived and heard thee, that made gape
The pine, and let thee out.

ARIEL
I thank thee, master.

PROSPERO
If thou more murmur'st, I will rend an oak,
And peg thee in his knotty entrails, till
Thou'st howled away twelve winters.

This was no way to treat a delicate and lovely spirit; and
Prospero is so harsh in his dealings with Caliban that he
inflicts more pain than it seems legitimate to inflict on
even such a loathly monster. But indeed this monster,
as Shakespeare indicates in some of his most subtly written lines, felt much of human yearning. Often he speaks
with the very voice of the unlovable craving love. He says
to Stephano and Trinculo (II.2.157):

I'll show thee the best springs. I'll pluck thee berries,
I'll fish for thee, and get thee wood enough.
A plague upon the tyrant that I serve!
I'll bear him no more sticks, but follow thee,
Thou wondrous man. . . .
I prithee, let me bring thee where crabs grow;
And I with my long nails will dig thee pignuts,
Show thee a jay's nest, and instruct thee how
To snare the nimble marmoset; I'll bring thee

To clustering filberts, and sometimes I'll get thee
Young scamels from the rock. Wilt thou go with me?

This is a lonely child seeking to win strangers as its play-
mates; and that this offer of self-surrender had been made
before, and the spirit had then been wholly of the
nursery, is proved by his reproach to Prospero (I.2.333):

>   When thou camest first
> Thou stroked'st me, and made much of me; wouldst give
> me
> Water with berries in't, and teach me how
> To name the bigger light, and how the less,
> That burn by day and night; and then I lov'd thee,
> And show'd thee all the qualities o' the isle,
> The fresh springs, brine pits, barren place, and fertile:
> Cursed be I that did so! All the charms
> Of Sycorax, toads, beetles, bats, light on you!
> For I am all the subjects that you have,
> Which first was mine own king; and here you sty me
> In this hard rock, whiles you do keep from me
> The rest o' the island.

In fact, Prospero had "colonized" (to use the word in its
pejorative sense) the island. His treatment of the indig-
enous population, even though it numbered only one,
would be hard to justify, according to the theory of
natural law, for one whose grievance against fate lay in
the infringement of a title recognised by that theory. His
excuse for introducing the color bar and peonage is not
congruous with his special wisdom (I.2.345):

> PROSPERO
>   Thou most lying slave,
> Whom stripes may move, not kindness! I have used
> thee,

> Filth as thou art, with human care, and lodg'd thee
> In mine own cell, till thou didst seek to violate
> The honour of my child.

But this episode only meant that Caliban manifested the same instinctive reaction toward the first nubile female he met which Miranda was later to manifest toward the first nubile male she met. Nobody would have expected Prospero to hand Miranda over to Caliban, but the perfectly just and loving man should have remembered that gorillas will be gorillas. Prospero had found it necessary to warn Ferdinand, in terms so explicit as to be comic, not to "give dalliance too much the rein," lest he should find himself anticipating the marriage ceremony, although he had reason to know, from the young man's meekness under his own crabbed treatment, that he possessed unusual power of self-restraint. Obviously a "freckled whelp hag-born, not honour'd with a human shape" could still less be expected to swear a vow of chastity. When Prospero curses and oppresses Caliban on this pretext he is putting himself on the same level as an ignorant mother who beats a child not yet house-trained, and this is strange conduct in a character who is depicted as the representative of the Renaissance intellectual, the modern artist and scholar, who has passed beyond the stage of simple submission to experience and is now learning to comprehend and control it.

But it would be naive to feel surprise because Shakespeare shows such "a paragon of animals" as acting hideously and unreasonably. It would seem to him impossible that such " a piece of work" should behave after any other fashion. In many plays Shakespeare had shown that political power destroyed the man who wielded it; and in this play he showed that artistic power also was a sword which corroded its sheath. This was logical enough. It was his case that power, of whatever kind, engendered pride, because the governing man, his will unfettered, feels superior to the governed man (who must needs wear some shackles) and begins to believe his relative strength absolute. This pride might well be ranker in the artist than in the man of action, because his medium imposes fewer restrictions on him. It cannot be said with any meaning that it is easier to write a poem or paint a picture or compose a piece of music than to put an army into the field, but it certainly arouses less material resistance. The artist is therefore freer than the man of action to let his will fly free, and with the higher flight there comes a stronger illusion of godhead.

It is a cruel dilemma, in life and in art: those who are the children of light are irresistibly drawn to assume a task which changes them to the companions of darkness. Significantly, in *The Tempest* there is only one person who thinks of power as if it might be innocently exercised, and speaks of the possibility of governing the island gently and initiating a golden age on its rocks; and that is the twaddling Gonzalo, the King of Naples' platitudinous counselor, a respectable cousin of Polonius. He could not conceivably be called to be a ruler anywhere. But Prospero's lordship cannot be questioned—even Caliban has to concede it in the end. Yet he himself revolts against it. That is quite clear, though *The Tempest* is the most behavioristic of the serious plays, and in it Shakespeare virtually abandons the soliloquy; when Prospero meditates, he records an intention or an emotion and does not dig out its cause from the deep mines within himself. But there is the constant assertion that the bewitchment of the shipwrecked men is the last throw of his magic, that he will let the spirits go their way as soon

57

as he has attended to the business (here, as always, regarded by Shakespeare as supremely important) of restoring the rightful succession of the state. There is the speech of renunciation, reticent but final as nightfall (V.1.50):

> But this rough magic
> I here abjure; and, when I have required
> Some heavenly music—which even now I do—
> To work mine end upon their sense that
> This airy charm is for, I'll break my staff,
> Bury it certain fadoms in the earth,
> And deeper than did ever plummet sound,
> I'll drown my book.

There is also that epilogue, that astounding epilogue, which purports to be a request to the audience for applause, but sounds so much as if it were directed elsewhere:

> Now I want
> Spirits to enforce, art to enchant;
> And my ending is despair,
> Unless I be relieved by prayer,
> Which pierces so, that it assaults
> Mercy itself, and frees all faults,
> As you from crimes would pardon'd be,
> Let your indulgence set me free.

This epilogue has been said by some to be an addition by another hand: but even so it would be a significant response to the ambiguity of *The Tempest*.

5 *The Unresolved Historical Argument*

Shakespeare carried this intellectual baggage on a long journey through a changing countryside. He first expressed certain ideas about power in his realistic and straightforward and historical plays; they are implicit in the purely imaginative great tragedies and in such indeterminate works as *Troilus and Cressida* and *Measure for Measure;* and they emerge intact in *The Tempest*, where fantasy opens its wings as widely as in any work in English literature. All of us would be surprised to find those ideas held today by any but some highly insulated, and perhaps lunatic, group. We do not feel, as Shakespeare did, a peculiar horror of all attempts on the part of subjects to rid themselves of rulers who have been called to the throne according to the customs of their peoples. We think that such an action might be bad or might be good. It is obviously regrettable when state machinery which is working well is smashed by rebellion, but when it has not worked well there is a reasonable case for dismantling it. All of us would think it natural for Brutus to feel shame and fear when he was visited by Caesar's ghost; but we would find it hard to blame Bolingbroke for taking the throne from Richard the Second when he had threatened the safety of his people. We are tempted therefore to think that, when Shakespeare showed such strong sympathy with Bolingbroke for feeling tainted by the performance of this dreadful act, he was writing as a child of his age, and that that is how his age felt about the monarchy.

This feeling is supported by the transcripts of historical records which furnish the material for so much of

the plays. The lines in which Shakespeare most passionately denounces the dethroning of monarchs, the speech
of the Bishop of Carlisle in *Richard the Second,* is a
paraphrase of a speech in fact delivered by that Bishop,
as reported by Holinshed (IV.1.121):

> What subject can give sentence on his king?
> And who sits here that is not Richard's subject?

But the Bishop of Carlisle was on the losing side, and
defeat had come to him over a hundred and fifty years
before Shakespeare was born. The situation had changed
since then, but Englishmen were still against the Bishop.
Historians have great difficulty in telling us precisely
what these Englishmen thought, for here we are explor-
ing a peculiarly inaccessible district of the past. We can
gain a clear picture by going back over two thousand
years and reading Plato and Aristotle; but if we go back
four or five hundred years we find it hard to understand
what Englishmen were thinking about the state. Our ancestors were trying out certain political ideas on an em-
pirical basis and improvising theoretical justifications for
them with tumbling fluency and exquisite subtlety; and
we have since fitted those same ideas, in a developed
form, into a framework of logical theory never envisaged
by their earlier exponents. It is very easy to fall into error
regarding the attitudes of the past, particularly the error
of assuming that when our ancestors took sides regarding
certain ideas which are still current today, those sides
are the same as those we take today. But, remembering
this need for caution, we can surely say that Shakespeare
and his contemporaries looked back with interest and
approval on the process which had destroyed the disorderly feudal system, with its splitting of sovereignty
into a thousand warring factions, and replaced it by the

monarchical system that gave a single person power to speak and act in the name of the law. Shakespeare was probably one with his contemporaries in wanting this single person to be given great but not absolute power. But where he was surely not one with his contemporaries is in his lack of sympathy with the contractual theory of the English monarchy; for surely if he had been aware of this idea, and pleased by it, he would not have harbored his eternal obsession with the usurper.

An English king becomes a king because he enters into a contract with the English people. In the coronation service, it is the anointment of the subject which transforms him into a monarch, but the subject is not anointed until he has taken the oath to govern his territories "according to their respective laws and customs" to "cause Law and Justice, in Mercy, to be executed in all your judgments," and "to maintain the Laws of God and the true profession of the Gospel." The statute book makes it clear that a monarch's status depends on the keeping of this oath. The King's subjects owe him allegiance, only because he gives them protection. If he fail them, they owe him no allegiance. It is true that this is to present the situation in terms too much in accord with our modern mode to be an exact description of a medieval complex. Many held that a king was as much a king before coronation as after, provided he were the true heir to the throne; as such he was regarded as a potential taker of the oath, a potential object of anointment, and thus passed into the category of kings. It is also to be noted that a subject who challenged the king for failing to provide protection was not acting in the spirit of a ratepayer suing a County Council for negligence, but was thought of as fulfilling a duty to an objective legal order which had been disturbed by the unworthy king and must be restored. It is not irrelevant that the arm of the administration termed the Crown could not be sued in tort until well into the nineteenth century. But then, as now, the English people were guided by their relationship with the monarchy by a broad principle which declared it to be called into existence by the sealing of a contract and maintained by the performance by both parties of reciprocal duties.

Long before Shakespeare's day this had been announced in terms at once supremely matter-of-fact and supremely impressive. It is really very odd that, despite his interest in constitutional history, he made no reference to Magna Carta in *King John*. It would have seemed certain that he would have found the perfect text for a dramatic crisis in the famous sixty-first article, in which the king himself admitted the right of his subjects to resist him if he failed in his duty toward them, and decreed the coercive machinery which they were to apply for the purpose of restraining him.

Since, moreover, for God and the amendment of our kingdom and for the better allying of the quarrel that has arisen between us and our barons, we have granted all these concessions, desirous that they should enjoy them in complete and firm endurance for ever, we give and grant to them the underwritten security, namely, that the barons shall choose five-and-twenty barons of the kingdom . . . who shall be bound with all their might, to observe and hold and cause to be observed . . . the peace and liberties we have granted . . . to them by this our present charter, so that if we . . . or any one of our officers shall in anything be at fault towards anyone, or shall have broken any one of the articles of the

peace or this security and the offence be notified
to four barons of the aforesaid five-and-twenty . . .
the said four barons shall repair to us . . . and peti-
tion us to have that transgression redressed without
delay. And if we shall not have corrected the transgression . . . within forty days . . . the said four
barons shall refer the matter to the rest of the aforesaid five-and-twenty barons, and these five-and-
twenty barons shall, together with the community of
the whole land, distrain and distress us in all possible ways, namely by seizing our castles, lands, possessions, and in any other way they can, until redress
has been obtained as they deem fit, saving harmless
our own person, and the persons of our queen and
children; and when redress has been obtained they
shall resume our old relations to us. And let whoever
in the country desires it, swear to obey the orders of
the said five-and-twenty barons for the execution of
all the aforesaid matters, and along with them, to mo-
lest us to the utmost of his power; and we publicly
and freely grant leave to every one who wishes to
swear, and we shall never forbid anyone to swear.
All those, moreover, in the land who of themselves
and of their own accord are unwilling to swear to the
twenty-five to help them in constraining and molest-
ing us, we shall by our command compel the same
to swear to the effect aforesaid.

Of course the article was great nonsense. Though it
sought to preserve the country from continual change
by forcing bad kings to reform instead of deposing them,
it might on the face of it have legalized a combined action
of magnates tantamount to permanent revolution, under a
buffeted marionette wearing a crown. But it was the

63

best the times could do. It built the right of resistance into the constitution, and it wrote a program for Parliaments to come, and though it may have flattered the hopes of barons longing for a second heyday, it was in line with the thought of the philosophers who wanted to contrive a holier future. St. Thomas Aquinas, a little later, approved revolt against tyranny, both in the *Summa Theologica* and in the parts of the treatise *De Regimine Principium* which are credited to his pen:

> First of all, if to provide itself with a king be among the rights of any society, it is not unjust that the king set up by such a society be destroyed or his power subjected to limitation, should he abuse his power and become a tyrant. It must not be thought that such a society is breaking faith in deposing such a tyrant, even though it should have previously vowed allegiance to him, since, by his misgovernment, he has broken faith with society. (*D.R.P.* 1. 6)

He lays it down that "to proceed against the cruelty of tyrants is an action to be undertaken, not through the private presumption of a few, but by public authority," but he asserts definitely that such proceedings may serve the highest morality, pointing out that St. John the Evangelist was brought back from Patmos when the Senate cast out Domitian.

Nearly three hundred years later, when Shakespeare was a child, a Frenchman wrote a letter which showed how that political theory had stood the test of time and had determined its value. François de Montmorin, Governor of the Auvergnes, addressed Charles the Ninth in these terms:

> Sire, I have received an order from your Majesty directing me to kill all Protestants residing in my

province. I respect your Majesty too much to believe that this order is genuine. But if, which God forbid, it should be so, I respect your Majesty too greatly to be able to obey it.

It is a magnificent letter. Indeed, it is Shakespearean in its magnificence. Yet it might not have been to Shakespeare's liking, for it is bluff, and though he described the Bastard Faulconbridge and Harry Hotspur and Henry the Fifth with delight, he plainly does not believe that bluffness is the style in which ultimate wisdom expresses itself. Magna Carta, too, is bluff; and it is even possible that Shakespeare might have reproached St. Thomas Aquinas for being on this subject too direct. Not so would have been written the secret which Prospero failed to find in his book, but believed he might yet find elsewhere.

But if the right of resistance was not in consonance with Shakespeare's peculiar prepossessions, neither was its opposite. The doctrine of the divine right of kings, which had slowly emerged as the middle ages died, was not the nonsense modern minds sometimes suppose. It was a reasonable enough answer to the claims of Papal supremacy. If the Pope claimed that as the Vicar of Christ on earth he must have power over temporal affairs and that, since God had entrusted him with this task of government, none should dare to resist him, it was reasonable enough for the nations, seeking independence, to declare that as their kings owed their kingship to a rite of anointment derived from the Scriptures and performed by the Church, they too were sacred and should be obeyed. The doctrine had against it the initial disadvantage of conflicting with the theory of natural law, which was presumed to be the authority above all men, kings, barons, and commoners alike. Later, the doctrine of divine right ran head on against the power of Parliament, though for a time Henry the Eighth held its ground for it. He desired to be an absolute monarch, and often enjoyed a similar condition, but was always careful to get what he wanted through Parliament; yet at the same time his political pamphleteers poured out a stream of propaganda in favor of an unrestricted monarchy. But it is a striking difference between the classical and the modern world that the idea of divinity is not now felt to be compatible with a plurality of mates, and the theory of divine right fell into temporary abeyance after the reign of Henry the Eighth and the disorderly succession caused by his marriages. For the time being the doctrine disappeared, and its place was taken by the doctrine of nonresistance, which preached the duty of obedience to all kings and princes, whether good or bad. But there was nothing mystical about that doctrine. Often it put on a theological robe, and its advocates maintained that God used tyrants to chastise sinners and to enable the pious to win salvation by sharing the sufferings of Christ. But fundamentally it was as bluff as a doctrine of resistance. It was called into being by need and it smelled of reality. England wanted the civil order and the comparative toleration which could continue only if Elizabeth felt safe in undisputed power. The court poets were able to compose their hymns to Gloriana because humbler men were writing this sort of doggerel (Thomas Brice, *A Compendious Register* . . .):

> When John Newman and Thomas Fusse
>   At Ware and Walden made their end:
> When William Harles, for Christ Jesus,
>   With breath and blood did still contend,

66

> When he at Barnet was put to death,
> We wished for our Elizabeth.

There was also the still more urgent danger of invasion by enemies who could only be routed if the defensive power was solid in unity. In fact those who upheld the duty of nonresistance were as bluff and hearty as those who upheld the right to resistance, and might have expressed themselves in the spirit of Faulconbridge, in the words of:

> Now these our princes are come home again,
> Come the three corners of the world in arms,
> And we shall shock them. Naught shall make us rue
> If England to itself do rest but true.

This, too, is not in the style of the secret sought by Prospero.

6 *The Resolved Theological Argument*

Certainly Shakespeare was not, in his notions about monarchy, holding up a mirror to his times; and we must recognize a paradox in his refusal to pick up that mirror. He was out of sympathy with the doctrine of resistance, and he was out of sympathy with the doctrine of non-resistance, though it would seem impossible to disbelieve in the one without believing in the other. But we have already noted that the two political assumptions which govern his imagination are in fact irreconcilable: he thought power so dangerous that no man born of woman could exercise it without falling into sin, but at the same time he regarded with horror all attempts to take power away from any monarch who had been entrusted with it according to the laws and customs of his country, no matter how sinfully he may have misused it. Hence kings and usurpers, though moving in opposition, are equally immoral. This is not clear political thinking. Perhaps it is not political thinking at all. If Shakespeare talked nonsense about kings, and at the same time we know that he did not talk nonsense, but such sense that humanity has been compelled to listen to him through the centuries, it might be that he was discussing the sovereignty not of this world but of another. He may be thinking inconsistently because he is thinking not only of politics but of religion, a subject which, by its own nature, precludes consistency, since it depends on our sense that there exists, outside this world, a system of values different from any established by humanity, and that this system is superior to ours, and that no knowledge we possess of the world around us is so important as this obscure and doubtful perception.

The word "symbol" has during the last century or so acquired the unattractive character which comes of being used for different purposes by many authors. But Yeats gave the term a valid meaning when he wrote of the Great Memory which humanity has developed by its life and its art, and pointed out that, like the lesser memories of individuals, it has developed a network of associations, and now links certain objects with certain events and moods and persons and that to mention one of these objects, these symbols, is to throw the light of consciousness on a complex of experience. To say that Shakespeare used any object as a symbol is, of course, not to say that he used it with the intention of conveying an indirect meaning. Criticism which pretends to tell us what was in the conscious mind of an artist during the act of creation is an enterprise of the same order as filling in football pool coupons or telling fortunes by tea-leaf readings. All we can say is that that pattern of a work arouses certain associations in the reader's mind, and as these associations are common property of reader and writer alike, it is possible that some part of the writer's mind was stimulated by the same associations during composition. With these reserves, it may be suggested that Shakespeare, thinking of power, used a king as a symbol of power, wrote of courts as places where power is exercised, and wrote of courtiers as symbols of the persons who submit to the exercise of power or contest it. But perhaps he pushed his journey still further into the dark continent of the interior life. Perhaps the king is a symbol of the will, the court a symbol of the personality containing it, the courtiers symbols of the other elements in that personality which are integrated with that will, or are in conflict with it.

If Shakespeare practiced this symbolism, and if he had

come to believe, either spontaneously or as the result of his observation, or as the result of theological teaching, that humanity is tainted with original sin, but nevertheless has knowledge of God, the two assumptions which governed Shakespeare's imagination are not inconsistent. The king must govern; man must use his will. God would not have given him his faculties if he were not to use them; and being born to love others he must make moral decisions in order to protect them. But his nature is corrupt, and therefore his will is dangerous when it turns an invisible thought into a visible deed, with infinite reverberations in the moral universe. So kings do evil: Vincentio abandons his responsibilities and Prospero does that and worse, bullying his delicate Ariel. Reform is impossible, for if we repent and try to remake ourselves, we can only use our will, which must still be a part of our corrupt nature. So usurpers, too, do evil: Angelo is worse than Vincentio, Antonio is worse than Prospero. They are bound to be worse, because the belief that they can grow better through their own efforts encourages pride, which makes them ride roughshod over persons and principles. Hence the answer of Antonio, when he was asked about his conscience: "But I feel not this deity in my bosom." Treated as a matter of religion and not of politics, Shakespeare's obsession with usurpers becomes interesting as sound argument and as prophecy. It is a poor piece of historical analysis. Even the most passionate legitimists must recognize that Cromwell was not worse than Charles the First and the House of Hanover not worse than the Stuarts, in this particular way. But Shakespeare's work gives impressive testimony against a heresy which had been revived by the Renaissance and was steadily to gain adherents till it triumphed in the nineteenth century: against Pelagianism. It was

70

an array of evidence against the theory that man is free equally to choose between good and evil, and that, should he choose good, his own natural ability will enable him to reach moral perfection, and that our race could be changed and made innocent without search for a higher authority and submission to it. This is not to regard Shakespeare as a religious writer. If he called on God, his cry was private. But his work is like the mold used for taking copies of sculpture, a form surrounding an empty space, which is enclosed by the negative impression of the object. He describes a world which is hollow, and its hollowness is the negative impression of God. This is man without grace; so can we understand what grace must be.

7 *The Moral Reason for Misreading* Hamlet

Surely the attraction of *Hamlet* lies in the refinement and strength and width of reference shown in its treatment of these problems, which is remarkable even for Shakespeare. The position of Hamlet is peculiarly favorable to the unfolding of the king-and-usurper theme, because he is neither; he is like that part of us which stands aside and watches what we say and do. Hamlet is not the king, but he is a potential king. The Danish succession was elective, and he had been a candidate after his father's death, though his uncle and stepfather, Claudius, had been preferred (V.2.64):

> He, that hath kill'd my king, and whored my mother,
> Pop't in between th'election and my hopes.

But Claudius has expressed a wish that on his death Hamlet should be elected. Again Hamlet is not a usurper; but he is a potential usurper. If he obeyed his father's ghostly command and killed Claudius, he would, in a sense, be the destroyer of a duly elected king (though Claudius' title to the throne is tainted, as there would have been no election had he not murdered his brother). It is to be observed that in Claudius there is a curious looking-glass reversal of Hamlet. Just as Hamlet was neither king nor usurper, so Claudius was both. On this earth nothing is clear; because of our corrupt nature no man's title to respect is impeccable. All that can be said on our behalf is that we do not let this confusion engulf us, we insist on surviving, on maintaining the act of creation which produced us; but we can survive only by continual compromise, which means surrender to evil in varying degrees.

72

This dilemma is harshly illustrated in a scene—usually omitted in performance but extremely important, for it has the whole force of Shakespeare's long political pre-occupation behind it—in which Hamlet and Rosenkrantz and Guildenstern come on Fortinbras' army as it marches toward Poland. Hamlet asks a captain the purpose of the expedition and is told (IV.4.14):

> THE CAPTAIN
> Truly to speak, sir and with no addition
> We go to gain a little patch of ground
> That hath no profit but the name.
> To pay five ducats, five, I would not farm it
> Nor will it yield to Norway or the Pole
> A ranker rate, should it be sold in fee.
>
> HAMLET
> Why, then, the Polack never will defend it.
>
> THE CAPTAIN
> Yes, it is already garrison'd.

Then Hamlet reflects with snarling irony that if men go to war for so little then, by their standards, he, with his far greater reason for violence, should be ready to carry out his father's murderous commands. But he makes it quite plain that he thinks these standards degrading, "Examples," he says, "*gross as earth*, exhort me" (IV.4.46). There is no question but that he thinks that Fortinbras is doing a dreadful thing in leading this expedition (IV.4.47):

> Witness this army, of such mass and charge,
> Led by a delicate and tender prince;
> Whose spirit with divine ambition puft,
> Makes a mouth at the invisible event;

73

Exposing what is mortal and unsure
To all that fortune, death and danger dare,
Even for an eggshell. Rightly to be great
Is not to stir without great argument
But greatly to find quarrel in a straw
When honour's at the stake. How stand I, then,
That have a father kill'd, a mother stain'd,
Excitements of my reason and my blood,
And let all sleep?, while, to my shame, I see
The imminent death of twenty thousand men,
That for a fantasy and trick of fame
Go to their graves like beds; fight for a plot
Whereon the numbers cannot try the cause
Which is not tomb enough and continent
To hide the slain?

Yet when Hamlet comes to die, and should be most conscious of the terrors of death, and solemnly takes thought
for the future of his people, he names Fortinbras as the
best possible king for Denmark. The repulsion he felt
regarding this expedition had to be disregarded because
it would have been impossible to find a king not involved
in the cruelty of war. We are members of an imperfect
society, and when we cooperate with it, we are committed to imperfection, because we are all imperfect beings and cannot conceive a perfect thought or act.

The peculiar force of *Hamlet* lies in its contention that
there is no escape from this guilt. Our imperfection cannot be sweetened by our acts or limited in its effect by
our caution. Hamlet is exquisitely accomplished, but it
does not aid his moral power. He is an egotist and annuls
his natural affections so that he achieves no valid relationship: he is a disobedient son to his father, he defiles

his mother, he is a querulous and fugitive lover, he is not a husband and not a father, and he treats Horatio as a listening ear rather than as a friend. Yet in this detachment he is responsible for the perpetuation and extension of evil. When the play opens, the crime which stains the court is the theft of the throne by the fratricide and regicide Claudius; but when the last curtain falls the stain has spread. Hamlet has killed Polonius and Rosenkrantz and Guildenstern, Ophelia is drowned, and Claudius has dipped himself in other crimes and has made an assassin of Laertes. These things have happened as the result of Hamlet's refusal to bind himself by the same ties of the flesh which have, through the ages, been generally blamed as the sources of sin. To our species all gates to innocence are barred.

The pessimism of *Hamlet* is indeed extreme. It is Calvinist in its allegation of total depravity, and indeed there are echoes of Calvin's voice all through this play, never more strongly than in the "What a piece of work is man" speech. For Calvin had the same sense as Shakespeare that man is an extraordinarily beautiful creature. "So hath God marvellously garnished the heaven and the earth with so absolutely perfect plenty, variety and beauty of all things as possibly might be, as it were a large and gorgeous house furnished and stored with abundance of most finely chosen stuff, last of all how in framing man and adorning him with so goodly beauty, and with so many and so great gifts he had shewed in him the most excellent example of all his works." (*Institutes of the Christian Religion,* I, 14, par. 20.) Again and again he extols man as a token of God's glory, replenished with infinite miracle. There was much divergence between Shakespeare and Calvin when they came to examine the flimsiness of this pretty toy of creation. The quintessence of dust, Shakespeare called him, and Calvin spoke of a cottage of clay. But Calvin promised that some of this clay would be translated to predestined glory, while Shakespeare is silent and leaves his damned world damned forever on his page.

It is therefore not at all surprising that later generations have substituted for the reality of the text of *Hamlet* a mitigating legend. They could not expel the work from its place in literature, for it is too beautiful. It has the patent beauty of a court, of courtiers dressed for great intricate ceremonies, of sword-play and pavanes and strolling players, of a mad scene with strewn flowers, of lovely, doomed young people. It draws its beautiful cartoon of Renaissance man in his prime; and the deep beauty of its verse makes our love of life take up arms refreshed. Though it is pessimistic, it does not diminish our courage but increases it, for to state despair so fully is to initiate hope. The delight we find in art amounts to recognition of a saving grace, to an acknowledgment that the problem of life has a solution implicit in its own nature, though not yet formulated by the intellect. The play was therefore kept in the library by enchanted readers, and in the theater also by enchanted audiences and by actors and actresses who found it gave them as much fame as they had power to take. There was no way of getting rid of this formidable work of art.

But if one were not a pessimist, and if one were a Pelagian, and believed that to be happy one had only to be good, and that it was possible to be very good indeed, there was really nothing to do with the play but put on a bold and fraudulent face and pretend that its meaning is something quite other than what actually lies on the page. This was not a very hard task, given man's power to persuade himself of anything that gives him comfort; and what mechanism was employed for this purpose can be seen by examining the position of Goethe. He was the arch-priest of the theory that Hamlet was a good man whose only fault was that he was not a robust specimen of his type, and could not bear the weight of the "great action" which his father had laid on his shoulders. "There is an oak tree planted in a costly jar, which should have borne only pleasant flowers within; the roots expand, the jar is shattered" (*Wilhelm Meister*, Bk. IV, ch. 13). Goethe could hardly lay greater emphasis on the element of irresolution in Hamlet's character: "He winds and turns and torments himself, he advances and recoils; is ever put in mind, ever puts himself in mind of his purpose, but at last all but puts it out of his thoughts, yet still without recovering his peace of mind" (ibid.).

Goethe was able to fly in the face of the text because he was the child of his time. He had revived for the late eighteenth century and early nineteenth century the conception of Renaissance man, fitting it into a philosophy which might be called, with reservations, pantheism. His contemplation of nature so satisfied him that he achieved an exquisite serenity which is beautiful in itself, but cannot be taken seriously as a philosophy because it is by no means certain that it would have remained intact had he been forced to take into account the proceedings of that part of man known as man in the twentieth century. The truth is that he was calm not so much because he was contemplating nature as because he was contemplating nature worked on by the bourgeoisie in their finest hour.

> Wo kam die schönste Bildung her
> Und wen sie nicht von Bürger wär?

> Whence does the finest culture come
> If not from the bourgeoisie?
>
> (*Zahme Xenieu,* Bk. IX)

he asked, and only the fanatic would seek to contradict him. "The bourgeoisie has been the first to show what man's activity can bring about. It has accomplished wonders far surpassing Egyptian pyramids, Roman aqueducts, and Gothic cathedrals. The bourgeoisie draws all nations into civilization, and in its rule of scarce one hundred years, has created more massive and colossal productive forms than have all preceding generations." This is, of course, an excessive tribute, but it was written not by Goethe but by Marx and Engels. Goethe, being a great poet, would have been more moderate, but he too was awed by the transformation of the world which had taken place since the rule of law and the advance of science had enabled industry to establish itself under the guidance of a new class inspired by this opportunity which was also a revelation.

Now, this had certainly altered the European conception of morality. Happy people whose happiness was due to their prosperity, which was due to their diligence in some form of labor, were naturally inclined to place high in their ethical code the duty of every man to find out what he could do and then do it. Irresolution would never help the wheels to go round in a factory or clear the shelves of a shop or fill the vaults of a bank; and, though the connection between Protestantism and early capitalism has been grossly oversimplified, the thesis that all activities, secular as well as sacred, of the elect redounded to the glory of God did in fact give a solemn majesty to honest trade. This gave action itself a status resembling that accorded to the virtues. Goethe was

78

credulous regarding the idealistic quality of Napoleon's actions because of their quantity; and in his "Maxims and Reflections" we read: "How can a man know himself? Never by observation, but through action. Try to do your duty, and you will know what is in you. And what is your duty? Your daily task!" Goethe was plainly unwilling to accept anything so alien from his historical situation as Shakespeare's terrible conviction that man could indeed know himself through action, and that the knowledge would always be shameful. But as an artist Goethe could not jettison Shakespeare. He could only pretend that his plays were as a man of less disturbing genius might have written them two centuries later.

But Goethe gives us a clue to another element in *Hamlet* which historical change had by this time made unacceptable. It is to be noted that when Goethe makes Wilhelm Meister plan an adaptation of *Hamlet* for performance by the strolling players, it is remarkable for its omissions. He suppresses most of the references to the disturbances in Norway, the activities of the young Fortinbras and the settling of the feud with the Danish house, Fortinbras' march to Poland, and his appearance at Elsinore, as well as the dispatch of Hamlet into England, his capture by pirates, and the death of Rosenkrantz and Guildenstern; and for these he substitutes an over-incidented and insignificant imbroglio with Norway. Though the supreme interest of the play was for him its human relationships, he intended these omissions to emphasize that the tragedy of Hamlet was the tragedy of a king as well as of a man, but in fact their effect is to diminish the international importance of the Danish court, and even its national importance, and to obscure the vital function of the king, whose duty it was to maintain the law by his domestic and foreign policy.

There is manifest a huge historical difference between Shakespeare and his adaptor. Shakespeare had, for one thing, a great deal less constitutional history to master, and consequently he knew it better. He had in his mind, bright as a new-minted coin, the conception of the English monarchy as it had emerged since the end of feudalism, created in order to end that system's tally of disorder. But since Shakespeare's death absolutism had triumphed in some European areas, and in England, where it had been defeated, the situation was confused by the long debate between the confused upholders of the divine right of kings and the equally confused upholders of an anointed monarchy working in double harness with unanointed Parliaments; and the French Revolution, which had actually erased the remains of absolutism as it existed in an unhappy symbiotic relationship with an imperfect form of representative government, had been simplified by the popular mind into a pure attack on absolutism. The situation was a great deal more difficult to grasp than it had been in Shakespeare's time. It was natural therefore that at the beginning of the nineteenth century many readers should think of a king as a supremely privileged person who, as the saying goes, "enjoyed" power, who had the first call on the wealth and obedience of his subjects, and who had no need to fear or envy anybody. A court, therefore, was in their imagination a happy place. It is to be noted that Goethe writes of Hamlet's father's murder and the son's perturbation as if these were disturbances of a normally relaxed and placid atmosphere.

But Shakespeare cannot have seen a court as a happy place, or conceived of a king as "enjoying" power. He could conceive of a king as being infatuated with power and rushing to embrace it, but it would be for him an act like rushing on a sword. He would have been astonished to talk with the many people in our world who tenderly imagine royalty as troubled only by a segregation from the ordinary joys and sorrows of humanity, which makes them (by a compensatory process not too direct) long to milk cows at the Petit Trianon. To Shakespeare a king was a man who had been appointed by fate, by a force half within him and half outside him, to be the custodian of an idea, and to exercise this function in the midst of a mob of barons who were rarely if ever entirely loyal to him or the idea, because some part of even the justest among them must regret the old days of feudalism when they could riot and thieve unchecked. To Shakespeare a king rocked backward and forward on a vertiginous see-saw. For he was bound to the law and had therefore to submit to the limitation of his monarchical power; but at times of crisis he had to resort to absolutism for the purpose of presenting a united front to whatever enemy was at the moment attacking his realm, since the machinery of Parliamentary government was not yet sufficiently developed to meet such emergencies. The king had then to seek the support of the barons, which meant that he must eliminate those who opposed him—which might bring on him the charge of tyranny, deposition and death, whether he deserved it or not.

This sort of king was never safe. We know from the historical plays that Shakespeare recognized danger as the climate of courts, and it follows that he saw the palace at Elsinore as a place of tension, where it might well be that Hamlet was much less tense than the people around him. He was above all the onlooker, who is detached and preserves his detachment even when he is involved in action. He was in fact detached from the Danish royal situation; because the electors had passed over his candidature he was not sitting on the throne, he was standing beside it, he was not involved in the struggle between the Danish people and their nascent institutions. He was also the new-born Renaissance man, whose liberated intelligence had given him a form of self-awareness which differed from the earlier forms of introspection, because it had no tinge of the confessional about it. When Hamlet soliloquized, he really was talking to himself, and taking pleasure in a recently acquired accomplishment. There could be no greater mistake than to see Hamlet as the only troubled figure in a court that was otherwise wax-work calm in the arrogant composure of an imaginary absolutism. Readers who see him thus must mistake the theme of the play, and see it as the failure of a weak human being to restore a pleasant status quo. But Shakespeare was writing about the failure of a strong and gifted man to alter a repellent situation, for the reason that he is tainted with the same guilt which has caused others to produce that situation.

If we are not loyal to our duty of finding out what it was that Shakespeare actually wrote, because our timidity or our ignorance makes us recoil from his commemoration of misfortune, we deny ourselves the opportunity of seeing how prodigiously fortune favored his genius. That writer is happy whose age helps him to find the proper mold for his substance, and in this respect Shakespeare was very happy. When he looked about him he saw many things, and among them was this situation, which he had observed either in the material world or in imagination, of the two men, both of considerable stature, both ready to justify their existence by the use of the will, and both doomed to failure, one after the other, because they were made of the same clay— which, nevertheless, was glorious stuff. When Shakespeare wanted to tell this story, the dominating political process of English history, the establishment of the monarchy, suggested an appropriate form for the telling. He was able to make the first man a king and the second a usurper. The phase of history which was his pattern offered advantages which we should note as peculiar. During this phase there were debated the vital issues which are written of in the Bible and which face every man in his time, making demands which vary according to his condition but which always seem excessive, and the debate was gloriously comprehensible. There were not so many deeds by then that they crowded the chroniclers' pages; the story was relatively easy to follow. As for words, though the Tudor pamphleteers had by Shakespeare's day degraded controversy, the bulk of the causes which had arisen had been debated by contenders who argued from the same premises, and who, since they were born to the status of disputants, were trained in disputation. But, more valuable still, this phase of history gave an example to any artist who concerned himself with it, in the field of the artistic process itself. For it was a movement toward simplicity. It sought to unify complicated and disordered things. It stretched out its hand to command moderation, though its origin was in exuberance. It directed its attention from the chaotic mob to the small significant group, to one single supremely important figure. That the single figure was a king, like a king in the fairy tales, gave a sense of familiarity, but what was done by this king in each of his manifestations was always new, or it would not have satisfied the hitherto unsatisfied need which history was continually creating and the political life was continually trying to satisfy. In fact, England was acting as an artist works, preserving tradition and at the same time adding to it; and the ultimate value of the state was the prime ingredient of literature, the individual. In every age writers have used the public life as a symbol of the private life, and have described the government of the state as they conceived it when they were thinking of man's attempts to order his nature, but few were as fortunate as Shakespeare in the material they found to their hand.

84

PART TWO

The Crowded Court

1 *The Great Optimist*

In following any issue raised by Shakespeare and treated again by writers of a later age, it is usually necessary to quit the field of the drama. Nobody has ever been able to explain why quite a number of English writers in the reign of Queen Elizabeth and King James were able to produce poetic dramas which were works of genius or of high talent, and why no writer in English has since then produced any important work in this form. The descent from Shakespeare, Marlowe, Ben Jonson, Ford and Webster, to Sheridan Knowles and W. G. Wills and Stephen Phillips has sometimes been treated as if it were due to a change in the practice of poetry, but surely the cause lies in something recalcitrant within the dramatic form itself. It is much more difficult to pretend that there is a thing called the drama which is not just a number of plays, than it is to pretend that there is a thing called poetry which is more than a number of poems, or that there is a thing called the novel which is more than a number of novels. It is an error to suppose that there exist in literature the equivalents of biological species, which comprise numbers of specimens alike enough to be considered as variations of the same pattern, and which reproduce their kind; but it is almost impossible to imagine the drama to be such a species. It follows no laws. We might contemplate the fact that Stephen Phillips, at the beginning of this century, wrote poetic dramas much inferior to Shakespeare, and decide that this justified the conclusion that people had stopped being able to write dramas in verse, were it not that at the same time dramatists such as Henry Arthur Jones

87

and Pinero were writing plays in prose even more inferior to the works of Congreve and even Sheridan than Stephen Phillips' plays were inferior to the works of Shakespeare. It might be tempting to try an alternative conclusion that men of talent were not attempting then to write for the theater; but that conclusion does not hold water either, for Tennyson, Browning, Swinburne, Henry James, and George Moore all wrote plays which were still worse than the work of Henry Arthur Jones and Pinero. Whatever page is turned in the history of the drama, it is always inscribed with a conundrum. To visit the exquisite little theater in Bergen, where Ibsen's plays were first presented, is to wonder how it happened that a writer who had no experience save of the provincial stage in a small country should write plays which have ever since challenged and gratified the technique of the most accomplished actors and actresses in the countries possessing the longest and richest theatrical tradition; while, at the time he wrote, those countries were listening to the clodhopperies of Tom Robertson and Sardou. And again, why did Oscar Wilde write one delightfully expert farce and a number of ridiculously amateurish melodramas? And why did Shaw and his audiences consider him a dramatist of ideas when he had few and his strength lay in the evocation of character? How does it happen that Sartre has written several exciting and amusing plays when he is a dull and unoriginal novelist?

But humanity is never more sphinxlike than when it is expressing itself. Though we can sometimes understand why people have performed momentous actions, it is very rarely that we can tell why they have produced momentous works of art. This blank wall surrounding the artistic process exasperates most when we come to

88

ask why great writers ceased to choose the poetic drama as their medium and turned to the novel, because it was a tragic step. They have never been able to produce as momentous works of art in the new field, and this was inevitable, because the poetic drama gives certain facilities to the writer seeking to describe the inner life which must be denied him by the novel. To begin with, poetry lifts from literature the handicap which bows it down while the other arts go free. The paint that a painter uses on his canvas is not the same sort of paint which we put on our houses to protect them from the weather, and the sounds with which musicians charm the air are not the same we use when we toot our horns to warn pedestrians that our automobile is coming, or when we call the cattle home. But the writer uses words, the same words that are used to make out a laundry list, to frame an advertisement for a baby-sitter, to draw up a deed of partnership. This use of language to secure the satisfaction of our material needs must create a narrowing predisposition on the part of everyone who reads or listens to a verbal communication. In a laundry list one must state exactly how many garments one has sent to be washed and describe them accurately; if one wants a baby-sitter, one must make it plain when one wants her and for how long; and contracts must name the parties and define their mutual obligations; and above all there is no occasion for excitement, and it should be done as briefly as is decent. Now, the writer who is describing the inner life of our kind must use language even more precisely than is customary in these utilitarian communications. But whereas nobody would send a thousand pairs of stockings to the laundry, it may well be that a man might feel a thousand desires, a thousand discontents; a woman might want not a baby-sitter

89

but a friend, a lover, a king, and he and she might seek to bind each other by exorbitant conditions, too exorbitant to be fulfilled, of a quality hard to realize on this earth. It is impossible to avoid excitement in rendering a just account of this ambitious thing, the inner life, and in no art is there any particular necessity to be brief. There is no more reason that a book should be short than that a picture should be small.

Therefore it is meet that an author must announce at the first possible moment that he is engaged in an enterprise quite different from the writing of a laundry list, an advertisement, or a legal document; and he can best do this by putting his language into the court dress of poetry. This is, in some countries, done by simple people in the course of daily life when it takes a turn toward grandeur. Montegrins, for example, deliberately resort to blank verse when they are entertaining strangers or are relating stories of their ancestors and their battles; and when the Balkan countries were newly liberated from the Turks and the inhabitants were proud of their new Parliaments, statesmen with important speeches to make made them in the same meter. In the nineties the ministers of finance in Serbia and Bulgaria always introduced their budgets in blank verse. The writer of a poetic drama at once intimates by his choice of medium that he is dealing with a subject which he and the spectators will recognize as solemn, and declares that he is making up his spiritual budget, he is balancing profit and loss, as in the sphere of his inner life.

It is true that there are two great dramatists, neither of them English, who dealt with the inner life in prose plays and convinced their time, and look as though they are convincing posterity: Ibsen and Chekhov. But Ibsen was a poet, and believed the plays he wrote in verse to be his best work; and as he grew older his prose plays showed such discontent with their condition that the last of them are almost as far away from daily life as *The Tempest;* and Chekhov confirms our fears that the dramatist has lost much by abandoning poetry. Now, when we go to see a Chekhov play, we all know what we are going to see; but those of us who were present at the first English performances of *The Seagull* and *The Cherry Orchard* remember that audiences not familiar with the text found it difficult to gather from the first act whether they were going to see an amusing copy of a specially incoherent sort of life or a serious interpretation of life which would reduce its incoherence. Chekhov, moreover, gives us another reason why the flight of the dramatist from poetry was regrettable, for though he had a genius for the creation of character, the fact that he is writing in prose denies him the resource which Shakespeare used for the underlining of character when he made Othello speak a special sort of music, rolling and splendid and unintellectual as thunder. We know how Madame Ranevsky spoke to her lover and her family and her friends and her servants, but we know what she said and how she said it rather than what she was as she said it, and it is hard to say how we could be given that additional information save by the evocative power of verse.

When we see how much dramatists have lost by their emigration to prose, we must suspect that writers have sacrificed far more by devoting themselves to the novel, which is now emphatically a matter of prose. Theoretically there is no reason why realistic accounts of the lives of men and women should not be written in verse, and Chaucer certainly managed it very well. But in recent centuries hardly anyone has succeeded in this

91

field except Crabbe; and numerous efforts such as *Evangeline* and *Aurora Leigh* suggest that this is an enterprise from which, to borrow a phrase from the pious, "blessing has been withheld." But the novel, though committed to prose, is not a medium which any but the bigoted perfectionist will despise. Many novels have been written to which no sensible and sensitive person would deny the title of greatness, and the form shows its biological fitness by its sturdy survival through the centuries to the present day. All the same there are tests which it cannot pass; and this is true even when we turn to the novels of Fielding, who, in the largeness of his creation, is most like Shakespeare. He would inevitably come under notice in an enquiry into the use of the public life by writers whose interest is in the private life, for he was as much committed to politics as he was to the imagination.

It is better to examine *Amelia* rather than *Tom Jones* for our purpose, because, whatever the respective merits of the books, *Amelia* begins with a *tour de force* which has never been surpassed. There is depicted, with the truthfulness and the tender anger characteristic of Fielding, a London prison, crammed with the diseased and pitiful and debased creatures who were its normal inhabitants. Into this dreary hell there enters a young army officer, Billy Booth, who has been charged with assaulting a watchman, simply because he had been walking home at night and had come on two men cruelly beating a third, whom he tried to rescue. But when the watch came up he arrested Billy Booth, for no other reason than that the young man had come out with empty pockets and the two hooligans had money on them and could raise a bribe. In the prison Billy Booth meets an old friend, a young woman named Miss Matthews, who has been brought in for stabbing to death her faithless lover. By the same art which Fielding exhibits throughout *Tom Jones*, it is perfectly conveyed that these two people are both in a state of glowing health and happy instinctive living, which affords an extreme contrast with the miserable wrecks round them. Miss Matthews has money on her and is able to buy the comfort of a private apartment, and there the two settle down and tell each other just how it happens that each has come to this present pass, why she had murdered her lover, and why he had no money in his pockets. Miss Matthews tells a story of violated innocence, to which Billy Booth listens sympathetically, with many expressions of assent and astonishment. However it is borne in on the reader that Miss Matthews' innocence can never have been violated, for no man could ever move speedily enough to forestall her own amorous intentions, and that Billy Booth knows this quite well but is accepting the story out of an innate kindliness, which feels that if she finds it easier to live on these assumptions she might as well be allowed to do so. The reader also learns that Miss Matthews will probably betray this kindliness, for she is not only a humbug, she is well on the way to becoming a harpy. When Billy tells his story, it is apparent that he is deeply in love with his wife, Amelia, and that she is deeply in love with him, and that Fielding considers this marriage as of great moral importance. Yet as the conversation between Billy and Miss Matthews continues, it can be seen that as soon as these two people stop talking they will fall into each other's arms; and this, Fielding conveys, inflicts an injury on Billy Booth's marriage, but cannot touch its essence.

This dazzling introduction leads into a realistic study of the hideousness which the eighteenth century imposed on both rich and poor almost as lavishly as it dispensed beauty. We now take it for granted that an educated man can, except in time of war, get himself out of the way of gross hazards, but it was not so in Fielding's age. Billy Booth was an educated man, who took a great joy in the classics, and he deeply longed for a quiet life with his Amelia, who was all he thought her, gay and good, like a hummingbird with moral genius; but his world would not permit it. It is the habit of critics to condemn Billy Booth as a weak sensualist who had only himself to blame for his troubles, but he lived in a world so dangerous that it encouraged the anodyne indulgences. The conception of honor, which in earlier times had been a helpful recognition that the pleasure-pain principle was not enough, had produced the bloody and boring pedantry of the duel. Poor Amelia was forever in danger of being left a widow because of this idiotic practice, and it would be absurd to pretend that Billy's courage was so great that he was made more stable by this constant risk of death. Even when life was preserved it was hard to maintain. The expansion of trade and finance had upset the bookkeeping system of society, and people who had been launched into the world in a state of economic overconfidence, because there always had been a living for their privileged kind, might find themselves without means of support and would fall into debt, which in those days meant dropping through a trap door into the underworld. That was a savage place indeed. Society had not learned how to keep its expanding cities clean or how to bring their increasing populations under the law; and more and more people lived by urban parasitic occupations, which gave them no sense of process and therefore allowed them to lack a healthy fear of destruction. In times of insecurity the class which

94

finds itself dispossessed always turns to gambling, and the London underworld was glad to go into the service of this or any other vice. Strong degenerative forces were pitted against poor Billy Booth, and would have been victorious had it not been for Amelia, and for Sergeant Atkinson, who, though a bumpkin married to a pretentious slut, was a good man, and so could work the same miracle that Amelia did. For it was Fielding's belief that, squalid as the world might be, the virtues of human beings could transform it and absolve it.

In fact, Fielding was engaged in the same argument as Shakespeare, but was on the opposite side. He had been born only ninety-one years after Shakespeare's death, and their preoccupations were much the same, in spite of a fundamental disagreement. Fielding was as interested as Shakespeare in the monarchy but made no fanciful adaptation of the problem to suit his genius; he took it as he found it in the real world about him. He was there faced with the legitimate king, in the person of the Young Pretender, and the usurper, George the Second, and he settled without the slightest disturbance of his spirit in favor of the usurper, because he accepted without reserve the contractual basis of monarchy. If a king did not govern well he must go, it was as simple as that; and with that simple principle to guide him he became a vigorous anti-Jacobite. What sort of king he wanted is shown in a digression in *Tom Jones* (Bk. XII, ch. 12). There he admits that mankind has never been so happy as when the greater part of the known world was under the rule of five successive princes who were absolute monarchs (Nerva, Trajan, Hadrian, and the two Antonines) and that a benevolent autocracy is obviously the ideal form of government, but goes on to proclaim the impossibility of finding autocrats of guaranteed benevolence. He makes a robust answer to the doctrine of the divine right of kings:

> In short, our own religion furnishes us with adequate ideas of the blessing, as well as curse, which may attend absolute power. The pictures of heaven and of hell will place a very lively image of both before our eyes; for though the prince of the latter can have no power, but what he originally derives from the omnipotent Sovereign in the former, yet it plainly appears from Scripture that absolute power in his infernal dominions is granted to their diabolical ruler. This is indeed the only absolute power which can by Scripture be derived from heaven. If, therefore, the several tyrannies upon earth can prove any title to a divine authority, it must be derived from this original grant to the prince of darkness; and these subordinate deputations must consequently come immediately from him whose stamp they so expressly bear. To conclude, as the examples of all ages shew us that mankind in general desire power only to do harm, and when they obtain it, use it for no other purpose . . .

He goes on to express his confidence in Parliament:

> In this case it will be much wiser to submit to a few inconveniences arising from the dispassionate deafness of laws, than to remedy them by applying to the passionate open ears of a tyrant.

At this point his logic has failed him; if it be true that "mankind in general desire power only to do harm," then parliaments, which through the years aim with increasing urgency to represent "mankind in general," must desire power only to do harm. But it is really not worth while making that point against him. His political passions were based on experience of a kind which we must all respect. Because Fielding's father was a thriftless donkey, Fielding sought, in his adolescence, with all the simplicity of Billy Booth, to earn his bread by writing pornography and political squibs that were quite insincere and were aimed at attracting patronage. But he was to learn all he could from libertinage and then forget it in one of the happiest marriages the great have ever achieved; and in the course of turning over the carcass of politics to see where he could cut off a slice for his own coarse feeding, he gradually became aware how the carrion stank and what an ugly thing it was compared to its own self, as that might be were it living and unmutilated.

He became infatuated with the idea of good government and saw it in the simplest terms, in Shakespearean terms: as a movement of honest people against First, Second, and Third Murderers, who, when Banquo said, "It will be rain tonight," answered, "Let it come down," and stabbed him. Such crime had for him associations which evoked his deep personal emotion, and so did its remedy, politics. That can be seen in the strange book, *The Life of Jonathan Wild the Great:* strange in that it is written with a passion that one would think that no man could lavish on any but his own child. Yet the theme is the parallel between the famous thieftaker Wild and the prime minister, Sir Robert Walpole and this was not his own—it had already been done to death by the Grub Street pamphleteers. It was as if he liked to contemplate the equal corruption of the despised and the honored, as if he had that appetite for eating earth which doctors used to call pica. The dark life of the London streets, with their runnels of sewage, and their parallel streams of violent acts, the hideous roughhouse fun of

Newgate Prison, where even the minister of Christ was a drunken humbug and a buffoon, the death on the scaffold, as lonely and graceless as if it were a rat that died: all these were to him that reality which was, to use the word in its literal sense, charming, which compelled his attention, which insisted on being the medium of his action and his thought.

This preoccupation with crime lasted all his short life. When he was made a magistrate, in 1748, at the age of forty-one, the appointment brought him a slight relief from his financial cares; but it also brought him spiritual satisfaction. During the six years which remained to him he was so tormented and crippled by gout that he might well have drawn his pay and done as little work as was allowed. But just at that time there was a strange outbreak of crime which presented a curious parallel to the gangsterism of our own days. Robbery and murder became so common in the urban streets and on the highways that people of any property hardly dared leave their houses even in broad daylight, and on this structure of simple crime the more intelligent criminals began to form elaborate organizations with as much confidence and competence as if they had been honest enterprises. Fielding himself believed that he had dealt with a conspiracy to kill the Lord Chancellor which had been formed by three gaming-house proprietors whose premises he had closed. He went into the attack on this outbreak as into a holy war, wearing himself out with the performance of duties far greater than would be laid on a magistrate today. It is as if a contemporary novelist, of the highest rank and still practicing (for Fielding was yet to write *Amelia*) was also to sit on the bench at Bow Street, act as Commissioner at Scotland Yard, and be a journalist specializing in penal matters. Fielding tried

98

his cases and encouraged the public to seek the protection of his court, and put an end to the intimidation of witnesses; he strengthened the police force and introduced such innovations as a register of convicted persons which was the nucleus of the existing Criminal Record Office at Scotland Yard; he himself, sick man though he was, took part in police raids; and he poured out pamphlets and essays on the reform of prisons and the criminal law.

In theory and in practice he often showed the most high-handed disregard for the civil rights of the persons involved, and it would be possible to make out a case for considering him the first enthusiast for the police state in England. But that would be grossly unhistorical. At that time the development of parliamentary power must have seemed, particularly to a Whig like Fielding, a guarantee against all forms of tyranny. There can be no question that his intentions were benevolent. The treatises he wrote recommending schemes for the extirpation of crime are full of a desire to protect the innocent from violence and to induce the criminal to abandon his aggressions, and he felt humanitarian rage against the state of the prisons. But he was not one of those reformers who regarded the criminal as a helpless victim of ill luck. He saw him as one in the grip of a loathsome form of evil, which might have been attracted to him in the first place by his misfortunes, but which he must have invited to remain with him by some consenting act of the will. He believed that the criminal has rejected salvation.

Fielding conceived the means of salvation in a fashion that is strangely familiar to us. Though he was a passionate and even bigoted Protestant, his work is saturated with the idea of the female who intercedes for the sinning soul and raises it to the skies. This is evident in *Jonathan Wild*. There Wild has set himself to ruin an honest jeweler, Mr. Heartfree, and after arranging for his gang to rob the poor man of most of his possessions, gets his creditors to arrest him and send him to prison. Then he induces Mrs. Heartfree to go to Holland with the remainder of her husband's stock, which he means to have stolen from her when she is alone and friendless abroad. This enables him to see to it that Mr. Heartfree is charged with another and more serious offense, with having sent his wife out of the country with his goods in order to defraud his creditors; and by plots and perjuries he gets Heartfree convicted and sentenced to death. The unhappy man is being led out to execution when suddenly Mrs. Heartfree appears before him, and while she faints in his arms news comes that he has been reprieved, because an accomplice of Wild's has confessed. Mrs. Heartfree has brought back her husband's jewels intact, with, added to them, a marvelous diamond presented to her in the course of some unforeseen adventures by an African chief much impressed by her resistance to his advances; and she and her husband are able to start life again as happy and honored citizens, while Jonathan Wild goes to the scaffold. Now *Jonathan Wild* is an extravaganza, a farce, a political squib, a tract on penal reform; and Mrs. Heartfree's story of her journey is a double parody of contemporary travelers' tales and romances in which the heroine resisted temptation not now and again, but again and again and again. Fielding had seen too many innocents twitched into lifelong misery, or even toward their death, by the stupidity of a magistrate or the communal tolerance of an obsolete law, to write without irony that Mrs. Heartfree considered it "the surest truth, THAT PROVIDENCE WILL, SOONER OR LATER, PROCURE THE FELICITY OF THE VIRTUOUS

AND INNOCENT" (*Jonathan Wild,* Bk. IV, ch. 2). Yet surely there is a certain seriousness in his treatment of the Heartfrees' marriage; and it is a picture that he painted in all his novels, each time with increasing gravity. Joseph Andrews would be nothing if he were not true to his Fanny; Tom Jones would be a brute and a boor if he proved unworthy of Sophia Western; Billy Booth would sink down into the world of Jonathan Wild were it not for his Amelia.

All these redemptory women must have been associated with some principle which Fielding had observed as operating in the universe, and which he approved. Sophia of "Tom Jones" must, in fact, be truly named and must represent Heavenly Wisdom; and Fielding more than once identified that principle for his readers. He thought that it was manifested within the human being and took the form of Good Nature, which he counts as the most valuable of attributes. Now, it would again be easy to regard Fielding as superficial in this view; but to tax him with this fault is always to be guilty of superficiality oneself. He is not shallow in his choice of this virtue, as he shows in a passage relating to false amiability in *An Essay on the Knowledge of the Characters of Men*:

> Men are chiefly betrayed into this deceit by a gross but common mistake of good humour for good nature. Two qualities so far from bearing any resemblance to each other, that they are almost opposites. Good nature is that benevolent and amiable temper of mind, which disposes us to feel the misfortunes and enjoy the happiness of others; and, consequently, pushes us on to promote the latter, and prevent the former; and that without any ab-

101

stract contemplation on the beauty of virtue, and without the allurements and terrors of religion. Now, good humour is nothing more than the triumph of the mind, when reflecting on its own happiness, and that perhaps, from having compared it with the inferior happiness of others.

This is, of course, quite Pelagian. It is true that in quoting a description of God as "the best-natured Being in the universe" he raised the possibility that he might consider Good Nature as the result of the operation of Grace. But he continues:

The more therefore we cultivate the sweet disposition in our minds the nearer we draw to divine perfection; to which we should be the more strongly incited, as it is that which we may approach the nearest to. All His other attributes throw us immediately out of sight, but *this virtue lies in will, and not at all in power.*

It is to be remembered that he several times specifically rejects the doctrine of total depravity. This quality of good nature is a human achievement, and it is conditional on intelligence; for Fielding comes to the conclusion:

That, as good-nature requires a distinguishing faculty, which is another word for judgment, and is perhaps the sole boundary between wisdom and folly; It is impossible for a fool, who hath no distinguishing faculty to be good-natured.

This explains the importance he attaches to classical studies, which he believed would make men's minds exact, just as many people today hope that scientific studies will perform the same task. Obviously, the more intelligent a man was, the more good-natured he would be. So in his argument with Shakespeare his position was that something, but not everything, was wrong with the court of Elsinore, and that Hamlet would certainly be able to set it right because he was the most intelligent person there.

Shakespeare disagreed, and showed it once and for all by making Hamlet send unshriven men to their death. But neither settled the argument, and it is continuing today. Graham Greene is even now pursuing Pelagianism round the landscape with an axe, and might very well write a modern version of *Amelia,* with Billy Booth and his brother officers and Miss Matthews translated into civil servants, while Amelia would be represented as the really bad person in the book, because by her beautiful cultivation of the natural affections she was disguising the advanced putridity of life, while Jonathan Wild was borrowed from his volume to play the part of the sort of human being which does not do that disservice to God, Who would certainly not be represented as the best-natured Being in the universe. This reflection forces on our attention the essential impurity of literature. For we know that in this contention the victory goes to Shakespeare, against Henry Fielding and Graham Greene, because his plays are greater than their works, and that as between Henry Fielding and Graham Greene, a victory lies with Fielding because, though *Brighton Rock* and *The Heart of the Matter* are good novels or *The Quiet American, Joseph Andrews* and *Tom Jones* and *Amelia* are still better. It is obvious, however, that this is only one sort of "victory," and there are other victories to be won in other fields. Quite apart from their aesthetic merit, in the conduct of this argument the authors score different degrees of success in approaching the truth in their argument about the salvation of man. Yet, again their books as obviously owe their importance largely to the fact that they are engaged in this argument.

There is no reason to suppose that this situation can be clarified beyond a certain point; but there is a pleasant clarity about Fielding's artistic situation. He was a self-conscious artist who was aware of his own struggles with his medium; and he discusses them freely, most notably in the first chapters of each book of *Tom Jones,* an achievement which makes us wonder whether literature is not too tightly corseted today. A contemporary author would receive cold looks from his publisher if he submitted a novel which, like *Tom Jones,* was eighteen times interrupted by short essays on the method of composition he had followed, and the critical theory behind it. A few of the essays in *Tom Jones* do deserve cold looks, but in most of them he makes a very fair business of writing an equivalent to Aristotle's *Poetics* for the novel. He was of the opinion that a critic who was that and nothing more should restrict himself to reviewing and leave the establishment of critical theory to creative writers, who alone could know of what they spoke. He felt that noncreative critics tended to declare that they had discovered laws when they had only detected precedents. "Little circumstances," he wrote, "which were perhaps accidental in a great author, were by those critics considered to constitute his chief merit, and transmitted as essentials to be observed by all his successors" (*Tom Jones,* Bk. V, ch. 1). Magnificently, he claims to regard such prescriptions as impertinent. "As I am, in reality, the founder of a new province of writing [which he defines as "prosai-comi-epic writing" or the "heroic, historical prosaic poem"] so I am at liberty to make what laws I please therein" (Bk. II, ch. 1). He is in fact claiming to have liberated invention from the confines of adventure and set it loose on the wider field of experience; and his claim is justified, though it may be disputed by the admirers of Richardson. For Fielding's aim was to give an objective picture of his characters, a God's eye view, while Richardson, by telling stories in the form of letters, falsifies all his main characters by showing them in the falsifying attitude of a letter writer, who puts pen to paper with the express purpose of imposing on his correspondent a certain impression of himself. The author may give away the truth behind the falsification; but it is as much a limitation as if a portrait painter were to depict all his models looking from behind a veil.

Fielding promises that he will make the laws of the new form with a kindly consideration for the capacity of human attention, and to that end he will be guided by two principles. But these turn out to be only one, for the first proves to be the Principle of Selection, and the second the Principle of Lively and Varied Presentation, and it is hard to imagine an author selecting material without regard for its vitality. Fielding submits that before an author can apply these principles successfully he must be endowed with four gifts. The first is Genius, which he defines as "that power, or rather those powers, of the mind which are capable of penetrating into all things within our reach and knowledge and of distinguishing their essential differences" (Bk. IX, ch. 1). He emphatically states a preference for observation over what he calls "a creative faculty," and thinks common sense to be very important indeed; and it is clear that he is trying to urge the claims of imagination which keeps in touch with reality, against the tradition of fancy, which had been developed by the romance-writers and was no more than doodling. In addition to Genius, the writer must have learning ("a competent knowledge of history and of the belles lettres is here absolutely necessary") and he must have "the sort of knowledge beyond the power of learning to bestow and this is to be had by conversation:" by this latter he means that the ideal author must be what Dryden called Chaucer, "a man of a most wonderful comprehensive genius." He must also have "what is generally meant by a good heart, and be capable of feeling" (Bk. IX, ch. 1). He must, in fact, be able to analyze experience and synthesize his findings in a form that favors the continuance of society.

The novelist who is applying the Principles of Selection and of Lively and Varied Presentation, by the light of his own genius, his learning, his comprehension of human nature, and his good heart, must follow four technical rules. He must keep his plots within the bounds of Possibility: no ghost, no elves, no fairies. He must keep within the bounds of Probability: no people who are ebony black in guilt, none who are snow-white in innocence. He must also keep his characters from performing actions which are beyond their capacities or incongruous with their natures. "I will venture to say that for a man to act in direct contradiction to the dictates of his nature is, if not impossible, as improbable and as miraclous as anything which can well be conceived (Bk. VIII, ch. 1)." The aim of these restrictions can be realized in a phrase in his gloss on the last of them. "Should the best parts of the story of M. Antoninus be ascribed to Nero, or should the worst incidents of Nero's life be imputed to Antoninus, what would be more shocking to belief than either instance?" (ibid.). A phrase trembled on his lips which was not to be uttered till a man then unborn spoke of the "willing suspension of unbelief for the moment, which constitutes poetic faith."

But even as we read Fielding's happy defense of the new form, knowing how triumphantly he and many others were to use it, the proof appears of its inferiority to the poetic drama, its incapacity to produce an equal faith. Prose keeps so close to the utilitarian use of language that it constantly arouses in both writer and reader associations with the real world which draw them away from the imaginary world where they should remain. It was bound to happen that Fielding constantly interrupted his analyses of the experiences of Tom Jones and Billy Booth in order to tell us about the routine of gaming-house or the defects of the bail bond system, and that everything practical in the reader should join in the distraction. The novel is always ambushed by the temptation to become informative on matters of fact, and this is not as great a disability as its comparative failure to give information on more relevant matters. We must note again that a prose writer is under a grave handicap because he can create a character only by describing him or her and making him perform actions and utter expressions congruous with his nature, and cannot underline his conception of that nature as a poet can, by suggestions arising from the music of verse. But a still greater handicap is the loss of the poetic soliloquy, which is uniquely potent as a revelation of the inner self. Dialogue can rarely go as deep, for what any person says in the presence of others is to some degree conditioned by his relationship with them, and is thus deflected from candor. Skillful dialogue may achieve candor by implication, but that is a sleight-of-hand performance which is not solemn. The writer's comment is too remote; and the interior monologue, has, except in the hands of one great writer, failed to achieve intensity and has too often appeared as a droning reverie. None of these resources can convince

107

with the power of a soliloquy, a self-analysis forced out of character at a moment which poetry certifies to be of supreme importance.

If writers know that the form they are using will not permit them to express the deepest truth about their characters' natures, it may well be that they will not trouble to find out what that deepest truth is. Thus a limitation is imposed on the novelist which narrows his Genius, and limits the area of his "reach and knowledge," often at the point where he must carry conviction to his readers. For it often appears to readers that a man is acting in "direct contradiction to the dictates of his nature" for the reason that they have not sufficient information about that nature. They think that an Antoninus is being saddled with a Nero's story because they have falsely identified characters with Antoninus and Nero; and the author must be hampered, by comparison with the poetic dramatist, in furnishing them with sufficient information to correct their error, because his more slender resources have actually left him knowing less than he should. It is the special defect of the novel that it often does not wield the requisite authority.

2 *Optimism and Compromise*

To many of us it seems that there is one English novel which can be classed with Shakespeare's plays, and that is Emily Brontë's *Wuthering Heights*. That transcended the limitations of prose because it was written by a poet who had spent her years of apprenticeship in the writing of romances, much of them in verse and all of them set within the framework of a poetic cosmos; and she conferred on herself a great benefit by not having this early work published, and thus remaining exempt from criticism by the reviewers who were then imposing the standards of prose on an age of poetry. It was fortunate that a woman of genius had been born in isolation at a time when the romantic movement had loosened the inhibiting powers of the intellect and had stirred up dynamic forces long subdued, and she was able, fearless and undisturbed, to contemplate her visions. Among the inhabitants of her visionary world was the Byronic man, a vaguely troubled Hamlet, not quite sure what ghost it had seen. But the court meant nothing to her. She was as apolitical as an eagle on the moors. Yet she was a participant in the same argument that engaged Shakespeare and Fielding, coming in on Fielding's side. She believed that incorrupt will existed, and could save mankind.

It was as if in her isolation she practiced a forgotten art and made a new myth, with the same conviction as those who at the dawn of history first weaved tales to account for their kind and the universe, with no touch of timidity due to the defeat of the individual by civilization and its constant demand for caution and restraint.

The two households, the homes of the Lintons and the Earnshaws, can be conceived as forming an assembly of gods, who exist in harmony until one god, out of too careless benevolence, brings into the divine company a dark being, evil itself; and Mr. Earnshaw takes into his home the little Heathcliff. The goddess who is the most potent embodiment of good in this group of immortals consorts with the embodiment of evil, loving it, for love does not disdain evil—but it destroys her. Catherine Earnshaw loves Heathcliff and is killed by her involvement with him. Miraculously, from the slain goddess there springs up a new goddess, who is invulnerable, who cannot be slain, and who slays evil without a weapon, and releases its victims from their chains. Young Catherine, Catherine Earnshaw's daughter, defies Heathcliff, and by her love for her cousin Hartley she raises him from the serfdom that Heathcliff has imposed on him. Her marriage with the young man brings back the money out of which Heathcliff has swindled the two families into its rightful channel. That is a symbolic victory of great moment, for the money represents the orderliness now once more the rule of life in this territory, which had been laid waste and is now to blossom again.

In its cunning technique (so intricate that for a long time bumbling criticism mistook it for confusion) and in its exhaustive disclosure of its characters, *Wuthering Heights* is as yet unsurpassed. Emily Brontë brought something to the novel which was not known to Fielding, who for many years must have lain unsurprised in his grave. That is her miracle. She was the sole and glorious innovator in his field. But when Jane Austen had emerged, fifty years after his death and forty years before *Wuthering Heights* was written, he must have felt a progenitor's pride. Jenny James in *Amelia* is not so exquisitely drawn as an Austen character, but she has the same blood in her veins (Bk. IV, ch.1):

> "And lastly, she is both too short and too tall. Well, you may laugh Mr. James, I know what I mean, though I cannot well express it—I mean, that she is too tall for a pretty woman, and too short for a fine woman.—There is such a thing as a kind of insipid medium—a kind of something that is neither one thing or another. I know not how to express it more clearly; but when I say such a one is a pretty woman, a pretty thing, a pretty creature, you know very well I mean a little woman; and when I say such a one is a very fine woman, a very fine person of a woman, to be sure I must mean a tall woman. Now a woman that is between both is certainly neither the one nor the other."

But that conversation ends with Jenny, at the price of a longer season in London and a present of two hundred guineas, offering to help her husband seduce Amelia, and Miss Austen would have had nothing to do with such squalor. An abyss divides her from Fielding, cleft by the difference in their circumstances, sex, and period. Fielding had been a Bow Street magistrate when the spirit of the eighteenth century was half Ariel and half Caliban, and he had seen many darker things than came the way of a lady of good family living in villages and resorts in a later age, quite committed, so far as ladies were concerned, to refinement. But there was a deeper difference than that. Jane Austen was unable to feel any interest in woman as a redemptory figure leading man up to heaven; there was nothing of the pre-Sumerian mythmaker about her. What preoccupied her was the lot of Sophia Western's grand-daughters here on earth. They were doing not so badly and not so well. The magnificent simplicity of Tom Jones would no doubt have been too simple for Elizabeth Bennet, and keeping the complicated Mr. Darcy in order gave her a delicious opportunity for gay "conversations of steel," as the French used to call foil-bouts. Billy Booth would have been neither so intelligent nor so stable as Elinor Dashwood would have demanded (though he was better educated than she was), and Edward Ferrars must have given her a pleasant and solvent life from the beginning. Yet the change was not all that could have been hoped. It is good that women should be neither raped nor seduced but led to the altar after a reverent courtship; and it is good that the fathers of innocent girls should not feel free to behave in their homes like the lewd-spoken bumpkin Squire Western. But respectability is not enough. Jane Austen did not want to be raped or seduced, but she thought it was also bad to be jilted. Though she felt that Marianne made too much fuss over losing Willoughby, she recognized that the girl had been stabbed close to the heart. If she would have disliked to be Squire Western's daughter, neither did she esteem Mr. Bennet's barren cynicism or Mr. Woodhouse's selfish sickliness. She was revolted by the humiliation inflicted on Catherine Morland when General Tilney, after having invited her to his house, tried to turn her out of doors for no other reason than that he had discovered her not to be the heiress he had supposed and therefore not a desirable daughter-in-law. She wrote that blandly terrible sentence describing the emotions of Fanny Price, the poor relation who is asked in marriage by the son of the house: "Let no one presume to give the feelings of a young woman on receiving the assurance of that affection of which she has scarcely allowed herself to entertain a hope" (*Mansfield Park*,

112

ch. 48). The essential worth of a woman could then guarantee her little more than the vague respect of the community. Her fate was decided by the financial position of her parents, by the whims of her suitors, and by her success in suppressing positive opinions and impulses.

But the condition of all human beings was ridiculous. The best of them were endowed with gifts which should have endowed them to live freely according to the principles of love and justice. But they were all of them, good and bad, at one and the same time immortal souls and pieces in a game played by society. They were pegs which had to be fitted into holes on a board or thrown away; and the holes were far too few in number, and in size and shape ill-adapted to the pegs. Jane Austen has often been reproached as a chronicler of small beer on the ground that her works contain no mention of the Napoleonic wars, but she was obviously moved to this omission for the sound reason that she had nothing to say about them. She was not apolitical, for she had much to say about those parts of the social structure which she had opportunities to observe, and noted its worst feature, which was the inequality presumed among people who were in fact equal, and who had to be dishonest to ignore their equality. The rich despised the poor, and men despised women, and the poor were too anxious to please the rich, and women too anxious to please men.

It had always been so, but the contempt and complaisance were now present in an exaggerated form. The idea of status was dwindling away, and the idea of power was more and more dissociated from service and associated with money. Life had in many ways been much worse. No young woman in Jane Austen's world was in the precarious position of Katherine Howard; even if she lost her head in a metaphorical sense she still kept it physically. But there were a great number of people who knew themselves entitled by education and by birth to respect and who were despised because they were neither landowners nor shareholders, nor the daughters of such; and in their insecurity they formed a desire to attach themselves to the secure, by whatever suckers they chanced to find on their tentacles.

The terrible feature of Jane Austen's world is her best characters' complete realization that they must never live candidly and seek salvation by faithfulness to a moral code which set principle above opportunism. She was helped in bearing the consequences of this situation by her special and lovely gifts. Her sense of comedy so delighted in the absurdity of human beings that she could not want them different; and she believed in the impregnability of the private life and its power to balance the books which had been disordered by society. It seemed to her that a woman whose mind was honest could not be degraded by any falsehood to which she consented under duress, and that the game of being picked up and dropped by philanderers and fortune-hunters could be annulled by sober love. But it is also true that the situation, in itself, did not appall her. She did not find it intolerable that individuals should be obliged to arrive at a compromise with society and at many points, often of the greatest importance, disobey the voice of morality as they heard it and follow the impure and interested social code. Indeed to Jane Austen and to many intelligent people of her day, compromise itself was morality. But she held this belief in a form suggesting an underlying faith that the survival of society was more essential to the moral purpose of the universe than the survival of the individual. She must have thought of society as consisting of individuals and something else, and that something else a collective will that was working for salvation.

Jane Austen's view of the courtiers of Elsinore would have been as unfavorable as Shakespeare's, but she would have felt confidence in the court itself. Nobody in the story of Hamlet had behaved according to protocol, and it was no wonder they had come to grief. If another generation should keep the rules, if Ophelia had been more like Elizabeth Bennet, everything would turn out all right. People might not be happy, but they might be moderately so, and they certainly could be innocent and amused, provided that they never forgot to make a dignified compromise with society. This did not prove her light-minded. She is indeed one of the most religious of novelists. She does not pray in public, but her work is suffused with a desire that it should not always be with men and women as she describes it. She knew a discontent which was not peevish: a hope that one day there might be an end to this constant prudence and candor may be not a rash lapse but a serene eternal habit. But she recognised that we were not yet entered into eternity. In the meantime, she was morally alert, she preferred good to evil, she believed that man could be saved by the exercise of his own will; and since she had, being observant, been depressed by failures of the individual will, she looked for a better and more potent will exactly where a number of other people were looking for it, in the group.

Chapter 3 of *The Bride of Lammermoor* has for a heading a poem in praise of action:

> Look thou not on beauty's charming,
> Sit thou still when kings are arming,
> Taste not when the wine-cup glistens,
> Speak not when the people listens,

115

> Stop thine ear against the singer,
> From the red gold keep thy finger,
> Vacant heart and hand and eye,
> Easy live and quiet die.

Those readers of today who cannot understand why Sir Walter Scott was and is considered not only an entertaining but an important writer should meditate on the implications of these lines. A man free from earthly involvements would be, they tell us, an inert object of contempt. But was the man who became involved an object of respect? It is interesting to go over the lines with reference to Shakespeare. "Look thou not on beauty's charming"—ah, yes, *Antony and Cleopatra.* "Sit thou still when kings are arming"—ah, yes, all the historical plays and *Troilus and Cressida.* "Taste thou not when the winecup glistens"—ah, yes, any of the minor characters round Falstaff and a scene in *Othello.* "Speak not when the people listens"—ah, yes, *Julius Caesar.* "Stop thine ear against the singer"—ah, yes, Hamlet and Prospero had heard all the singing of the age in which they lived. "From the red gold keep thy finger"—ah, yes, *The Merchant of Venice* and *Timon of Athens.* Though Scott's first appeal is, of course, derived from his capacity for creating character—"his most wonderful comprehensive genius," to use Dryden's phrase again—the secret of his power lies in the side he takes in this moral argument, in which he is on the opposite side from Shakespeare. He did not believe the human will to be corrupt, and his belief was so strong that it embraced the largest kind of deeds, and he thus enjoys and approves the whole historical process. Not only is he for Fortinbras because he will be a good king, he is for almost any Fortinbras,

116

because to him any king is a good king, for the reason that the disputes of kings produce gallant deeds.

There is to be observed in the work of Scott a paradoxical feature which can also be found in other nineteenth-century novelists, and is disquieting. The "prosai-comi-epic" form which Fielding had initiated was inspiring in the writers who used it an extraordinary gift for the creation of character, which far outstripped his own, so far as width of range was concerned. They approached and even exceeded Chaucer's span. But at the same time their respect often seemed to pass from the individual to the group, to the mass, to society, and a convention was established that to write of institutions was a more dignified enterprise than to write of persons. This was true even of Charles Dickens, who, in spite of his failure to create a great tragic figure, his lack of feeling for form, and his excess of a vehemence incompatible with tragedy, was a colossal genius in his creation of real people. It is true that his books are sometimes so closely packed with characters of great liveliness but no significance that they recall the extreme but not exciting fertility of a cod's roe. But at other times in the completeness of his creative achievement he far surpasses the more genteel modern masters who were free from the handicap of hurry and uncertain taste. It is interesting to read in succession *Dombey and Son* and Thomas Mann's *Buddenbrooks,* and ask oneself which treats better their common theme: the unreliability of those bourgeois characteristics which are considered by the superficial to be eternally reliable. It is Dickens which gives the most convincing account of how those characteristics take a family at full speed to success, but refuse to regard that station as a terminus and start again and carry them on a journey to

117

disaster. It is interesting, too, to read in succession *Our Mutual Friend* and any of Henry James' nervous studies of outsiders trying to force their way inside the social barricade. James never surpasses the veneerings; very simply and briefly Dickens conveys the biological discomfort suffered by these two parasites who have married because each wrongly supposes the other to have money, as it might be two liver-flukes, who, failing to find a convenient sheep as host, attempt to sustain life upon one another. But every now and then Dickens ceases to take a primary interest in his characters, and shifts his attention to the institutions of the society in which they live and we feel that a natural process has been inverted. He did not create Little Dorrit and send her to Marshalsea Prison because that is where her destiny would have taken her; he created Marshalsea Prison and had to insert into it a frail and innocent person to serve as a measure of its tough squalor, as architects put a human figure in their drawing of a building to give a livelier sense of its proportions than a scale could give. To take a more gross example, *Oliver Twist,* under the thick sugar icing of its style, is a masterpiece written on the theme of professional crime, of adult mischief, of the black nursery where children never grow up and firmly go on saying to an invisible nurse that they are not sorry. But though some of its parts survive by their own life, the whole carries no conviction because the plot defies belief. Dickens has flouted those rules which Fielding drew from his ancient master concerning the necessity of keeping within the bounds of possibility and probability. *Oliver Twist* shows us a band of criminals pursuing a helpless child with a malignity which obviously must have some specific cause behind it. As the story goes on, a cloud of unreality descends on his pursuit, though the pursuers are real enough; and the reason for this lies in the inadequacy of the specific cause which Dickens has imagined. It is possible that a wife who hated her dead husband might also hate his mistress and their child, even though she and her husband had been separated long before he met that mistress; and it is possible that the wife might practice a crude kind of vengeance on the mistress while the girl lived, and after her death on her child, and that her own son would join her in this. But it is improbable that they would be inspired to follow a course which inflicted considerable personal inconvenience on them both, out of resentment against the husband's last will and testament, which left them annuities amounting to sixteen hundred pounds a year (which in those days was quite a considerable income) and named the mistress and her then unborn child as residuary legatees; for the wife had destroyed the will, and in consequence had inherited all her husband's fortune and had had the satisfaction of knowing that the mistress, destitute, had given birth to her son in a workhouse and died. But it is really impossible to believe that after the wife and her son had thus slaked their appetite for vengeance, they would have put themselves to the trouble of "a year of cunning search" in order to make an elaborate attempt to ruin her child's life. Shakespeare did not represent Iago as engaged in a subsidiary conspiracy against Othello's little brother. It is just possible that the wife should on her death-bed make her son swear to "spit upon the empty vaunt of that insulting will" and hunt down the mistress' child till he dragged him to "the very gallows' foot"; but if she did, it is extremely dubious whether he would have kept his oath, and condemned himself—while he was still in possession of six thousand pounds—to the extreme discomfort of the life he is

119

represented as leading throughout the book, frequenting insanitary Thameside premises in order to engage in schemes that might have taken him to Newgate at any moment. It is not that people are never so wicked as this; it is that they are rarely so indefatigable.

Fielding made no such mistake in *Amelia*. The causes he assigns for the unhappy position of the Booths are entirely credible. Billy, who lacked the armament of commonsense, was the target of two different types of assault. Miss Matthews, the terrible lettered courtesan, was hunting him down like an unchaste Diana, and Colonel James felt double hatred for him, because he himself lusted after both Miss Matthews and Amelia; and the pressure these two lechers apply to the situation is commensurate with the degree of energy commonly possessed by human beings. It was no effort for Fielding to invent these credible motives because his power of creation had brought these two characters into full existence, and there was nothing in their minds which was not known to him. Dickens, however, never troubled to create Oliver Twist's half-brother and persecutor, Edward Leeford; he "had sullens," to borrow a phrase which Shakespeare put in the mouth of Richard the Second, and was otherwise a blank. If Dickens had really wanted the drama played out by human beings, he would not have killed off Leeford's mother before the novel began; it is as if Shakespeare had killed off Gertrude before the curtain rose on *Hamlet*. But the spirit of the age had whispered in his ear that if a novelist took care of his workhouses, his characters would take care of themselves. What seemed to Dickens and his readers of the first importance was that Oliver Twist should be presented first as a victim of society, and then as a beneficiary of the same society, which shows itself repentant.

120

For we are back once more in an argument about salvation. Dickens like Emily Brontë, like Jane Austen, like Scott, believed that the human will is not corrupt; and unlike Fielding and Emily Brontë, but like Jane Austen and Scott, he believed that the human will was most capable of attaining order when it was exercised through a group. In the ideal situation, an unfortunate person was lifted out of want and misery by a person who was fulfilling the purposes of society so well that he had been rewarded for his cooperation by wealth. The picture of the Cratchetts' virtue in *A Christmas Carol* has not an absolute value; its significance, like the virtue of all Dickens' poorer characters, is relative. The Cratchetts are doing something good in itself, but what is really important is that Scrooge is not doing the same thing, for he is rich. This is quite a logical view once one has agreed to lay emphasis on the group instead of the individual; it matters very much that the stronger members of the group should be as virtuous as the weaker. Nor are these considerations absurd, for there is indeed great beauty in the idea of the kingdom of heaven being established on earth by the increasing holiness of a reformist state. But when this ideal is made manifest in imaginative literature, certain difficulties appear. The individual, the prime ingredient of literature, is forgotten.

These difficulties are disguised from the reader in Dickens' novels because his overriding difficulty seems to be his lack of taste, which every now and then blows his style to pieces, and his theme with it. What Dickens was trying to say about Bill Sikes' Nancy is very much the same thing that Dostoevsky says about Sonya Semyonovna in *Crime and Punishment*: both are writing of a woman who has been given a degrading status by society and annuls it by her own worth. The chief difference is that the Westerner makes Nancy gain salvation by works in the form of decisive and courageous action, and the Orthodox believer makes Sonya save herself and Raskolnikov by, to give Orthodoxy its correct translation, the right worship. But Dickens appears to be engaged in a far inferior enterprise, to be saying something false and nonsensical, because he develops Nancy's situation in inept dialogue. When Nancy tells Rose Maily that she cannot leave the band of criminals whom she detests, because one of them is her lover, Rose asks her, "Why do you wish to return to companions you paint in such terrible colors? If you repeat this information to a gentleman whom I can summon in an instant from the next room, you can be consigned to some place of safety within half an hour's delay." The reader is tempted to assume that, if he is troubled by the works of Dickens, it is because they contain many passages like these.

Dickens' troubling characteristics were due to his detachment from the tradition of the novel; but his great contemporary, Thackeray, was nearly as troubling, though he was faithful to that tradition. Thackeray was one of the most paradoxical of writers. Fielding was to him a god. He admired him and was influenced by him, and far more than that; he copied him, playing "the sedulous ape," as Stevenson put it, not only in his youth, when such imitation is natural and a useful exercise, but throughout his life. The most conspicuous example of the debt is his attempt at a second Amelia Booth in Amelia Sedley of *Vanity Fair;* and Billy Booth can be met in his pages again and again. A hundred years divided the two men. There are people today who write novels in imitation of Trollope, who is divided from us by the same distance, but they are not particularly gifted writers, and it is surely odd that a man who had such great powers as Thackeray should have followed so closely in the tracks of another writer, particularly when he had an imperfect understanding of him. Thackeray wrote two books about criminals, *Catherine* and *Barry Lyndon,* which are both obvious imitations of *The Life of Mr. Jonathan Wild the Great,* and in both he shows that he has missed the point of his model. What gives Fielding's book its strange palpitating life is the political parallel: Jonathan Wild is a wicked man, and he is like Walpole. It appalled Fielding, and at the same time delighted his sense of the comic, to see that wickedness ran right through the world, and that society is sometimes not to be distinguished from its enemies. Hence those puzzling, provoking speeches in Newgate Prison, which seem to be echoed from the stone walls, though that cannot be the explanation, for what the echo says is not quite the same, though nearly so; somehow we are listening to speeches delivered on the other side of London, in the Palace of Westminster. Hence those ambiguous conversations between the prisoners and their Ordinary, talk of the Common Room heard in a dream. "With all the opportunities you have had," Fielding said to the rich, "you are as base as the poor that have had them not." But *Barry Lyndon* and the criminals in *Catherine* are simply the enemies of society and nothing else.

It is indeed hard to understand how such an intelligent man as Thackeray, educated and of wide interests, was not overcome with boredom long before he finished the hundred and fifty thousand words of *Barry Lyndon,* a retelling of a true and disgusting story which tells us nothing we did not know before of the vices it describes and never from start to finish gives us a hint of an underlying and significant pattern. Yet he thought of himself as a more moral writer than Fielding, and so did Char-

123

lotte Brontë, who declared in the preface to the second edition of *Jane Eyre*: "He resembles Fielding as an eagle does a vulture: Fielding could stoop on carrion, but Thackeray never does." We will find Thackeray's reasons in his essay on his idol in *English Humourists;* he has to interrupt his tribute with some qualifying clauses, because he disapproved so deeply of Tom Jones, particularly in his relations with Lady Bellaston. Also he thought Fielding's art had been poisoned by his life, which he believed to have been debauched. (Here he may have been wrong in his premises, misled by a tradition built on the mistaken belief that dropsy, the disease which killed Fielding, was caused by dissipated habits; it is not at all certain that Fielding lived riotously except in his youth, or that even at that time he went beyond the custom of his age.) Charlotte Brontë makes clear her reasons for believing Thackeray superior in comparing him to the prophet Micaiah, in a passage which the student of the novel should keep by him, for it has its relevance to other authors and other periods (*Jane Eyre,* preface to 2d ed.):

> There is a man in our own days whose words are not framed to tickle delicate ears; who, to my thinking, comes before the great ones of society, much as the son of Imlah came before the throned King of Judah and Israel; and who speaks truth as deep, with a power as prophet-like and vital—a mien as dauntless and as daring. Is the satirist of *Vanity Fair* admired in high places? I cannot tell; but I think if some of those amongst whom he hurls the Greek fire of his sarcasm, and over whom he flashes the levin-brand of his denunciation, were to take his warnings in time —they or their seed might yet escape a fatal Ramoth-Gilead. Why have I alluded to this man? I have al-

124

luded to him, Reader, because I think I see in him an intellect profounder and more unique than his contemporaries have yet recognised; because I regard him as the first social regenerator of the day— as the very master of that working corps who would restore to rectitude the warped system of things; because I think no commentator on his writings has yet found the comparison which suits him, the terms which rightly characterise his talent. . . . His wit is bright, his humour attractive, but both bear the same relation to his serious genius, that the mere lambent sheet-lightning playing under the edge of the summer-cloud, does to the electric death-spark hid in its womb.

This is manifestly absurd. *Vanity Fair* is a masterpiece, but it is not a true satire. Neither in that book nor in any other of his writings did Thackeray attack anything which anybody would defend; and satire is essentially an attack on some person or institution or movement unworthy of the support which he or she or it is receiving from society. The picture he paints of Queen's Crawley is merciless: the ancient estate which "had never recovered the heavy fine imposed on Walpole Crawley, first baronet, for peculation in the Tape and Sealing Wax Office" (ch. 9), but still had its uses as a rotten borough which sent to Parliament that miserly old boor, Sir Pitt Crawley, who "was such a sharp landlord that he could hardly find any but bankrupt tenants," and who took a hand in various enterprises that the expanding economy put his way, yet still was ruined since "for want of proper precautions, his coal mines filled with water, the government flung his contract of damaged beef upon his hands; and for his coach horses, every mail proprietor in the kingdom knew that he lost more horses than any man in the country from underfeeding and buying cheap." But for years before the time Thackeray painted this picture nobody had had a good word to say for Sir Pitt Crawley. Two centuries earlier, the illiterate skinflint landowner had been a stock figure in Restoration comedy; and opposition to him had long ago overflowed from the world of art into the world of fact, and the politics of Victorian England were prizing open his grip on English power. In attacking him, Thackeray was not a prophet, he was not announcing that someone was going to die, he was talking about somebody who was dead, and he could do it safely; he need not fear the fate meted out to Micaiah, of whom Ahab said, "Put this fellow in the prison, and feed him with bread of affliction and with water of affliction, until I come in peace." He was completely acceptable to his generation, as an artist of such exquisite accomplishment would naturally be.

Oddly enough, what prevents our generation from taking the proper delight in that exquisite accomplishment is an uncertainty about his moral position. There is too much double talk in Thackeray's work. Dickens also indulged in double talk, but his was a not very grave aesthetic fault. If he described the death of a child he was apt to insert some sentences which in affect said, "Look, I am describing the death of a child, and it could hardly be more pathetic"; but it would turn out that his description was in fact deeply and honestly pathetic. Thackeray's double talk was more complicated and more sinister. When he describes the virtues or calamities of the poor and unimportant, he always conveys the feeling that his readers might have expected him to be too worldly to recognize merit or sympathize with sorrow on such a lowly level, but here it is, the proof that he has a true and unspoiled heart. When Colonel Newcome dies, Thackeray writes of him with a heavy, prodding pressure, as though he were pointing out that he could not be more sorry if the Colonel had been the premier duke instead of a poor old man living on charity in an almshouse. This feeling is ground out in paragraph after paragraph, and it appears in the famous description of the old man's last moments:

> At the usual evening hour the chapel began to toll, and Thomas Newcome's hands outside the bed feebly beat time. And just as the last bell struck, a peculiar sweet smile shone over his face, and he lifted up his head a little, and quickly said, "Adsum!" and fell back. It was the word we used at school, when names were called; and lo, he, whose heart was as that of a little child, had answered to his name and stood in the presence of The Master.

There is something too much there, if it be only the epithets "peculiar, sweet." Thackeray is able to create an old man who must be liked by the least maudlin, and to build about him such a vile prison as is in fact often built round the gentle-hearted people in this world. But he cannot trust us, or himself, to like or pity Colonel Newcome, and in his efforts to persuade us and himself makes Colonel Newcome almost unlikable and his conditions melodramatic.

This curious trait is explained by one of his obsessions. Thackeray published something over five million words, and it is fair to say that about a million deal with the subject of snobbery. *The Book of Snobs,* which is as monotonous as *Barry Lyndon,* alone accounts for a hundred thousand words, and he constantly reverts to the subject. Like Jane Austen, he saw that human beings were not only immortal and aspirant souls, they were also pieces in a game played by society, pegs which had to be fitted into holes on a board or thrown away. But Jane Austen and he differed in their attitude to this duality. Both were aware that it necessitated a moral compromise, but Jane Austen felt the necessity to be regrettable. It is always assumed in her pages that there exists a system of values differing from that held by society, and sometimes antagonistic to it; and her affection for her characters depends on the degree to which they induce society to accept this other system. She believed that the courtiers would run riot if they did not regulate their wayward lives by the rules of the court, but she never confused the court with the courts of heaven. She recognized the absolute importance of the individual and the relative importance of society. But Thackeray's convictions were not nearly so definite. He was painfully aware that humanity had to go on playing this game, that whether men and women were pegs or not, if they did not pretend they were pegs, and find holes in the board for themselves, they would be thrown away; and he was appalled by the distance and violence with which they were thrown.

Nearly all Thackeray's novels are records of financial disaster: in *Vanity Fair* the Sedleys lose their money and the Crawleys, Sir Pitt in one way and Rawdon in another, are in a constant tangle of loss and debt; *The Newcomes* and *The Adventures of Philip* are studies of prolonged corroding descents into poverty; *Pendennis* is a wrestling match with mean and pretentious want; gambling losses make the plots of *Henry Esmond* and *The Virginians;* and most of the people in the background of his stories and essays are the prey of financial anxiety. We are wrong in supposing (as many writers tearfully do) that the insecurity of the middle classes is peculiar to our age. There has never yet been a time when the lion and the lamb lay down together; there has never yet been a time when the bank manager and his client have been as the turtledove and its mate. The financial disorders of Fielding's age had been lessened by the better actuarial organization of the state; the maintenance of officers in Thackeray's day was not left to chance and private fortune as much as it had been in Billy Booth's day. Nevertheless it continued to be true that the rate of interest on invested capital and the expansion of trade were not so perfectly adjusted to the rate of increase in the population that it was possible for all the children of every middle-class couple to enjoy the same standard of living as their parents; and thus it happened then, as it happens now, that a high proportion of the middle classes had to seek employment and would have liked to find such employment in the professions, but were prevented because the amount of professional care a community needs and can afford is not nicely adjusted to the number of persons who would like to furnish it.

The situation was as depressing to the nineteenth as it is to the twentieth. The gap between the figures which in ideal conditions should match was not so wide then as it is now, but it was the only gap our ancestors knew, and it was quite wide enough to make them dislike it very much. Moreover, the world had some time before emerged from a state of almost perpetual war into a state of almost unbroken peace, and, though we now find it amazing how little eighteenth-century wars interfered with trade, the early Victorians believed that peace was going to cause a huge increase in the wealth of the nations. Thackeray and his generation had seen that hope realized to some extent, but not enough to save many of their own kind from bankruptcy and a loss of privilege which were felt to be not only bad things in themselves, but also breaches of a promise given by society. Not at all unreasonably, he was all for stability. He felt that at any cost the social system should be preserved as it was: the game should be played according to the rules and the board held steady, so that none of the lucky pegs which had found holes would drop out and roll away on the dusty floor. It was as if he felt the existence of the species was at peril and one must make broad arrangements for its survival, and abandon for the moment the study of the individual. Let us see what he does to the most living of his individuals, Becky Sharp. We know her physically, we respond to her troubling, ignoble, yet spirited appeal. We recognize her mixture of stupidity and intriguing, farsighted intelligence that makes her never know when to stop, we are convinced by the meanness which made her keep Steyne's money to herself when her young husband had to go to a spunging-house, and the not really inconsistent generosity that made her at last tell Amelia the truth about her dead husband and set her free to marry Dobbin. If we love her strange sweet-sour tawdry authenticity, we are loving her maker. Yet it is difficult not to hate him for the way he treats her. From the beginning he nags and scolds her because she is a poor woman of no family who has forced a gate into the enclosure reserved for the fortunate. It is not what she does there that he really resents, it is the fact of her presence which he finds intolerable.

It is the measure of the difference between Jane Austen and Thackeray that the shadow of fear passes over Jane Austen's serenity when it seems likely that someone who has enjoyed the benefits of the enclosure is to be expelled from it, as Lydia Bennet might have been had

Wickam not married her, but what rouses Thackeray's apprehension is the prospect that someone extra may be brought in (as Jane Austen's Emma tried to bring in Harriet) to share those benefits, of which there were hardly enough to go round. He attacked snobbery (*Book of Snobs*, "Concluding Observation"): "I am sick of Court Circulars, I loathe *haute-ton* intelligence, I believe such words as Fashionable, Exclusive, Aristocratic, and the like, to be wicked, unchristian epithets, that ought to be banished from honest vocabularies." He genuinely hated these things and because he recognized the soundness of the tradition which made the artist's first loyalty go to the individual. Nevertheless his own first loyalty went to society, and the proof of that lies in his virtuous characters, who, unlike Jane Austen's favored children, had no reserves. They had no private lives which were free of control save by their own quiet selves; and they possessed the conforming virtues and none other. This is not too grave an accusation, for our race would perish if it could not conform. But on the other hand it would not be worth keeping alive if it did not produce an Antigone from time to time.

The story of Antigone is not the only plot. There are many others, and Thackeray has developed some of them superbly; and it might be that he was able to forsake the tradition of the artist's fidelity to the individual without damage to his art. But there are signs that, great artist as he is, he suffered some injury by his extroversion. We are right to be shocked at the passages in which he belittles his novels by a nodding, winking admission to his readers that not a word of them is true. "Come, children, let us shut up the box and the puppets, for our play is played out," are the last lines of *Vanity Fair*, and at the end of *The Newcomes* he tells us: "As I write the

131

last line with a rather sad heart, Pendennis and Laura, and Ethel and Clive, fade away into Fableland. I hardly know whether they are not true; whether they do not live near us somewhere," and so it goes on for some hundreds of words. "But for you, dear friend, it is as you like. You may settle your Fableland in your own fashion. Anything you like happens in Fableland. Wicked folks die apropos (for instance, that death of Lady Kew was most artful, for if she had not died, don't you see, that Ethel would have married Lord Farintosh the next week?)." It is possible that Thackeray may have made these curious assaults on his readers' condition of belief in imitation of the interpolated essays in *Tom Jones*, which certainly make the same attack on illusion. But there is an important difference. In those essays Fielding discussed the technical devices by which an artist can convey to his readers a discovery of his own which he believes to be true; and that he should put it before them in the form of a fable simply means that he is availing himself of one of these technical devices. He never suggested that what he was doing was as unimportant as a puppet-show for children, or that what happens in Fableland is arbitrary. Always he insisted that art is tethered to reality and must not be mere doodling. In fact he explicitly states that it must be "discovery, or finding out," and goes on to say that by this he means, "to explain it at large, a quick and sagacious penetration into the true essence of all the objects of our contemplation." It is not surprising that his characters are as real as reality, and that Thackeray's characters, with the exception of Becky Sharp, who leapt out of his hands and ran away from him, always have a doll-like quality and are arbitrary in their natures.

What happens to the artist who conceives his art as a celebration of society rather than of the individual is seen even more clearly by turning to the works of Trollope. This is no hardship, for if Thackeray is a great writer Trollope is in some respects a greater. His taste (in his long novels) is usually perfect, his knowledge of his characters complete. It was his own injunction to a novelist that "on the last day of each month recorded, every person in his novel should be a month older than on the first" (*Autobiography*, ch. 12), and he obeyed it himself. "The objects of his contemplation," to use Fielding's phrase, were as numerous as Fielding's own, and he had the same strong, competent hold on practical matters, which made him as good a civil servant as Fielding was a magistrate. In 1863 he wrote for his chief in the Post Office a minute expounding the paradoxical truth that promotion in the civil service must go by seniority and not by merit, for the sake of both merit and mediocrity; and its sound observation and its logic and its trimness still make it enjoyable reading. He was bound to feel happy in his work, since it had given him prosperity for which he had not hoped, having known an insecure and shamefaced childhood as the victim of a father who, not content with the deep degree of poverty which can be attained by an unsuccessful barrister, sought concurrent failure as a farmer in the outskirts of London, and then sought further financial distress by devoting himself in his tumbledown farmhouse to the composition of a Dictionary of Ecclesiastical Terms. Trollope had had every reason to fear that he might be one of the pegs for which there was no hole and no hope of anything but falling off the board to the dusty floor. Therefore he was very glad that the game was continuing in his time and that he had found a hole for himself in the English Civil Service, which is indeed one of the administrative glories of the world and was then in its pride. Fielding had been grappling with administrative problems in a form that had been fixed in 1660, when administration had been cut off from its direct relationship to the monarchy through the King's Privy Council and its ancillary organizations, and had been put under the power of the King-in-Parliament at Westminster, with the local justices of the peace for instruments. There the matter had rested for a long time. The eighteenth century knew nothing of various central artifices for controlling administration which we now regard as almost natural objects; in Fielding's day there was no Home Office. It took a famous speech on economic reform by a spendthrift and incompetent of genius, Edmund Burke, to create a sense that the chaos of sinecures and unsupervised labor which composed the public services must be brought to order. Step by step, there was established a new system of administration which was orderly and subject to check by the central government, and in the middle years of the nineteenth century it was committed to sweetness and light by an eccentric of violent temper named Sir Edwin Chadwick. There is great charm in the contrast between these reformers and their own unreformed condition, but there was no occasion for poetry. There are no situations in the history of the Civil Service which would inspire a poet to make any Burke or Chadwick or any of those involved in this nascent triumph cry out such words as "Give me the glass and therein will I read. No deeper wrinkles yet? Hath

sorrow struck So many blows upon this face of mine
And made no deeper wounds?" (*Richard II*, IV.1.275).
The establishment of the Civil Service Commission in
1851, with its initiation of the principle of open competition for all but certain exceptional posts, was an event
of great moment, but it is hard to imagine a commem-
orative line which could match, "This day is called the
Feast of Crispian." The social landscape of the nineteenth century did not lend itself to poetry, and Trollope
was so much a part of that landscape it was inevitable
that he should be a novelist, and that his novels should
be extremely prosaic.

But it is not to be assumed that because Trollope
turned his back (or had his back turned for him by the
spirit of the age) on poetry that he followed naturalism.
His novels are for the most part pure fantasy. All the
Barchester series describe cathedral towns that never
were on land or sea. He says so himself (*Autobiography,*
ch. 5):

> I may well declare at once that no one at their com-
> mencement could have had less reason than myself
> to presume himself to be able to write about clergy-
> men. I have been often asked in what period of my
> early life I had lived so long in a cathedral city as
> to have become intimate with the ways of a Close.
> I never lived in any cathedral city—except London,
> never knew anything of any Close, and at that time
> had enjoyed no peculiar intimacy with any clergy-
> man. My archdeacon, who has been said to be life-
> like, and for whom I confess that I have all a parent's
> fond affection, was, I think, the simple result of an
> effort of my moral consciousness . . . but in writing

about clergymen generally, I had to pick up as I went whatever I might know or pretend to know about them.

It is only necessary to consult the biographies of Victorian ecclesiastics (which exist in vast numbers; it is one of the departments of literature of which there is enough to go round) to realize that what Trollope knew about clergymen amounted to very little indeed. There is the initial fault that none of the ecclesiastics of Barchester is shown as practicing his devotions with any intensity or as engaged in theological researches of any depth. The canons met Mr. Slope's hostility to ritual with well-bred resistance, and some manifest a gentle piety, and Mr. Arabin flirted with Roman Catholicism but extricated himself from the dubious entanglement, and that is all. Yet the life of the Church of England was then turbulent with passion. The first of the Barchester series, *The Warden,* was published in 1855. The fervent Oxford Movement was only twenty years old; in 1852 Browning had written "Christmas Eve and Easter Day," with its picture of the contending High Church, Low Church, and Liberal Church Movements; and *Essays and Reviews* the famous volume of papers by seven Liberal churchmen was to be published only five years later. It was not that only a few clergymen were agitated by these matters. Many were so deeply moved by them that, often at great sacrifice, they gave up their places in the Church and to meet the needs of such cases an Act was passed making it lawful for a clergyman to relinquish his orders. But it is not only its omission of contemporary religious issues that makes the Barchester picture false. The quality of the ecclesiastics is too poor. The Church of England was then full of fine classical scholars and maybe some scientists; Bishop Colenso, for example, who was then working his way toward a heresy trial, was a first-class mathematician, and Pelham Dale, who was to go to prison for his ritualism, was one of his best pupils. But the Barchester ecclesiastics could hardly have matched quotations with Billy Booth, and their concern with figures was administrative and domestic but not scientific. As for Mrs. Proudie, there are available to us a fair number of letters and diaries written by Bishop's wives, and these forbid us to suppose that any of them (particularly one who was the niece of a Scottish earl) would say of a troublesome and disabled guest at a reception, "Lame, I'd lame her if she belonged to me" (*Barchester Towers*, ch. 11). She might have said worse things than this, but not in that idiom.

Trollope's version of the scene is wrong, but not false. Everything in this superb phase of Trollope's genius is true. When he interrupts his novel to speak directly to the reader over the heads of his characters, he is not as Thackeray at such moments; he is not saying with a nervous laugh that of course all his story is "made up" and as trivial as a children's game. He is as Fielding, who discusses with his readers whether he is using the best technical devices for conveying to them the truth as it is his individual discovery. "This narrative is supposed to commence immediately after the installation of Dr. Proudie," Trollope writes, "I will not describe the ceremony, as I do not precisely understand its nature" (ibid., ch. 3). In other words, he can tell the reader what he wants him to know without obscuring it with facts of no importance; and later he steps out of the story with as sensible a technical purpose, to give the reader an assurance that Eleanor Bold is not going to marry Mr. Slope, and no one need hurry on to get that news and thus miss the fine touches by which the reality of Eleanor and her suitors is established. All the characters in Barchester may be wrongly labeled, but they are real. Mr. Harding is the true likeness of the good man who cannot accept the necessity for compromise in this world, for the reason that it casts a reflection on the Maker of the Universe. Archdeacon Grantly is the true likeness of the good man who can accept the necessity for compromise in this world, and is the true martyr of the two, since propinquity with such absolutists as Mr. Harding makes him look not wicked, which could perhaps be borne, but ridiculous. Mrs. Proudie may not speak with the accents of a bishop's wife or a Scottish earl's niece, but somewhere that upas tree grew high and blasted all living things for miles around.

The situation is defined in a sentence to be found in Chapter eleven in *Barchester Towers* which describes the lamentable end of Mrs. Proudie's first reception. Bertie Stanhope asks the bishop, "Is there much to do here, at Barchester?" in a tone which Trollope particularizes as one "that a young Admiralty clerk might use in asking the same question of a brother acolyte at the Treasury." Almost all the conversations in the Barchester series might have the same gloss. These are really novels about the Civil Service, furnished with an ecclesiastical background and trappings. Trollope gives this away in the passage in his *Autobiography* when he describes how he came to write *The Warden*, as a consequence of a visit to Salisbury in the course of his duties as a Post Office surveyor (*Autobiography*, ch. 5):

> . . . Whilst wandering there on a midsummer evening round the purlieus of the cathedral I conceived the story of *The Warden*—from whence came that

138

series of novels of which Barchester, with its bishops, deans, and archdeacons, was the central site. . . . I had been struck by two opposite evils—or what seemed to me to be evils—and with an absence of all art-judgments in such matters, I thought that I might be able to expose them, or rather to describe them, both in one and the same tale. The first evil was the possession by the Church of certain funds and endowments which had been intended for charitable purposes, but which had been allowed to become incomes for idle Church dignitaries. There had been more than one such case brought to public notice at the time, in which there seemed to have been an egregious malversation of charitable purposes. The second evil was its very opposite. Though I had been much struck by the injustice above described, I had also often been angered by the undeserved severity of the newspapers towards the recipients of such incomes, who could hardly be considered to be the chief sinners in the matter. When a man is appointed to a place, it is natural that he should accept the income allotted to that place without much inquiry. It is seldom that he will be the first to find out that his services are overpaid. Though he be called upon only to look beautiful and to be dignified upon State occasions, he will think two thousand pounds a year little enough for such dignity and beauty he brings to the task. I felt that there had been some tearing to pieces which might have been spared.

In fact, he looked at Hiram's Hospital as if he were a Civil Servant, strongly affected as all intelligent civil servants were by the movement toward administrative reform, preparing a minute. He himself thought this made *The Warden* a bad book, for the reason that he tried to be fair and fairness had no place in literature (ibid.):

> But I was altogether wrong in supposing that the two things could be combined. Any writer in advocating a case must do so after the fashion of an advocate—or his writing will be ineffective. He should take up one side and cling to that, and then he may be powerful. There should be no scruples of conscience. Such scruples make a man impotent for such work.

Here Trollope was speaking half in jest, mocking the crudity of the public mind, but he was certainly half in earnest and trying to account for the failure of an exquisite book to create quite the effect that it should have done, given the beautiful character of Mr. Harding and the art with which it is displayed. But its very slight degree of failure is surely due to its attempt to be at one and the same time a realistic novel and a satire. The reader cannot suspend his disbelief in order to sympathize with Mr. Harding, and a minute later laugh at Dr. Pessimist Anticant and Mr. Popular Sentiment, who are caricatures of Carlyle and Dickens, which he is invited to regard with something much less than total belief. In fact, Trollope had to state both sides to establish the theme of the novel. When the Whig reformer revealed to Mr. Harding and the public that an undue amount of the endowment of Hiram's Hospital, far greater than the founder had intended, had been diverted from the maintenance of the pensioners to the stipend Mr. Harding drew as their warden, he resigned. After that the stipend was adjusted so that the warden drew no more than the founder had intended; but it was then too small to afford anybody without means a livelihood, and nobody with private means would choose to give up his leisure to attend to so small an enterprise. Hence the beautiful little hospital fell into decay, and the poor old men dragged out their lives, neglected both in body and soul. Trollope shows us how true it may be that institutions founded in the past cannot be kept alive without injustice to the present, yet must be preserved, since even when an institution operates without full regard to the rights of any section of the community, the people in that section may be the worse off if the institution should collapse altogether, because they will lose the partial regard it accorded their rights. Trollope had a great understanding of the morphology of society.

There is a similar admixture of the true and the false in such of his novels as give a brilliant account of the structure of England in his time, particularly those called "the political novels," which owe a superficial unity to the appearances in all of Plantagenet Palliser, afterward the Duke of Omnium, and his wife Lady Glencora. Here Trollope paints a true picture of a territory long occupied by the fortunate, which is being subjected to an invasion, disagreeable but not undeserved. The aristocrats, the landowners, were the original ascendancy, but now the industrialists had come to share their power, and every day were taking a larger share. However, that was not the only battle. There were all sorts of ways by which people, not themselves landowners or industrialists but in good relations with what is now called "the establishment" could stake out their claims to a share in the good fortune of the country. There were the offices which not only afforded a livelihood but conferred a distinction; if a man were a member of Parliament or held a conspicuous post

141

in any of the bureaucratic institutions, among which the Church had to be included, he enjoyed general respect, could lead an interesting social life, and improved his chances of marrying a bride with money and useful connections. But the middle classes were increasing, and for these offices there was with every generation fiercer competition. The bulk of Trollope's work consists of accounts of conflicts between people who wanted to maintain the power which had been their birthright and people who wanted to maneuver themselves into the possession of power to which they had no title; and the situation was complicated for Trollope by his recognition that even the people who had power as their birthright had no clear title to it. He believed that they had a right to it which was difficult to define, because it was at once hereditary and contractual; they had been bred for the virtues, and particularly for the virtue of public spirit. Nevertheless he could not close his eyes to the fact that as a result of enjoying this birthright they had become proud, narrow-minded, and humorless. The old Duke of Omnium was ridiculous to the point of danger; even his nephew and heir, Plantagenet Palliser, though a good man dedicated to the service of his people, was absurd. When Lady Glencora, at the end of *The Prime Minister,* suggests that her husband should cheer himself up after his political defeat by giving a houseparty at one of his country seats where they have both known the extremity of defeat and unhappiness, it is said that "he hardly yet knew his wife well enough to understand that the suggestion had been a joke." To hold power on the terms Palliser had been given it a man should be able to understand not only his wife, but everyman.

Yet Trollope understood the structure of his society, if not the substance. In the beautiful Oxford edition of certain of his works, edited by Michael Sadleir and Frederick Page, the preface to *The Prime Minister* is written by that brilliant English politician L. S. Amery, who was born in 1873, two years before *The Prime Minister* was published, and went into politics twenty-three years later, as the secretary of a member of Parliament, and stayed in it all his life, holding important positions in both wars. Nobody knew the political scene better than he did, and he writes:

> Trollope in his *Autobiography* is scathingly contemptuous about Disraeli's novels. He sees in them only "pasteboard and tinsel . . . a smell of hair-oil, an aspect of buhl, a remembrance of tailors, a feeling of false jewels." For him they are essentially "false." Making all allowance for personal prejudice, this criticism, true of some aspects of Disraeli's style, is even more symptomatic of Trollope's complete incapacity to be interested in, or understand, political issues as such. *Coningsby* is profoundly suggestive even now because it discusses the perennial problem whether a political party lives by following the tide of current opinion or by principle. No one can understand the psychological background of our social and industrial problems today who has not read *Sybil*. In it are to be found both all the essential facts on which Marx based his political philosophy and the effective practical answer to Marx's false conclusions. In their profound insight into the realities behind politics Disraeli's novels are far less "false" than Trollope's sketches of a political world with the politics left out.

This pronouncement would have broken Trollope's heart, for he himself had censured Dickens for being "marvelously ignorant" of "the political status of his own country" and had added that Thackeray had never studied the

143

subject either, and he had as much right to think he spoke with authority as came of being an unsuccessful liberal candidate. But it is true. It is impossible to deduce from the "political novels" either the intellectual quality of Victorian Westminster, which was very high, or the material on which it worked.

Go into a library stocked in our great-grandfather's time, and take down from the shelf, say, the historical essays written by the third Marquess of Salisbury, who in Trollope's day was twice Secretary for India and later Foreign Secretary. In those essays there is displayed a richly allusive mind: he was delighted to note that Dr. Strauss (the author of *The Life of Christ,* which George Eliot translated and which destroyed her orthodoxy) had published a lecture denying the historical existence of Christ, which he recommended to his fellow countrymen by stating that it was delivered for the benefit of a fund for building a German fleet by private subscription. Salisbury's mind was not only amusing and well-furnished, it was penetrating and prophetic; it considers such international problems as those arising out of the contiguity of great and small states, particularly when the small states number among their inhabitants minority groups akin in blood to the inhabitants of the great states. He observed Germany ingesting Schleswig-Holstein as, seventy-five years later, it was to ingest Czechoslovakia, and perceived such a meal to be a threat to the world. Or, in the same library, you may come on *Greater Britain, a Record of Travel, in English-speaking Countries, 1866-7,* which Charles Dilke published when he was twenty-five, in the same year that he was elected member of Parliament for Chelsea, and there you will find that the idea of the trusteeship of backward peoples, put forward in the writings of Burke and his great quarry, Warren Hastings, is developed with a power and enthusiasm not unworthy of them. Tory and Whig, there was more to the men in St. Stephen's than Trollope allowed; and it was not lack of understanding or incompetence which made him fail to convey it, since he was an able civil servant and as a novelist he was a virtuoso.

Trollope wrote of the structure of society and not its substance, of the Church without religion and of Parliament without political ideas, because he was distracted from the discussion of what appears to be his subject by his absorption in the long argument about the salvation and damnation of man. We are back with Shakespeare in his deliberations on kingship. The Duke of Omnium and Plantagenet Palliser, like English kings, had a split title to power. They were born to rule because they had been born into a ruling family, because they had gone through the prescribed forms of election, and because they had promised to give the people protection in return for allegiance; and like kings they were corrupted by power. It is said of Lady Glencora when her husband was prime minister that "the turmoil in her husband's mind, the agony which he sometimes endured when people spoke ill of him, the aversion which he had at first genuinely felt to an office for which he hardly thought himself fit, and now the gradual love of power created by the exercise of power, had all been seen by her" (*The Prime Minister*, ch. 66). She herself had been moved by that same ambition to what her husband had reluctantly to condemn as "vulgarity," and to actual brutality when the Duke of Omnium showed signs of making a senile marriage and it became possible that her husband might not inherit the Dukedom. If the king does not exercise his power properly, a usurper will come in and exercise his power for him, and Trollope is of the same opinion as Shakespeare that usurpers are a necessary but dubious breed. To him the Tories were the rightful kings, and the Whigs were the necessary usurpers; and there were terrifying creatures, usurpers without hope of right, who came in from the outside and tried, without the justification of any connection with "the establishment," to get a share of the good things which were being distributed to the elect insiders. Even Thackeray's hatred for Becky Sharp is not so intense as Trollope's hatred for Ferdinand Lopez, which is so furious that he paints him far too black for his own purposes. Lady Glencora was indiscreet but not demented, and no sane woman would have admitted such an obvious scoundrel to her world.

But Trollope's time made it difficult for him to think of power: of a king, of a court, of courtiers. What Shakespeare saw was a single figure that was three figures, fused like Laocoön and his sons, into a sliding, changing shape: the anointed king who could do no wrong, the contractual kind who had taken the oath to his people and must do no wrong, and the usurper who was blaspheming the rite of anointment and defending the sanctity of the oath, all in the grip of this strange necessity, the conception of kingship. By Fielding's time it looked as if power were becoming a simpler entity, for there was but one king at court, a solid, material, contractual monarch, and though the other two royal figures had been brought back by the Jacobite rebellion, they were as ghosts, and Fielding helped to lay them. But this is what Trollope saw, as he describes it in a letter written to an Australian friend in 1872:

> Of course I admit your theory of government upon which all our parliamentary practice is founded—but

in this as in many other matters our Constitution is worked by usage in direct opposition to the theory. The Crown by its prerogative is the controlling power of the Army, but the Army is controlled by Parliament—and it is because these apparent contradictions are admitted, so that a gradual development of the power of the people is enabled to go on without abrupt changes in our traditional theories, that we have no revolutions and remain loyal and contented . . . The loyalty which thinking men at home are able to feel for and to show to the Crown, rests on the knowledge that the sovereign can do no act of government. Were it not so, the loyalty would be impossible, because we are all agreed not to entrust the power of governing us to any one person. Could the Queen act on her own responsibility, tens of thousands of us who pride ourselves on our loyalty would be rebels tomorrow. But in regard to this great act of choosing a responsible minister, we know that the sovereign asks advice and acts upon it. No one dreams that were Gladstone to resign tomorrow the Queen would do other than ask his advice as to what she would do upon his resignation.

The king had gone from Trollope's court and there was not even a usurper in his place, or rather there were so many usurpers that the eye could not take them in.

To conceive of a court at all, in the sense of a seat of power, the observer had to turn his back on Buckingham Palace and look at the much more involved Palace of Westminster and the members of the House of Lords and the House of Commons, who by their hundreds thronged and congested its architectural confusion of old and

147

new. But what the usurping Parliament was doing was rarely visible to the naked eye, for the Cabinet system had been introduced; and more and more of the business of government was carried on by the Civil Service which, even for an expert like Trollope, was hard to fit into the eye-span, for it was scattered all over London in ministries and municipal buildings and all over the country in councils. Trollope was under an obligation to note all he could of this huge and crowded scene, for like Thackeray, he was for the court, and indeed exceeded him in his enthusiasm, for he was indifferent to the tradition which made the artist's first loyalty to the individual. He did indeed believe that some of the courtiers were good, but this cannot be taken as meaning that he did not think the human will incorrupt, because he was so conscious of the group that his moral judgments of the individual were perfunctory.

He had some characters who are certainly virtuous, such as Mr. Harding and Mr. Crawley, but this is no testimony in favor of the human will, for they are people in whom the will and most positive attributes are present in only very small quantities. It is as if Trollope believed that there were not only deficiency diseases but deficiency forms of health, and took it that these men were good because they were nearly nothing. Shakespeare came near to this view when he made the twaddling Gonzago the one man on Prospero's island who could envisage the innocent use of power. There are other Trollopean characters whom their author favors for the same reason that made Thackeray prefer certain of his own creations: they conform. But Trollope goes much further than Thackeray in his estimation of the extent to which conformity should be allowed as an excuse. Thackeray thought it could be taken as a license for vacuity, but hardly asked for more. But Trollope gave the conformer a vastly wider range of fault. Phineas Finn is an empty-headed and empty-hearted adventurer, only admirable for his half-stupid, half-courageous hardihood and imperturbability, and Trollope knew he was of no great value, for he was a composite portrait of an unhappy suicide and a notorious lady-killer, a rascal. He had his point of virtue, which was of the same nature as the one good deed that Shakespeare allowed Hamlet. It was political. Phineas Finn resigned his hard-won office because he thought the tenant-right system of land tenure was right for his native country, Ireland, and the administration of which he was a part was opposed to it. But hardly anything could redeem him from the charge implicit in his marriage.

After the extremely disingenuous love-life of his early years had come to a close, he married Madame Goesler, one of the most repulsive characters in fiction. She was a schemer of an order which makes Becky Sharp look like one of Wordsworth's simpler children. But she had the luck to be the wealthy widow of an Austrian banker, and she installed herself in London and by a mixture of cringing modesty and moneyed ostentation (she takes "a cottage in Park Lane") and cold discretion she interjected herself into London society. This would be of no great moment, for many harmless persons and some admirable ones, and even a few who have had great gifts, have enjoyed the life of great houses. But Trollope draws Madame Goesler, with power that could not have been exceeded by Balzac, as a damned soul. The old Duke of Omnium met her and formed a senile love for her, which she fostered, as indeed an ambitious young woman might do without planning any great mischief. The first time he called at the little house in Park Lane he was told she was not at home. "Her doors were not open to all callers; were shut even to some who find but few doors closed against them; were shut occasionally to those whom she most specially wished to see within them. She knew how to allure by denying, and to make the gift rich by delaying it. We are told by the Latin proverb that he who gives quickly gives twice; but I say that she who gives quickly seldom gives more than half." She then sends the Duke a little note of apology, "hardly scented, and yet conveying a sense of something sweet," and he forgives and calls again. Very soon he suggests that she should come to his villa on Lake Como, and she refuses. It would not be worth her while to be his mistress, but it might be worth while to become his Duchess. "There was the name of many a woman written in a black list within Madame Goesler's breast—written there (ch. 50) because of scorn, because of rejected overtures, because of deep social injury, and Madame Goesler told herself often that it would be a pleasure to her to use the list, and to be revenged on those who had ill-used and scornfully treated her. She did not readily forgive those who had injured her. As Duchess of Omnium she thought that probably she might use that list with efficacy."

As the result of her careful handling the Duke presently proposes marriage to her, and she sends him away for two days to wait for her answer. Before the time is up she receives a visit from Lady Glencora Palliser, who, as the wife of the Duke's nephew, the heir to his title and his fortune, is terrified lest Madame Goesler become the Duchess and produce a son. She grossly insults her, telling her that the projected marriage would "degrade" the Duke in the eyes of his fellows, although she is perfectly respectable because she has no rank. Madame Goesler sends her away, and comes to the decision that she will serve her own interests best if she rejects the Duke and puts it to Lady Glencora that in return for her friendship she will give him no further encouragement, and will protect him from further entanglements. For the next three years she is the constant companion of the old man, and is with him when he dies, when he says perhaps the most solemn thing he ever said in all his life: he wishes that he had met her earlier, "I could have talked to you about things which I never did talk of to anyone. I wonder why I should have been a duke, and another man a servant" (*Phineas Redux,* ch. 25).

There are elements in the situation which should touch a heart of stone, which have indeed touched the heart of stone which is man's, all through the ages. A senile passion must be tedious to its object, it may be disgusting if the flesh that feels it is too far gone in decay, but it is always pitiful. That a man about to die should try to turn his back on the grave and lay hold on life at its most living is an occasion for tenderness, and when a man who has made this attempt at escape is reclaimed by the forces which he fears, it is inconceivable that those who have watched his defeat should not feel emotion. But Trollope makes it quite clear that Madame Goesler felt nothing about the Duke. After his death she spends three weeks staying with her dear friend, Lady Glencora (ch. 30):

On her journey back to Park Lane many thoughts crowded on her mind. Had she, upon the whole, done well in reference to the Duke of Omnium? The last three years of her life had been sacrificed to an old man with whom she had not in truth possessed aught in common. She had persuaded herself that there had existed a warm friendship between them; —but of what nature could have been a friendship with one whom she had not known till he had been in his dotage? What words of the Duke's speaking had she ever heard with pleasure, except certain terms of affection which had been half mawkish and half senile? She had told Phineas Finn, while riding home with him from Broughton Spinnies, that she had clung to the Duke because she loved him, but what had there been to produce such love? The Duke had begun his acquaintance with her by insulting her—and had then offered to make her his wife. This,—which would have conferred upon her some tangible advantages, such as rank, and wealth, and a great name, she had refused, thinking that the price to be paid for them was too high, and that life might even yet have something better in store for her. After that she had permitted herself to become, after a fashion, head nurse to the old man, and in that pursuit had wasted three years of what remained to her of her youth.

The woman is a desert. She had made a handsome gesture: in the Duke's will he had left her twenty thousand pounds and all his jewels, but she rejected both bequests, and asked only for a small ring, with a black diamond, which the old man had always worn. But it had been made only for effect; and the situation for the sake of which she had produced it gives her no comfort, for it was barren:

Even in her close connection with the present Duchess there was something which was almost hollow. Had there not been a compact between them, never expressed, but not the less understood? Had

not her dear friend, Lady Glencora, agreed to bestow
upon her support, fashion, and all kinds of worldly
good things,—on condition that she never married
the old Duke? She had liked Lady Glencora,—had
enjoyed her friend's society and been happy in her
friend's company,—but she had always felt that
Lady Glencora's attraction to herself had been
simply on the score of the Duke. It was necessary
that the Duke should be pampered and kept in good
humour. An old man, let him be ever so old, can do
what he likes with himself and his belongings. To
keep the Duke out of harm's way Lady Glencora
had opened her arms to Madame Goesler. Such, at
least, was the interpretation which Madame Goesler
chose to give to the history of the last three years.
They had not, she thought, quite understood her.
When once she had made up her mind not to marry
the Duke, the Duke had been safe from her;—as
his jewels and money should be safe now that he
was dead.

Here we must take note again of the essential impurity
of literature. We must feel intense satisfaction in Trollope's creation of the episode and the involved characters,
which are indeed on a very high level, on a Balzacian
level. There is sublime mastery in the account of the
means by which Madame Goesler disposes of her self-
awareness when, at the end of her reflections, it grows
too uncomfortable a possession. "Instead of being borne
down by grief at the loss of a friend, she found herself
almost rejoicing at relief from a vexatious burden. Had
she been a hypocrite then? Was it her nature to be false?"
But nothing, it turns out, was her fault. "She had tried
to believe in the Duke of Omnium, but there she had

153

failed." Her egotism is absolute and so, by consequence, is her loneliness. But the episode leaves us unhappy about Trollope in his capacity as moralist. Madame Goesler marries Phineas Finn and continues to be linked with Lady Glencora, now the Dutchess of Omnium, in a friendship which Trollope seems to take too seriously, or rather, as something it cannot have been. There could be a kind of friendship, even of a touching sort, between two women who had met to bargain over an old man's bones: the comradeship of harsh and harried people who find themselves able to speak their mind to one another because each holds the same assumptions and is compelled to sympathy. But Trollope considered Lady Glencora and her husband as admirable figures. "I think," he wrote of them, "that Plantagenet Palliser, Duke of Omnium, is a perfect gentleman. If he be not, then am I unable to describe a gentleman. She is by no means a perfect lady:—but if she be not all over a woman, then am I not able to describe a woman" (*Autobiography*, ch. 20).

It is odd that Trollope should have imagined that Madame Goesler could like or be liked by a man who was really a gentleman, or a woman who was really a woman. But Trollope represents their friendship as a solid and gracious edifice. When in *The Duke's Children*, the Duchess is struck down in early middle life, it is Madame Goesler who is with her when she dies, and it is to her that the Duke turns when he needs someone to take charge of his young daughter Mary. Again, this is credible. Harsh people may be kind to each other. But it is odd that Trollope should write of this relationship as if it were composed of manifestations of sensitiveness, and there is a more fundamental oddity than that. The Duke is not a perfect gentleman. Madame Goesler refuses to take charge of Mary, and is, characteristically, moved to the refusal by two considerations, one of which she discloses, one of which she conceals, for reasons of cunning. The first, which she discloses, is her consciousness that she has no rank. The second, which she does not disclose, is her knowledge that Mary is in love with a poor commoner, and that her dead mother fostered the affair, although it would obviously be distasteful to the Duke. There is no reason why Madame Goesler could not have put the matter before the Duke in a way which would have spared his feelings, but she takes no risks and disengages herself. Nevertheless she cannot quite free herself, and though she behaves correctly in her dealings with Mary and the young man, she excites the enmity of the Duke.

He then behaves to her with barbarous insolence. This is artistically right. The narrow, inarticulate man behaves outrageously because he is distraught with grief for his dead wife. When he gets the letter in which Madame Goesler explains and completely justifies her actions, he resents it for many reasons (*The Duke's Children*, ch. 15):

> And then how wretched a thing it was for him that anyone should dare to write to him about the wife that had been taken away from him! In spite of all her faults her name was so holy to him that it had never once passed his lips since her death, except in low whispers to himself,—low whispers made in the perfect, double-guarded seclusion of his own chamber. "Cora, Cora," he had murmured, so that the sense of the sound and not the sound itself had come to him from his own lips. And now this woman wrote to him about her freely, as though there were nothing sacred, no religion in the memory of her.

155

It would have been true of this man that his sorrow, graceful as a mourner carved on some neo-classical memorial tablet so long as it had only an interior existence, should express itself in boorishness. But it is odd that Trollope should have considered a man whose expression was so crass as the examplar of a breed whose title to respect is its capacity for restraint. It even occurs to the Duke, in his rage against the woman who has been such service to his family and who was his dead wife's closest friend, that "he might just acknowledge the letter, after the fashion which has come up in official life, than which silence is an insult much more bearable." Such official letters are still written in our age, and surely anyone at the head of an agency which dispatches them can be regarded as a gentleman only if it be assumed that he is not aware of the effect they produce. It is odd, too, that Trollope should think of Madame Goesler's attempts to win an apology from this boor as a sign of self-respect, although they are inspired, like all her actions, by a double motive. She knows she has been unjustly accused by her dead friend's husband, and her husband's political interests might be prejudiced if the Duke were not obliged to own his accusation false. And her efforts take her to a point far beyond the frontiers of abjection.

But it would be absurd to think that Trollope has failed to notice these flaws in his characters. We notice them only because of his directing finger. He knows they are not valuable people, according to the criteria which we apply to individuals, but he believed that they derived a value from the part they played in society. This belief, however, was not so simple as may be supposed. He did not hold any infantile faith that the rich did the community a great service by being rich, and indeed in a quiet paragraph describing the death of the Duke of Omnium, Madame Goesler's suitor, he dismissed it as folly (*Phineas Redux*, ch. 24):

> There was not a club in London, and hardly a drawing-room in which something was not said that day in consequence of the two bulletins which had appeared as to the condition of the old Duke:—and in no club and in no drawing-room was a verdict given against the dying man. It was acknowledged everywhere that he had played his part in a noble and even in a princely manner, that he had used with a becoming grace the rich things that had been given him, and that he had deserved well of his country. And yet, perhaps, no man who had lived during the same period, or any portion of the period, had done less, or had devoted himself more entirely to the consumption of good things without the slightest idea of producing anything in return! But he had looked like a Duke and known how to set a high price on his own presence.

Trollope's attitude to social institutions was not dependent on any persuasion that they operated well or ill; he felt deeply that society would be a much more unpleasant place if the forces of revolution had their way, and for the most part he was as little interested in alternatives as the modern existentialist. Like Thackeray, he felt that society is playing a game of putting pegs in holes, with far more pegs than holes, and that, cruel as this game is, since the pegs have hearts and pride, and often families to keep, it would be still more cruel if the game were broken up, and some of even the lucky pegs rolled away on the floor. He felt this with great intensity. Reluctant as one must be to seek the explanation for an author's work in his personal life, since the greater he is, the more complicated the alchemic processes to which he subjects his experience, it is profitable to look for the cause of this special intensity in Trollope's early years. He spent humiliating years as a charity boy at Harrow, where, because his tutor announced this status in the classroom and because his clothes stank of his father's unprofitable farmyard, he was shunned and excluded from all games. One shocking day the boy was suddenly called to drive his sick father to the docks and put him on the Ostend boat, and returned home to find the house taken over by sheriff's officers. He was to endure misery in a great derelict house outside Bruges, where he watched beside his father, who was dying of a disease perhaps to be regarded as a complication arising out of bankruptcy, and his brother and sister, who were dying of consumption, while his mother scribbled the novels that kept them all, in such hours as remained to her after acting as both day-nurse and night-nurse. One who had lived through such a youth might well look on whatever was solvent and not sick and wish that it might flourish forever. So Trollope was for the court, because it gave an enduring and honorable shelter to the courtiers, of whom he had a divided view.

Again it is worth while going back to his own account of his early life because he spent much of it among the people who were later to be his material. He writes of the boys at Harrow: "I coveted popularity with a coveting which was almost mean. It seemed to me that there would be an Elysium in the intimacy of those very boys whom I was bound to hate because they hated me" (*Autobiography*, ch. 1). Here he was giving way to the masochistic malice of self-criticism. The child had not been mean but honest. He had observed that these boys, the children of the most attractive families in the country, had many delightful and admirable qualities, and could not shut his eyes to these because they were not displayed for his enjoyment. When he had later grasped that his schoolfellows had been obeying an instinct which made them show their hackles because his presence seemed to threaten a breach of the class system which gave them and their families the chance of cultivating their attractions, he still was honest. So he knew that people could be delightful and admirable, and owe their merits at least in part to privilege, which gave them demerits too. This was the education that gave him an exaggerated devotion to the group: a belief that the court was far more valuable than the courtiers. His view on the courtier is almost shocking. The power which saved him from squalid obscurity was his mother, of whom he wrote: "Of all people I have known she was the most joyous, or, at any rate, the most capable of joy" (ibid., ch. 2). These are heartbreaking words to be written of a woman who spent so much of her life contending with an irritable husband's self-dedication to ruin. But the last words Trollope wrote of her, closing the chapter, ran: "But she was neither clear-sighted nor accurate; and in her attempts to describe morals, manners, and even facts, was unable to avoid the pitfalls of exaggeration." What he meant was that she would not have made a good civil servant, and Trollope took this very seriously, for had he not been a civil servant he would have slipped back into the obscurity from which she had snatched him.

But for all that he was dismissing into the darkness someone of the sort that Fielding celebrated as Amelia. It is worth while turning to a passage in *Phineas Redux* which shows what kind of woman he really admired. When the Duke of Omnium owns on his deathbed that he, too, has had his revolutionary moments of doubt and has wondered why he should have been born a duke and another man a servant, Madame Goesler has her tactful answer ready (*Phineas Redux*, ch. 25):

> "God Almighty ordained such difference." "I'm afraid I have not done it well;—but I have tried: indeed I have tried." Then she told him he had ever lived as a great nobleman ought to live. And, after a fashion, she herself believed what she was saying. Nevertheless, her nature was much nobler than his; and she knew that no man should dare to live idly as the Duke had lived.

This is a curious passage. If it be accepted that to be noble means to be faithful to virtue, without regard to material considerations, Madame Goesler was not noble at all. Her whole being was absorbed in the struggle to acquire sufficient prestige to dazzle the world into forgetting that she was not an aristocrat. But Trollope's admiration of her was obstinate and it is to be supposed that he must have admired the one trait which distinguishes her from his other characters: self-awareness. Though she suppresses this when it grows too inconvenient, she is for the most part conscious of what she does, and Trollope seems to regard this as courageous, like her horsemanship. The same quality was Hamlet's chief attribute, and in him also it is part of a general audacity. It is as if Shakespeare and Trollope felt alike that since human beings are what they are, those are bold who dare to look within themselves. But Trollope was writing of an age which seemed to him so complicated and so perilous in its complication that self-awareness must be tinctured with self-interest. The court may be saving the courtiers from perdition but it does not bring them near salvation.

Trollope's view of the world as a necessary court crowded with necessitous courtiers made it difficult for him to present the essence of any man's life in a simple and shapely form. Shakespeare could tell the truth about a man by putting a group of people to act out a series of events in a palace, or a place under the shadow of some such seat of government; and he had the advantage that the status of the various people was clear to him and his audience, who also shared or at least were aware of certain fundamental assumptions about power, which were implicit in the current conception of kingship. Conditions were more complicated for Fielding, but he could still write about most of his characters in full faith that his readers would know what kind of people they were, so far as means and origins and habits and belief were concerned, and that he could regard these matters as understood and deal at once with their doings and feelings. But before Trollope could introduce his readers to a character, he had to do a great deal of description. He had to say in what part of the modern state the character had found security; and it was necessary to describe the degree of that security, whether the peg had been stuck firmly in its hole on the board or might fall out with careless handling, and this could often be done only by a careful account of his appearance, his way of speaking and dressing, his upbringing, his household. He had above all to describe the man's relations with the other inhabitants of the modern state, what place he held in their social hierarchy, and whether he was likely to go higher or sink lower, which was not quite the same as maintaining his security. This made for diffuseness and,

161

what was worse, for an unwholesome proliferation of characters. If a man was to be seen in this way, as part of a group, many samples of the group had to be given: the reader must be shown not only the people with whom he lived as equals, but the people with whom he could not live because they were his superiors, the people with whom, owing to a stroke of good luck, he succeeded in living, although they had formerly been his superiors, the people who remained his superiors, no matter what he did, the people who were his inferiors but rose to be his equals, the people who were his inferiors and remained so, and the people who were his inferiors until a stroke of bad luck reduced him to their level. The reader must even be shown people who had nothing to do with this man, so that it can be realized how vast was the forest in which this tree stood.

This is a temptation to the novelist. If he be worth his salt, it is a challenge which he can take up all too readily, and too often. In the last of the political novels, *The Duke's Children*, there is a Mrs. Spooner, of sinister significance though of genial nature, and a credit to her maker. With supreme artistry Trollope tells us all about her; how she "had been the penniless daughter of a retired officer,—but yet managed to ride on whatever animal anyone would lend her" (ch. 62), and had then married old Tom Spooner of Spoon Hall, and thereupon had hunted four days a week, "never flirted and wanted no one to open gates," and was "a good housewife, taking care that nothing should be spent lavishly, except upon the stable." We are given an economical but exhaustive account of her good heart and good sense, particularly as they manifested themselves in her horsemanship. But there is no reason why we should know anything about her at all. She plays some part in the hunting accident when Tregear falls at a rail and Silverbridge follows him too close, and his horse rolls on the prostrate man; but that episode could be perfectly well handled without her. The truth is that Trollope found it amusing to create her, and his readers found it amusing to make her acquaintance. But she harms the book, which is already bursting with superfluous characters, and, benevolent as she may be in herself, she may be thought of as the Hecate who presided over the novel in the dark years when it was within sight of ruin by overpopulation. Novelists found that when they created characters their readers were enchanted, and that when they did not trouble to create them, but merely invented them, those readers continued to be enchanted, with an obstinate fidelity which made it unnecessary to tether these characters to any theme. Readers did not insist on an interpretation of life; they were often satisfied with an imitation of it, and a clever writer, compiling a list of the superficial attributes of a character, could imitate life very brightly. Who were Lord Mussleburgh, Peggie Roslyn, Jack Duncombe, Oswald van Rosen, George Brand, Natalie Lind, Nana Beresford, Frank King, Sheila Mackenzie, Frank Lavender, Sir Anthony Zembra, Walter Lindsay, Lord Arthur Redburn, Will Anerly, Annie Napier? They were a few of the many characters invented by a Victorian novelist named William Black, who began publishing about fifteen years before Trollope's death, and was industrious for another twenty years after it. He had many colleagues (such as Sir Walter Besant) who were as prolific, and are as much forgotten.

Flaubert describes how Julian the Hospitaller, when his princely state had inflamed his baser nature and he had grown gluttonous on the pleasures of the chase, wandered one night into a strange forest, and found himself surrounded by the phantoms of all the poor beasts which he had unnecessarily deprived of life. They followed at his heels, fanning his flesh with their jungle breath. It can be imagined that an English novelist, going home through the darkness, might find himself followed by a trail of characters to whom he had unnecessarily given life, fanning his flesh with their insignificant breath.

4 *The Convention of Dissent*

The view of life to which the nineteenth-century novel was committed was unfavorable to the soliloquy or to any equivalent revelation of the self. The soliloquy supposed that what a man says to himself may be of supreme importance and that he may thereby submit his case to a higher court than presides over the conversations he may have with others. But this supposition cannot be accepted by a writer who thinks that man achieves his positive value only as a member of society—who is a Pelagian of the sort which believes that humanity can be saved by the efforts of its own will, provided that will is expressed through a group which, if one takes a quantitative standard, is strong, and not through the individual, who by that standard is weak. There is, of course, a Victorian novel which looks deeply into its characters, though the author was entirely convinced of the importance of the group and its capacity to work miracles. George Eliot's faith in the capacity of culture to improve on what had preceded it in time was a logical consequence of the belief in the redemptory power of the group, which since it was always doing well, must, since it enjoyed the benefit of the accumulations of its own virtue, do better and better. Her hope that the whole content of religion could be revised by modern scholarship, and her anxiety that the ethical code founded on religious belief should not deteriorate but improve as a result of the revision, were essential parts of her being, and she allowed them to interfere with the free flow of her imagination. They led her to speed up the journey of the universe toward perfection by insisting on harmonies which do not yet exist. In *Middlemarch* Dr. Casaubon neglected Dorothea on their honeymoon in Rome in order to pursue his researches, and later he turned out to be an indifferent scholar and his lifework a blunder. But any reader with some experience of life will know that a fine scholar might neglect his wife on his honeymoon, and that an indifferent scholar might be a most attentive bridegroom. It is also put to us that Dorothea was an idealist and a wise and thrifty house-wife, and that Rosamond Vincy was a materialist and a spendthrift, although many daughters of Minerva have let money run through their fingers and many daughters of Venus have been of a saving disposition. It cannot be taken that George Eliot is telling us that it was thus and so in the case of the particular people she was describing, for she has the air of pinning her faith to these con-gruities. She hardly would trouble to describe life were it not so consistent. Nevertheless, *Middlemarch* is one of the great English novels, firmly constructed and deeply felt. But it was written by a woman of genius who was the contemporary of Trollope—she and he and Dickens and Thackeray were all born in the second decade of the nineteenth century. Where the tradition they followed was leading was apparent in the next generation, when Mrs. Humphry Ward was acclaimed for novels which were at once crowded and empty, solemn and trivial.

Meanwhile another tradition was establishing itself in England. Meredith was born in the next decade, in 1828, and his first novels came out about the same time as Trollope's Barchester series, and Thomas Hardy was born in 1840, and his first novels came out about the same time as Trollope's political novels. Yet Meredith and Hardy seem to belong to the generation after Trollope, or even to the generation after that. Neither of them is widely read as a novelist today, and it would be safe to say that they survive rather as poets, and that this is just. No novel of Meredith's is as great as his poem *Modern Love;* and readers of *The Mayor of Casterbridge* and *The Trumpet Major* are pleased for many reasons, but perhaps most of all by recognition of the disciplined, cunning, yet untricked beauty, the shrewd and canny yet loving and trusting observation of human nature, which they have already learned to love in Hardy's poetry. Yet the novels of Meredith and Hardy are true works of art, which still delight—and will surely delight till time has broken the bridge between the future and our past—by their substance and their form, their perception and their expressiveness, and they were of great temporal importance. They were the inaugurators of a period in which the novel was to be chiefly a call of revolt. Indeed they were the mouthpieces of two rebellions, one particular and one general. They attempted to correct an abuse peculiar to their age; and they were also blowing a long blast on the rams' horns, at the sound of which all the people were to shout with a great shout, and the wall of the city of Jericho was to fall down flat, and society as they knew it was to perish and be rebuilt.

The contemporary abuse that Meredith and Hardy chiefly denounced was the indignity which had befallen women in the previous hundred years. The women in the works of Shakespeare and Fielding were far more free than the women shown us by Dickens and Thackeray and Trollope. The difference in their status can be grasped if one tries to imagine an interchange of their female characters. Dickens was tender to women in a lachrymose way, Thackeray liked them well enough, and Trollope was a feminist. But it would be astounding to find a Juliet in their pages. None of the three could have respected her

167

passion as Shakespeare respected it, for the double reason that it was beautiful in itself and that it had a right to exist, like her own body, like the lovely town about her, like lovely Italy, like all sound processes of nature. It would be equally astounding to find Agnes Wickfield or Amelia Sedley given importance in a Shakespearean play; he had dismissed them as born "to suckle fools and chronicle small beer" through the mouth of one to whom he would probably have attached Madame Goesler as a working partner, had he been obliged to handle her. As for Fielding's Amelia, no woman created by Dickens or Thackeray or Trollope cares to love and live so courageously; and that standard had fallen even during the half century that had passed since Jane Austen had written. She had been subject to some constraint, and it is impossible to imagine any of her women venturing on marriage with either Billy Booth or Tom Jones. But it would have been impossible for Dickens or Thackeray or Trollope to let any of their heroines use her wits in fencing with her future husband as Elizabeth fenced with Mr. Darcy. Indeed, Trollope was deeply shocked by his own Lady Glencora, because she teased her solemn husband on their honeymoon. It is true that he represents virtuous young women as being extremely disagreeable. The dialogue ascribed to Alice Vavasour in *Can You Forgive Her?* is invariably rebarbative. But humor is never present, and the surliness is evidently the response to an intensification of the situation which is described by Jane Austen. In her day a woman's safety from humiliation depended not on her own worth but on the solvency and status of her parents, her ingenuity in preventing herself from being compromised or jilted, and her success in disclaiming strength of intellect and emotion. But by Trollope's time the pitfalls before her had greatly increased, and a woman of pride and foresight had to put out so many defenses that she became as prickly as a porcupine.

This was partly due to a great change in the English attitude to money. The country was becoming saner about its wealth. The aristocracy had been idiotic in the use it made of its great fortunes while it lived and more idiotic in the carelessness with which it disposed of it when it died. Elizabeth Montagu, the first blue-stocking, who was born in 1720 and died in 1800, was one of those people who can live fully and yet remain isolated from the life of their time. She showed it in no way more clearly than the sobriety with which she faced the fact of her own great wealth. Her letters often break into complaint against her contemporaries who had no such vigilance of conscience in this matter, such as an octogenarian peer who died intestate, making no provision for the mob of helpless old pensioners in his great house, although the heir at law could take no steps to help them, since he was a not much younger brother of the dead man, himself senile and paralyzed. By the middle of the nineteenth century all this was altered, and the new concern that people felt for the maintenance of their families was reflected in various acts regarding testacy. And they had more to leave. Society was beginning to understand the principle of the joint-stock company, which had existed ever since the sixteenth century, but which had been confused even by financial experts with the idea of monopoly and had never been subjected to intelligent codification. All through the twenties and thirties Parliament was taking steps which gave investment a new security and respectability, and in 1844 there was passed the Joint Stock Companies Act, which laid the foundation for the British company law. While Dickens and Thackeray and Trollope were writing, progress was made in introducing the principle of limited liability, and in 1862 there was passed the Consolidating Companies Act, which gave English finance for the rest of the century its peculiar reputation for stability. All this had the curious result of making women seem as dangerous as if they were made of dynamite.

A man now felt that he was establishing his moral and social value when he made a fortune and transmitted to his descendants as much of it as would enable them to live in comfort and leisure and serve the state by public work. But he might be wholly frustrated in this effort to give his ego permanence if his daughter attempted to establish her moral value by insisting on her right to dispose of her own person in marriage. For a married woman could own no property. All she possessed as a spinster passed to her husband as soon as she married him, and all she acquired after her marriage became his automatically. Therefore, if she married a scoundrel or an incompetent, there was no means by which her father could be sure that the money by which he hoped to establish his own worth and hers would not be wasted. The chief subsidiary plot in *The Prime Minister* gives painful proof of this: the endless legal and financial complications, all of them attended by genuine unselfish distress, which were brought on Mr. Wharton by his daughter Emily's marriage to Ferdinand Lopez were in fact a real wrong inflicted on an upright and sensible and affectionate man. It was possible to rectify the situation by ingenious settlements, but this required the consent of the husband. That was done in the case of Lady Glencora's fortune, but Plantagenet Palliser was a paragon, and even so the arrangement gave rise to wounding moments. When she squandered vast sums on the realization of her

170

inflated dreams of the pomp appropriate to a Prime Minister, and Palliser rebuked her, there was bitterness. She thought to herself that he had no right to question how she spent her own money, and he thought to himself that it was her own money indeed, but only because he had relinquished his legal right to it, and that this should surely have made her more delicate about the disposal of it. There was no end to the injurious side effects of this horrid situation, which was not to be rectified until, through the advocacy of Dr. Pankhurst, a bill was passed which gave married women the right to own property.

The worst of these side effects was a morbidity which invaded even the most normal of relationships. The love of money comes from primitive elements in our nature, and so does the love of a father for a daughter. The confusion of these two obscure forces was apt to engender emotions which, even in the least barbaric of men, were not civilized. In *The Duke's Children* there is a brilliant analysis of how disadvantageously the situation affected even the correct Plantagenet Palliser. He has just left a friend who has told him that his daughter must go about in society, because she may forget the unsuitable young man of her choice, when "someone else has made himself agreeable to her" (ch. 11):

> The Duke as he went away thought very much of what Lady Cantrip had said to him; particularly of those last words. "Till someone else has made himself agreeable to her." Was he to send his girl into the world in order that she might find a lover? There was something in the idea which was thoroughly distasteful to him. He had not given his mind much to the matter, but he felt that a woman should be

171

sought for,—sought for and extracted, cunningly, as it were, from some hiding-place, and not sent out into a market to be exposed as for sale. In his own personal history there had been a misfortune,—a misfortune, the sense of which he could never, at any moment, have expressed to any ears, the memory of which had been always buried in his own bosom,—but a misfortune in that no such cunning extraction on his part had won for him the woman to whose hands had been confided the strings of his heart. His wife had undergone that process of extraction before he had seen her, and his marriage with her had been a matter of sagacious bargaining. He was now told that his daughter must be sent out among young men in order that she might become sufficiently fond of some special one to be regardless of Tregear. There was a feeling that in doing so she must lose something of the freshness of the bloom of her innocence. How was this transfer of her love to be effected? Let her go here because she will meet the heir of this wealthy house who may probably be smitten by her charms; or there because that other young lordling would make a fit husband for her. Let us contrive to throw her into the arms of this man, or put her into the way of that man. Was his girl to be exposed to this? Surely that method of bargaining to which he had owed his own wife would be better than that. Let it be said,—only he himself most certainly could not be the person to say it,—let it be said to some man of rank and means and fairly good character: "Here is a wife for you with so many thousand pounds, with beauty, as you can see for yourself, with rank and belongings of the highest; very good in every respect;—only that as regards her heart she thinks she has given it to a a young man named Tregear. No marriage there is possible; but perhaps the young lady might suit you?" It was thus he had been married. There was an absence in it of that romance which, though he had never experienced it in his own life, was always present to his imagination. His wife had often ridiculed him because he could only live among figures and official details; but to her had not been given the power of looking into a man's heart and feeling all that was there. Yes;—in such bargaining for a wife, in such bargaining for a husband, there could be nothing of the tremulous delicacy of feminine romance; but it would be better than standing at a stall in the market till the sufficient purchaser should come. It never occurred to him that the delicacy, the innocence, the romance, the bloom might all be preserved if he would give his girl to the man whom she said she loved. Could he have modeled her future course according to his own wishes, he would have had her live a gentle life for the next three years, with a pencil perhaps in her hand or a music-book before her;—and then come forth, cleaned as if it were by such quarantine from the impurity to which she had been subjected.

We are back with Ophelia: we see a human being treated as a thing because it happens to be female. It is alarming that her tormentor is not the Renaissance man, who by definition was dangerous, a creature with no more inhibitions than a new-born babe, who nevertheless lays about him with the strength and subtlety of a grown man. It is the Victorian man who is torturing her, although he is defining himself as civilized and morally mature. There

173

was some justice in the claim, for Plantagenet ultimately gave way, and Lady Mary had no need to end where a willow grew aslant a brook. But such progress related to external matters. Though this man desired to be good, and indeed was better than his fellows in many respects, there was still boiling in him a ferment of primitive emotions which would have preferred feminine flesh to have been uninhabited by any will.

It is out of the question to suppose that Trollope could have recorded the situation so honestly had he approved it. But he lacked the first requisite for replacing Ophelia by Amelia. Fielding was able to imagine a woman falling in love—that is, using her will in the most extreme way, which may upset all the arrangements that have been made by all men concerned with her—because he had a manly appetite for pleasure; and in the first chapter of Book VI in *Tom Jones*, which deals with love, he exposes the mechanism (ch. 1):

> First, we will grant that many minds, and perhaps those of the philosophers, are entirely free from the least traces of such a passion.
>
> Secondly, that what is commonly called love, namely the desire of satisfying a voracious appetite with a certain quantity of delicate white human flesh, is by no means that passion for which I here contend. This is indeed more properly hunger; and as no glutton is ashamed to apply the word love to his appetite, and to say he LOVES such and such dishes; so may the lover of this kind, with equal propriety, say, he HUNGERS after such and such women.
>
> Thirdly, I will grant, which I believe will be a most acceptable concession, that this love for which I am

174

an advocate, though it satisfies itself in a much more delicate manner, doth nevertheless seek its own satisfaction as much as the grossest of all our appetites. And, lastly, that this love, when it operates towards one of a different sex, is very apt, towards its complete gratification, to call in the aid of that hunger which I have mentioned above; and which it is so far from abating, that it heightens all its delights to a degree scarce imaginable by those who have never been susceptible of any other emotions than what have proceeded for appetite alone.

. . . Though the pleasures arising from such pure love may be heightened and sweetened by the assistance of amorous desires, yet the former can subsist alone, nor are they destroyed by the intervention of the latter. Lastly, that esteem and gratitude are the proper motives to love, as youth and beauty are to desire; and therefore, though such desire may naturally cease, when age or sickness overtakes its object; yet those can have no effect on love, nor ever shake or remove, from a good mind, that sensation or passion which hath gratitude and esteem for its basis.

It is quite clear that Fielding could write about men and women with serene power because he had faced all possible contingencies in their relationship and considered them in the light of his own philosophy. But Trollope, though he wrote constantly of the attraction between the sexes, submitted to the pressure of his age and disregarded some of the commonest features of life among the nubile. He was neither a prude nor a coward; *The Mayor of Bulhampton* is an attack on the convention by which the Victorians closed their doors on their erring daughters, while "for our erring sons we find pardon easily enough." But occasionally he would distort a story in the interests of propriety. The part played by Lady Laura Standish in the life of Phineas Finn is not credible unless it be assumed that Trollope is lying, and that she is a mistress who has lost her lover because her pervasive lack of harmony makes her passion burdensome, but who keeps a place in his life by her devotion and her manifest worth. It is, however, more important and more regrettable that Trollope's lovers are always mysteriously located outside the biological framework. They are forever marrying and giving in marriage, but a being from another planet who had only Trollope's novels to go on would never find out why. It is conceded, largely conceded, that a hunger was felt; but there is a lack of sensuous feeling and domestic warmth in his world, which means that he is not bringing whole men and women into his books. He is cutting down his courtiers to fit them into the court.

Meredith and Hardy both possessed, to a high degree, the quality which was so abundantly present in Fielding and so lacking in Trollope. They could bear to think of the whole field in which men and women have their being, and they revolted against the pretense that part of this field was empty space, and that women had been constructed without certain parts, including the will; and their revolt was so great that in memory their work appears as two long galleries filled with portraits of beautiful and rebellious women. Meredith's heroines are brave and usually well born. They hold their heads high, they perform splendid feats, using their sensuousness as an instrument of their courage. The pattern of a Meredithean heroine's great moment is Aminta's bathe in the North Sea, her strength bearing her up happily in "the region where our life is as we would have it be; a home holding the quiet of the heavens, if but midway thither, and a home of delicious animation of the whole frame, equal to wings" (*Lord Ormont and His Aminta*, ch. 27), while she swims out of her oppressive husband's irrational life, into the reasoned life of her lover. Hardy's heroines sat more quietly on the canvas, conditioned either by the need to earn their bread or to bide quietly with breadwinning husbands, or to carry out the duties which the sober sort of landowner felt it right to discharge. But, though his style was chastity itself, he put all his heroines back in the biological framework. How he disposes of them has its special value because of his decorum. It could be suspected that what Meredith said about women could not be accepted as evidence, by reason of his proneness to ecstasy; but Hardy had none of that. Quietly, without lust in his heart, though with a great capacity for love and a due recognition of its proper end, he watched the Wessex country women go by on their way to the byre and the dairy, and wondered how it went with them within their print dresses, or bowed over the hands of noble dames at the annual County Ball in the Assembly Rooms and tried to guess what was written on the obverse of the pride they wore like heavy antique lockets. He saw women as possessing imagination of a sort which never lit the clay of their menfolk, and he even set their power higher, as a magical gift.

In *Wessex Tales* there is a story which has a significance greater than lies on the surface. Ella Marchmill is the wife of a dull man, and mother of his dull children, who is herself a little brighter, being to a poetaster what a poetaster is to a poet. When the family is spending the August holiday at a watering place, she learns that a famous young poet is staying near by and tries to meet him, but is disappointed and has to satisfy herself by brooding over his photograph. After she returns home, she reads in the newspapers that the young poet has killed himself, and she falls into a state of melancholia and dies in childbirth in the following May. The child she gives birth to is so like the poet that when the husband finds the poet's photograph among his wife's possessions two years after her death, when he is clearing up the house before his second wife installs herself, he feels certain that the child is illegitimate. "Get away you poor little brat! You are nothing to me!"

There is something very characteristic of Hardy in the simplicity with which he bases this story on the old wives' tale of children born with the image of their mother's longings printed on them; it could be false, but time has put forward so much evidence in its favor that a shrewd countryman could not dismiss it. The story also makes a temperate and tender claim that a little lamp is better than total darkness and may be a pretty thing in itself. But it makes a wider reference than that. Meredith and Hardy were for the courtiers and against the court. They were definitely opposed to Shakespeare, who was against both courtiers and court, because their quarrel with the court was only temporary. Like him, they saw it as an imperfect institution which could be raised to perfection by the efforts of "good-natured" courtiers, and like him they believed that it was the ladies of the court whose efforts were most likely to reform it. But Fielding's conceptions of the perfected court and the redemptory female were quite different from theirs. Fielding's ideal society was the one he knew, changed only so far as just and merciful government would change it; and Amelia was to save Billy Booth by harnessing his sensual nature to the sentiments of "esteem and gratitude," by mak-

178

ing him and their home a source of benevolent rays which should warm the social atmosphere to the temperature conducive to the cultivation of justice and mercy. His ideal was in the possible range of the real.

But Meredith and Hardy were bound to think of the required redemption in quite another way, because the French Revolution had happened between Fielding's death and their birth, and it was nearer to them than they are to us; and they had lived through the intoxicating year of 1848. They cared not only for liberty and fraternity, which Fielding also had cared for, but also for equality, which he had only partially considered. The economic inequalities of society had indeed distressed him, but not its social inequalities, which he took for granted, although obviously the grosser sorts would be eliminated by "good nature." But Dickens and Thackeray and Trollope resented the poverty of the poor with a more impatient, even hysterical passion than Fielding had felt, because they had seen the success of the charitable and legislative efforts which he and his kind had inaugurated, and they wanted the task finished; and they were resentful of the class system on behalf not only of the poor, but of the class to which they belonged, the middle class, and of their own artistic kind. Thackeray spoke, for once, with greater candor than Dickens and Trollope when he expressed their common sense of insult in the last chapter of *The Book of Snobs*. "A Court system," he wrote, "that sends men of genius to the second table, I hold it to be a snobbish system. A society that sets up to be polite, and ignores Art and Letters, I hold to be a snobbish society." The younger men were more candid still. Meredith made the same complaint in *Evan Harrington,* which records the difficulties encountered by a young man who, being gifted and well mannered,

179

wished to be accepted as a gentleman but was (like himself) a tailor's grandson. Hardy makes the same complaint on behalf of his young architect (he himself was an architect and the son of a builder) whose social status is the operative fact in *Two on a Tower*. This situation the redemptory female could not remedy by imitating Amelia. But it was thought, and the thinking had a vague connection with the evolutionary theory which had burst on the world in 1859, that if women ceased to be the property of their fathers and were able to choose their own mates, their instinct would always lead them to seek out the healthiest and most gifted men, irrespective of their worldly state. Thus the class system would be destroyed, in the most romantic and enjoyable manner imaginable.

This was a crucial point in the history of imaginative literature. The novel was taking aboard a load of revolutionary thought which it was to carry as its chief cargo till our own day. The feminism of Meredith and Hardy was not an isolated force, but was bound up for them, and for their contemporary disciples, and for their successors, even to Shaw and Wells and Galsworthy, with a revolt against existing social institutions. There is a curious expression of this belief in Ibsen's remark that the future of Europe rested with women and workmen. Women were to break down the class system and also improve the race by choosing the fittest mates, and to kill superstition by practising a rational code of ethics which would permit them to leave mates who had proved themselves unworthy; while the working classes were to be given a large share of the national wealth, and government was to be conducted by all—there was to be no such thing as a governing class. All these things were in fact about to happen. Women were going to assert their capacity for independence and put an end to the made marriage; they were going to extort from Parliament legal permission to keep their own earnings, to own property, and to sign contracts, after marriage as before. Workmen were going to organize themselves in trade unions, the suffrage was to be extended, and the Labor Party was to become one of the two great political parties. These changes were all the inevitable results of the industrial revolution, the growth of the population, and the extension of education. But Meredith, Hardy, and their followers induced the cultured to accept these changes not only as innovations desirable in themselves, in the results they procured, but as examples of a process which ought to be repeated again and again, because it had the supreme value of destroying what already existed. They established the convention that the superior man must not only be ready to rebel against conditions which were inflicting some wrong on the community or a part of it, but also be a rebel as a second profession. It might have seemed obvious that he must sometimes be under an obligation to practice conformity, since it would be absurd if he did not acquiesce in some social arrangement, which he himself had initiated by rebellion. But this was disregarded. The convention demanded that he should be ready and willing to attack society at any moment.

This was not so illogical as it sounds. Both Meredith and Hardy had rejected the European religious tradition and were pantheists of the modern sort, who saw Nature as redeemed and given a soul by man's observation and interpretation. Meredith found this a joyous prospect, an eternal neoclassical *fête champêtre*. In *The Dynasts* Hardy used some odd supernatural machinery to express his grimmer version of this philosophy. The Spirits of the Years and of the Pities, the Spirits Sinister and Ironic, the

181

Shade of the Earth, and their immaterial attendants pass among the living persons who are acting out the Napoleonic drama, uttering discouraging comments on the lack of purpose in history; but these abstractions all meet together after Waterloo and come to a more favorable conclusion. The last chorus reads (Pt. III, After Scene):

But—a stirring thrills the air
Like to sounds of joyance there
That the rages
Of the ages
Shall be cancelled, and deliverance offered from the darts that were,
Consciousness the Will informing, till It fashion all things fair.

This appears at first sight to propound a ridiculous theory that man is a missionary to God, but of course Hardy was not so silly, nor Meredith either. They saw the human will as incorrupt, and therefore believed the courtiers capable of creating a court in which all things would be fair; but the courtiers were plainly handicapped by their ignorance, which century by century, decade by decade, was dispelled. The court as it was yesterday could not be so good as it was today or would be tomorrow; so reform was doomed to eat its children, and the reformer to become a rebel engaged in a permanent revolution.

The weakness of this plausible theory is its total belief in progress. The state of humanity has indeed improved with the passing of time: the care of children is, in most inhabited parts of the globe, more kind and efficient than it has ever been before; in large areas fewer people than ever before are cold and hungry; the treasures of art are accessible to more people than in any preceding age. But Aristotle and Plato and Aquinas are not dwarfed by our

182

contemporary thinkers, nobody is writing as well as Shakespeare, or painting as well as Titian, or composing as well as Beethoven. These people may be given their peers in the future, but the quality of human cerebration certainly does not improve steadily, in step with time. We cannot take it that any community knows so much more than its predecessors that it would be justified in assuming itself to be doing well when it destroyed their social arrangements, until it had taken the strictest account of whether the substitute it was going to bring into being was superior in its effect on human beings. But even if the quality of thought showed a steady secular development, that would not justify the cult of rebellion for its own sake. For the fact that children and the sick are cared for, that society guards against unemployment and destitution, and art galleries and concerts and public libraries are provided for the people is the result of the absorption of thinking which went on quite a long time ago. Good government depends on the recognition of certain principles (such as the necessity of suppressing physical violence and enabling every citizen full opportunities to be as healthy in body and mind as his constitution permits) which were discovered in the dim past, since they are so essential to good government that they emerged as soon as man tried to govern himself. For this reason antique institutions may serve modern needs, if they are rebelled against as soon as they operate in an obsolete manner, and if those who rebel against them conform as soon as they succeed in getting them modified, and stay quiet until the modifications are worked out in practice. It is therefore better when admiration is given to the man who can both rebel and conform, according to the needs of the time, and not to the man who can only rebel. But this obvious prescription was not realized by many novelists of the late nineteenth and twentieth century.

As time went on, it came about that every novelist who hoped to be taken seriously had to accept the obligation to be in opposition. When Robert Louis Stevenson died in the last decade of the nineteenth century, he left an astounding amount of enduring work, considering that he had lived a scant forty-four years, harried by sickness: *The Master of Ballantrae, Treasure Island,* and *Weir of Hermiston* are paragons in their own class. But the colleagues who survived him hesitated to admit his place among the immortals, not because they doubted his title to that place, but because he was not serious, which was to say that he was not a rebel. Actually Stevenson understood rebellion very well, but his was a historical understanding based on the Jacobitism of his native Scotland, and did not count with his contemporaries, whose hostility to institutions was an affair not of history but of ideology, in an atmospheric form. There was a vague connection between this vague revolt and Rousseauism, which itself is a vague entity. No discreet person would wish to write of Rousseauism without imperative cause, for it is so large a subject that a writer can easily seize on a part and be traitor to the whole. One of the best known and most influential books on Rousseau published in the last century is explicable only if it be supposed that it was written about another man of the same name, possibly the Douanier Rousseau. But it is a mark of the greatness of Rousseau that where his shadow fell it never passed away, but left a pattern on the earth; and in order to understand the English novelists and the novel readers of the nineteenth century, it is necessary to grasp the fundamental facts about the teachings of Rousseau.

Emil Faguet pointed out long ago that the principles

laid down by Rousseau in *The Social Contract* are not the same as those laid down in his other works, and indeed often contradict them. In *Emile* Rousseau regards civilization as a system of constricting outrages practiced on the natural man. "One is obliged," he wrote, "to choose between maiming a man and making a citizen, for one cannot make both at the same time" (ch. 1); and he declares that "everything is good when it leaves the hand of the author of nature; everything degenerates in the hands of man." *Julie* echoes this cry against the hardening of social pressure into tyranny over the spontaneous, and while not abandoning the conception of duty, the book recommends moral guidance by ecstasy and sentiment. It has often been pointed out that some readers have imagined that *The Social Contract* pleads the same case, because the famous first sentence runs "Man is born free, and everywhere he is in chains," and this sounds as if the author were describing a situation which strikes him as deplorable. But the rest of the paragraph and the whole of the book makes it clear that Rousseau thought it man's supreme good fortune that he should wear those chains, and is only concerned with establishing the legitimacy of the act which imposed them on him, and the best way of wearing them (Bk. I, ch. 8):

> The passage from the natural to the civil state produces a very remarkable change in man [he wrote], substituting justice for instinct as the guide to his conduct, and giving his actions the morality they previously lacked. . . . Although in this state he loses many of his material advantages, he gains so many in return, his faculties are exercised and developed, his ideas are broadened, his sentiments ennobled and his whole soul elevated to such an extent

185

that if the abuses of this new condition did not often degrade him beneath his former state, he ought unceasingly to bless the happy moment which wrested him forever from it, and turned him from a stupid and limited animal to an intelligent being and a man.

It is true that Rousseau takes back what he gives in the phrase "if the abuses of his new condition did not often degrade him beneath his former state," and that we get a further jar when we ask what "his former state" can mean. Had Rousseau, have we any knowledge of men not to some degree organized in a civil state? It is to be remembered that anthropology had got well on its feet during the eighteenth century, and was specially interested in the social organization of early peoples, as it wished to prove that the instinct to form civilizations was implanted by God. But later on, in the chapter on "real property," there is a footnote which blows up the book like a bomb: "As a matter of fact, laws are always useful to those who have property, and harmful to those who have nothing. It follows, therefore, that the social contract is advantageous only insofar as they all have something, and no one has any more than he needs."

This is obviously not true. To take a single example: in many areas, at many periods, the laws against murder have not been of any special service to the rich, or specially inconvenient to the poor, even in communities where some people owned no property and others owned far more than they needed. But even if it were true, what does this assumption make of Rousseau's enthusiasm for the social contract, which is now admitted to operate favorably only in conditions which have never existed? It suggests that Rousseau is dealing with the matter superficially in not first planning how economic equality is to be established, other than by a few simple prescriptions regarding land tenure. It is true that in 1762 there was a lot less economic science to be taken into account than there was a hundred years later, as one realizes when one reads the *Considerations on the Government of Poland and on Its Proposed Reformation*, which Rousseau prepared at the request of the Confederation of Bar, a body of Polish landowners who had banded together to make plans for restoring the independence of Poland after its virtual annexation by Russia. Rousseau was able to advise them to have no financial system at all: "Financial systems are modern," he wrote, "I cannot see that anything good or great came of them. The governments of antiquity did not even know the meaning of finance, and what they accomplished with men is prodigious" (*Considerations on the Government of Poland,* ch. 11). This was not to seem as absurd as it seems to us until the industrial revolution had had its way with the world. But the fact remains that Rousseau laid down an economic condition as necessary for the satisfactory fulfillment of the social contract which made it inapplicable to the nineteenth century, and it might have been thought that this would have limited the duration of his influence.

It is uncertain from moment to moment whether what Rousseau writes about the civil state is to be taken as the description of a historical phenomenon deemed to exist or to have existed, or a blueprint of one which might exist in the future, but the haze is only round the foundations. The structure itself is distinct enough. It is so necessary for man to be shielded by membership in a society that he must surrender all his rights to it; and society will return to him all those rights after having secured that he will not be able to use them in any way which

187

would jeopardize the absolute equality of all citizens. Equality is the chief end toward which any society should work. This will be effected by laws drafted by an élite which has renounced the use of force to impose its views, though not of deception. Rousseau was careful to make it plain that these lawmakers were not to be considered representatives of the people, for he was strongly opposed to the Parliamentary system (*The Social Contract*, Bk. III, ch. 15):

> Any law which the people has not ratified in person is null and void. The English people thinks it is free; it is very much mistaken. It is free only when it is electing Parliament; as soon as they are elected, it is enslaved and reduced to nothing. The use it makes of liberty, during those brief moments, shows that it well deserves to lose it. The idea of representatives is modern; it comes to us from a feudal system, that absurd and iniquitous government which degrades the human species. In the republics and even in the monarchies of antiquity, the people never had representatives.

That society was to keep its side of the bargain is guaranteed by the pressure of its sovereignty, which resides in the general will, which is not the same thing as the will of all. The latter "looks to private interest and is simply a sum of particular wills" (Bk. II, ch. 3), while the general will "looks only to the common interest." The exact operation of distinguishing between these two entities is explained thus: "If you cancel out from those same wills all the mutually destructive pluses and minuses, the general will remains the sum of the differences" (ibid.).

To preserve the general will, all cliques and secret societies were to be suppressed, for "the will of each

188

of these associations becomes general with reference to its members, and particular with reference to the state. . . . Finally when one of these associations becomes large enough to prevail over all the rest . . ." (ibid.) it impairs the balance of differences, and there is no longer a general will. It is impossible to exaggerate the degree to which Rousseau expects the citizen to sacrifice his being to the state. "The better the state is constituted," he wrote, "the more does public rather than private business preoccupy the minds of citizens." How far he carries this principle is shown when he counts among the most disruptive of these associations the Christian religion. He treats the difficulty of reconciling Church and State as if it were a sufficient reason for wishing the Church had never been called into existence. He professed to be a devout Protestant in *The Social Contract,* and calls Christianity "this holy, sublime and true religion," but he hedges by distinguishing between three sorts of religion: "The first, without temples, altars, and rites, and limited to the purely interior cult of omnipotent God and the eternal duties of morality, is the pure and simple religion of the Gospels, true theism, and may be called divine natural law" (Bk. IV, ch. 8). The second, is the state religion, to be found from earliest times, which expounds dogma and practices rites prescribed by law, and gives a nation tutelary deities. There "is a third, more bizarre sort of religion which, by giving men two systems of legislation, two rulers, and two countries, subjects them to contradictory duties. . . . Such is the religion of the lamas, the Japanese, and the Roman Catholics." He claims to be attacking only the third variety, but actually his complaint is made on a high level: "These were the circumstances in which Jesus came to establish a spiritual kingdom on earth, a kingdom which, by separating the theological system from the political system, deprived the state of its unity, and gave rise to those intestine divisions which have never ceased to agitate Christian peoples." He declares that the influence of Christianity is wholly bad from the point of view of the state. Rather oddly, he says that he knows of no good Christian soldiers.

> Christian troops are excellent, we are told. I deny it. Show me your Christian troops. I myself do not know of any. You will cite the crusades. Without questioning the valour of the crusaders, I shall point out that, far from being Christians, they were the soldiers of priests, and citizens of the Church. They were fighting for their spiritual country, which the Church had mysteriously transformed into a temporal kingdom. Properly speaking, this is a form of paganism. Since the gospels do not set up a national religon, no religious war is possible among Christians.

This is very odd, because Rousseau was writing only eighty years after the Siege of Vienna. There Christian soldiers had found themselves well and truly engaged in a religious war, because Mohammed had set up a militarist religion; and they had been victorious. But Rousseau conceived that Christians must always be an embarrassment to the state, even if their religion was private, because "instead of binding the hearts of citizens to the state," it "detaches them from it, as from all worldly things." He was indeed afraid of Christianity, because it "preaches only servitude and dependence," and "its spirit is too favorable to tyranny not to profit always by it." Now, this is inconsistent with his declaration that Christianity is "true," which must mean that he conceded it a supreme value, overriding all temporal considerations; but that inconsistency might be simple hypocrisy. Another inconsistency harder to explain lies in Rousseau's approval of "the founding fathers of the nations," such as Moses and Mohammed, who have declared that the laws they promulgated had been suggested to them by God, in order that the people might submit to them. Here Rousseau quotes a passage from Machiavelli (Bk. II, ch. 7): "Truly there has never been among any people any extraordinary legislator who did not have recourse to God, since otherwise his work would not have been accepted; for there are many things which a wise man knows, but the reasons for which are not in themselves sufficiently evident to enable them to persuade others." Rousseau adds that this imposture is, of course, insufficient by itself. The laws thus fraudulently recommended have to be good laws. "False miracles create a passing bond; only wisdom can make it durable." Let us leave the morality of this judgment on one side; this is not a topical question. What is more important is that it is inconsistent with his other pronouncements on religion. If legislators are to use the religious beliefs of the masses in order to persuade them to accept wise laws, religion cannot be treated simply as a tiresome trespasser in relation to the state.

But the ignorance of the masses which is here assumed draws attention to yet another inconsistency. Man in a state of nature was innocent, but had been corrupted by social institutions. It is not explained how innocent men created corrupt institutions; and though it might well be that institutions originally innocent might become corrupt in the course of time, because circumstances had changed, this theory would not have pleased Rousseau, who admired beyond measure the institutions

191

created by the past. This might not always be apparent. He detested English law and told the Poles how to do things in a better way (*Government of Poland,* ch. 10):

> You must have three codes covering constitutional, civil, and criminal law respectively: all three as clear, short, and precise as possible. These codes will be taught not only in the universities but also in all the secondary schools; and you will need no other body of law. All the rules of natural law are better graven in the hearts of men than in all the rubbish of Justinian. Just make men honest and virtuous, and I assure you that their knowledge of law will be sufficient.

But Rousseau really worshiped ancient laws more than most thinkers who are reputed conservative. He was always citing the customs of the Greeks and the Romans with the deepest admiration, and had a capacity for deriving comfort from recollections of the achievements of Numa Pompilius which has been withheld from the rest of us. One of the most vigorous passages in *Considerations on the Government of Poland* ends with these words: "Worthy Poles, beware! . . . Correct if possible, the abuses of your constitution; but do not despise that constitution which has made you what you are" (ibid., ch. 1). Indeed, his test of a good law (and hence of a good state) was that it was durable. "Why then do people pay so much respect to ancient laws? Precisely because they are ancient. We can only believe that it was the excellence of these ancient decisions that made it possible for them to last so long" (*Social Contract,* Bk. III, ch. 11). But at the same time durability leads to no happy end. Every state is bound to perish in the long run. "The body politic, no less than the body of man, begins dying from the moment of its birth, and bears within itself the seeds of its destruction." By seeds of destruction Rousseau did not mean that the state would encounter problems which it could not solve. He thought (as Spengler was to think a hundred and fifty years later) that there was an analogy between organic and inorganic nature which included the inevitability of death and extended to abstractions. It is true that Rousseau carries this analogy through to the point of claiming that a well-governed state will have a longer life than an ill-governed one, just as a healthy body will survive a sick one. But as he insists that only certain countries can ever be well-governed, because good government is practicable only in countries below a certain size, this is not a generous concession.

Many writers have tried to clear Rousseau of the charge of inconsistency. One of the most whole-hearted supporters of Rousseau's claim that his work was a harmonious and logical exposition of a principle was that attractive German writer, Ernst Cassirer, who saw Rousseau as having solved the problem of theodicy, as having justified the ways of God to man and cleared Him of the responsibility of creating evil. But what Cassirer sees as that solution is one of Rousseau's most obvious inconsistencies; his rejection of the doctrine of original sin, his claim that man was born innocent and has become corrupt as the result of the machinations of society— which, however, innocent man created; and his further claim that corruption can be banished from the world if men start afresh and organize another society with the intention of being virtuous, though that must have been their intention when they first organized society, since they were then innocent. This, of course, is far from solving the problem of theodicy, because even if it

193

worked out it would not absolve God from the responsibility of putting man on a globe where it is so difficult for him to live without sinning. It is indeed quite a vain task to try to argue out of sight Rousseau's inconsistency because it was part of the panoply he wore as incarnation of the spirit of his time.

A change had come over thought and its expression. If we turn back to Shakespeare's meditations over the conception of kingship, we find that he had an attitude to kings and to usurpers which was not strictly logical: he believed it inevitable that a king should be corrupted by the exercise of power, even to the point of being unable to keep his oath and protect his people, and yet regarded the usurper who seized power from the worst of such kings as somehow worse than the bad man he supplanted. This is an apparent inconsistency, though it resolves into reason, if it be understood that in his depths he was meditating on the sovereignty of the soul, and the spoiling of all its works by original sin. But the apparent inconsistency is only one of judgment. He does not ask us in one passage to believe that kings and usurpers do one thing, and in another ask us to believe that they do the opposite. But it would perhaps be fairer to make the comparison with a political writer. Jean Bodin gave himself to the study of sovereignty about the same time as Shakespeare. His style rambles among a thousand classical and biblical examples as he develops his thesis that the monarch should be subject to constitutive limitation but should enjoy absolute executive power, which he must exercise in harmony with the natural law. But there are no holes left gaping in the argument which catch the reader's eye; to criticize it makes the same serious demand on the attention that the writing of it must have made.

Surely we are noting a real secular variation in literature. There have been in every age writers who were poor and muddled thinkers, but it might fairly be said that before a certain period writers did not gain repute unless they carpentered their arguments. It would be difficult to fix the date of the decline in precision, for history is not geography and has no definite frontiers; and nothing can be more certain than that this change has nothing to do with an alleged dissociation of intellect and emotion. But surely Rousseau was the first writer of stature to win the homage of learned Europe by publishing work which was spotted with manifest absurdities. All of us still pay Rousseau homage for his *Confessions,* but the public which covered him with adulation had never read them. It was the author of *Emile* and *The Social Contract* who was worshiped, and the only conclusion which can be drawn is that readers were no longer shocked by inconsistency. Perhaps consistency is a quality hard to conceive in a world which is overcrowded with people and things and knowledge. In a world where politics included little else than the conquest of feudalism and the conflict between the Papacy and the monarchies, and ethics were tied up with a well-comprehended theological system, and economics and science were in their childhood, there was plenty of space round the objects man could discuss. It could be clearly understood that any theory regarding certain objects had to take into account what was already known about those and all related objects. But time has steadily presented humanity with more and more material for consideration. Some of the more sinister effects of this are obvious: when schools were split into "classical" and "modern" sides it was a terrible admission that in future no man could hope to grow up with all-round knowledge of his environment, and the develop-

195

ment of the arts and sciences has cut up every field of study into strips of specialization, so that the arts and sciences are now cultivated under the same disadvantages as are imposed by the manorial system of agriculture. But it may be that these excessive gifts of time have done still greater damage by distracting man from part of the necessary process of thought, the avoidance of inconsistency, the checking of every theory by reference to all relevant facts.

Let us never be ungrateful to the nineteenth century, for it gave us many and magnificent reforms. The trade union, without which industry would have become a shambles, was built up into a legal and efficient organization; women were emancipated to the point of being able to work in many fields which gave them a better living than before and to retain control of their property after marriage; there was steady progress in penal reform; many civil servants devised services which alleviated the horrible conditions endured by the poor in the cities, where the improvements wrought by Fielding and his fellows had hardly survived the pressure of the huge increase in the urban population; men and women gave away great fortunes to charity, and voluntary social workers subjected themselves to discipline and became armies of helpfulness. These were great days when the possessing classes made up their mind to the sharing of possessions which has begun in earnest in the Britain of our time. So steady was the advance toward social and economic quality, it is safe to say that had it not been for the first World War and the ensuing train of disasters, the West might have become the most civilized society that the world had yet seen. Yet the literature of the second half of the nineteenth century echoes with faint cries of shame and embarrassment, interrupted by wailed prom-

196

ises to do better in the future, which grew more clamant as time went on. The intellectuals of the period were talking like Rousseau and the middle classes were listening with the same spell-bound attention that Rousseau's admirers had given him. This is not to imply that any but an infinitesimal proportion of them had been influenced by actual study of Rousseau's works. Few seemed to be aware that Rousseau was firmly of the opinion that to weld society together all men ought to be compelled to practice a state religion and be killed if they broke away from it. Rather is it to be considered that any ingenious spirit, faced with the unmanageable complexity of the modern world, and taking fright at it, might well be apt to think like Rousseau, who, being a genius, had seen what the expansion of trade and the accumulation of learning and the increase of population was putting on man's plate. As the twentieth century dawned, the British atmosphere was saturated with Rousseauist discontent with all existing institutions, with the same feeling that man had been born innocent and now was being distorted and degraded by an artificial society, wholly alien from him. The only part of Rousseau's doctrine which was not absorbed was his reverence for ancient laws. The assumption at the back of the works of Shaw and Wells and Galsworthy was that there was no part of the existing structure of society which did not deserve to be razed to the ground, and that it would be quite easy to replace it by a substitute which could completely satisfy the needs of man. Let us repeat what is perhaps the most unrealistic thing Rousseau ever wrote:

> You must have three codes covering constitutional, civil, and criminal law: all three as clear, short and precise as possible. These codes will be taught not

197

only in the universities but also in all the secondary schools; and you will need no other body of law. All the rules of natural law are better graven in the hearts of men than in all the rubbish of Justinian. Just make men honest and virtuous, and I assure you that their knowledge of law will be sufficient.

This might have been written by George Bernard Shaw. It might even have been written by H. G. Wells. They were both capable of assuming that it would be possible to codify constitutional, civil, and criminal law in a form which could be taught to high school pupils, and that a number of such simplifications would put an end to war, poverty and unhappiness. But we hardly notice these follies in Shaw and Wells because they were both great men and great creators of character. When Shaw put Saint Joan on the stage, she was recognizably a saint; and when Uncle Ponderevo and Kipps and Mr. Polly bubbled to the surface of the ink pot, they were completely created of flesh and bone and cartilage, of blood and lymph and marrow. Let it be realized that we are following the treatment of a certain theme through English literature, but that works which treat it clumsily or which ignore it altogether may establish another value.

But the handicap under which the men of this generation labored, when they did treat this theme, can be recognized in the chief work of a writer who offers us less distraction because he was less gifted than Shaw or Wells: John Galsworthy's *The Forsyte Saga*. This depicts a family which owns property and is so dominated by the conception of property that its members think of all relationships in terms of owning and being owned. It is an attempt to deal with the moral aspects of power, as they appeared in the contemporary scene, by a man of

198

great seriousness. The family is portrayed because it illustrates another stage of the process which Shakespeare describes in his historical plays. Power corrupted the feudal lords and it passed to the monarchy, and when it had corrupted the monarchy, it passed to a capitalist democracy, the rise of which Trollope described; and now in its turn capitalist democracy was corrupted by power and was losing it. Now was the moment when the Forsytes, archetypes of the governing class under capitalist democracy, had been fully corrupted, and had they been kings should have surrendered their power to a usurper who smote upon the palace door. But the Forsytes had no palace; their name was legion; they were dotted all over Great Britain in solid Victorian mansions with well-stocked wine cellars, in villas with hard tennis courts, with stables and garages; nor had they been countable, or held accountable under a palace roof, could the usurper have smote upon its door. For what was usurping their power was a steadily mounting income tax, a huge increase in the social services, and a number of persons in the Houses of Parliament, the Civil Services, and various agencies of local government. Not possibly from this situation could a scene emerge when the usurper could possibly say anything comparable to the deadly words, "Go, some of you, and fetch a looking-glass," and a Forsyte could do nothing comparable to dashing the glass against the ground. It would be hard to unify this conflict of huge, interlaced, sluggish forces, covering immense areas, indeed covering all the social space we know, and running far back in to the past and promising no climax in the future, committed to the prosaic by reason of its involvement with our total social being even to its last drab dregs; and it would be hard to shape the picture of it into a pattern of events memorable for beauty. As a symbol of the conflict between the Forsytes and the vital principle which escaped them because of their corruption through power, Galsworthy used the unhappy marriage between Soames and Irene. But Irene is a character too limited to bear the weight of the significance assigned to her. She was not Amelia Booth, she was Amelia Sedley, who had gone on a diet and fined down, and had in obedience to the conventions of the day run away from her husband, instead of staying with him as the conventions of yesterday had commanded. But that hardly matters compared with the Rousseauist convention which makes Galsworthy blame the Forsytes because they did not—though it was the case against them that they were corrupt—take some step which would be the essence of innocence and would instantly give the signal for the establishment of a new heaven and earth. It was unfortunate that the course of the novel led the novelist of the late nineteenth and early twentieth century to concern himself with the public life under the guise of confused chiliastic myth.

PART THREE

The Castle of God

1 *Nonconformist Assenters and*
   Independent Introverts

Among the novelists writing in English at this period
there were some resistant personalities unaffected by the
Rousseauist influences of their time; but the greatest
among them were not English. There was Henry James,
who had come to England from his native America perhaps because his parents were affected by a Pelagian belief that a well-ordered court could save its courtiers by
ceremonial which tamed the blood and developed the
taste, and there were as yet a few traces of a like discipline
in his native land. In 1880 he wrote, in his study of Haw-
thorne (ch. 11, p. 43):

> One might enumerate the items of high civilization,
> as it exists in other countries, which are absent from
> the texture of American life, until it should become
> a wonder to know what was left. No State, in
> the European sense of the word, and indeed barely a
> specific national name. No sovereign, no court, no
> clergy, no army, no diplomatic service, no country
> gentlemen, no palaces, no castles, nor manors, nor old
> country-houses, nor parsonages, nor thatched cot-
> tages, nor ivied ruins; no cathedrals, nor abbeys, nor
> little Norman churches; no great Universities, nor
> public schools—no Oxford, nor Eton, nor Harrow; no
> literature, no novels, no museums, no pictures, no po-
> litical society, no sporting class—no Epsom nor
> Ascot! Some such list as that might be drawn up of
> the absent things in American life—especially in the
> American life of forty years ago, the effect of which,
> upon an English or a French imagination, would

probably as a general thing be appalling. The natural remark in the almost lurid light of such an indictment would be that if these things are left out, everything is left out. The American knows that a good deal remains; what it is that remains—that it is that remains—that is his secret, his joke, as one may say. It would be cruel, in this terrible denudation, to deny him the consolation of his national gift, that "American humor" of which of late years we have heard so much.

Henry James' work was largely an ironic criticism of this attitude; and he began his researches when he went to Europe as a boy of twelve in 1855, a year in which Thackeray was lecturing on "The Four Georges," Dickens was writing *Little Dorrit*, and Trollope published *The Warden*. He himself published his first book in 1875, the year in which Meredith's *Beauchamp's Career* was running as a serial in *The Fortnightly Review*, and Hardy was writing *The Hand of Ethelberta;* he published his last book in 1914, the year in which the first World War broke out, a year after Shaw's *Pygmalion* had been produced, and three years after Wells had published *The New Machiavelli.* He liked few of the changes that took place in this long span of years, and he would have liked to travel backward through time to avoid them, passing the eighteenth century, passing the seventeenth century, avoiding the huge serene effort of Fielding, to the Shakespearean days when the formality of a palace had a visible connection with salvation and damnation. But he could not write his books about the contemporary English court, for it hardly existed. The historical process, of which the beginnings were described by Shakespeare, had detached the crown from politics, and though that hardly mattered to him, for he was truly apolitical, it mattered to him that the widowhood of Queen Victoria had left the court a vacuum in the midst of English social life. But he took the English aristocratic life as the next best thing, and his novels assume that it should have been, and sometimes was, a school of virtue. His work consists largely of descriptions of the conflict which was bound to break out when those who were teachers and pupils in this school came in contact with those who lacked this education. That conflict took many forms: sometimes the untutored showed a simple virtue which put to shame those who had been schooled too well and had gone stale like overtrained athletes; sometimes the untutored showed a presumptuous incapacity to understand what it was they had to learn; sometimes the teachers had become so immersed in cultivating the refinements of their study that they forgot its elements and let some situation be stained by the presence of evil, which James, with a simplicity alien from his age, firmly believed to be a reality; and always the custodians of this redeeming cult were threatened by the eternal enemy, the usurper, in the shape of people who had not the right credentials, who had not a clear title, who were parvenus.

The extent to which Henry James identifies evil with vulgarity was extreme. Nearly all his works, with the exception of his lamentable plays, are impressive, and none more immediately so than *The Turn of the Screw*. That masterpiece conveys a sense of evil with which we are all familiar from childhood, since it lurks in fairy tales, in the person of the bad fairy or the dwarf or the talking crow, as dreadfully as it does in the doorways of cities depraved since the beginning of time: a sense of evil which is terrifying because it defies the dimensions, and is at once deeply entrenched in the flesh yet is half way to another and immaterial world. The incarnation of that evil, Peter Quint, who has come back from hell with the true Lucifer light about him, was a gentleman's gentleman, as valets called themselves in Victorian days, who would have been scorned by other gentlemen's gentlemen, for he stole his master's shirts. The converse of this argument is expressed in that great humanist version of the cry of hunger and thirst for righteousness, *The Wings of the Dove*. That story of a dying girl who finds herself the victim of a cruel and mercenary fraud and contrives to deal with this hideous situation so that it flowers in beauty is so told that her moral triumph seems to be vitally connected with the taste that takes her to die in a Venetian palace. This made Henry James' meliorist contemporaries regard him as lacking in seriousness, but they did him an injustice.

Henry James could not have been more earnest regarding the salvation of the soul, but he was historically unfortunate, as appears if his prefaces to the collected editions of his novels (published together under the title *The Art of the Novel*) are compared with Fielding's essays on the same subject in *Tom Jones*. Henry James shows agreement with Fielding in all essentials. He certainly held that genius lay in "that power, or rather those powers, of the mind which are capable of penetrating into all things within our reach and knowledge, and of distinguishing their essential difference," and that the novelist must have "the sort of knowledge beyond the power of learning to bestow and this is to be had by conversation"; and that imagination must be controlled by observation. But Henry James lays a peculiar stress, which Fielding would hardly have understood, on the need for a "lens," for the presence of a clear, balanced intelligence among the characters of a novel which, by

206

its obvious authority should impose on the reader a proper estimate of what is happening. He insisted on numerous occasions that the need for that unifying intelligence was really desperate; and so it was, for he had to guide complicated themes through a world which was not only complicated but confused, and thus inimical to the definiteness which he always sought. It is obvious that Henry James started at a disadvantage compared to Shakespeare, when we consider that no action in the world he described could give such radical information about the character who performed it as the withholding of the last sacrament from men about to die. But that disadvantage Henry James could overcome by his subtlety. A disadvantage far less easy to overcome was his lack of a framework for belief in the good, which Fielding found in his world of honest parsons and classical scholars. Henry James' gospel had to be passed by word of mouth from drawing room to drawing room in the London squares; and there was a curious insubstantiality about the guarantees which could be given in those mansions. He seems to have pinned his faith to the wrong society and got that wrong too. It seems conjectural, in the style of the models of brontosauri and pterodactyls which are constructed in plaster of Paris according to theories derived from the study of fossils. We cannot doubt his thesis that the court saves the courtiers, for the courtiers he shows us are living and are saved, but it is not quite possible to believe in the court.

There was Rudyard Kipling, who was almost as foreign as Henry James, though he was of English blood, for the reason that he was Indian born. Curiously enough, there was a strong element of Rousseauism in him, for he embraced those parts of the faith which are rejected by his meliorist contemporaries. He was with the philosopher, where Shaw and Wells and Galsworthy left him, in his enthusiasm for the training Sparta gave its youth, armoring them with courage and loyalty and asceticism, and teaching them contempt for self-interest, and in his belief that ancient laws must be the best, since it must be their excellence which has made them survive so long. There is of course a great deal to be said for both Spartan discipline and ancient laws, but unfortunately Kipling gave the impression that he was ready to go still further with Rousseau on this line of thought, and to agree with him that the development of the arts and sciences had destroyed the primitive virtues, and therefore ought to be destroyed in the form that we know them; and the ancient laws which he most admired seemed to be those which placed India under the tutelage of England, though these date back no further than the seventeenth century, and already in the eighteenth century Warren Hastings and many another had made it clear that they must be regarded as temporary expedients. But it has to be noted that Kipling expressed his admiration for Spartan discipline and the English occupation of India with a fire which would probably have burned less fiercely had it not happened that his contemporaries were so loudly denying the need for any discipline, whether Spartan or of any other kind, and so loudly affirming that the English were in India only for purposes of spoliation. Kipling was placed in time even less fortunately than Henry James, for in some respects he lagged behind his age and in others he was far in advance of it. He was the first important writer to feel the romantic charm of machinery, and this was taken as a mark of the permanent adolescence of his extrovert nature, though the same emotion was later to be held natural and laudable when the Americans rejoiced in their maturing industry and the Russians in their nascent industry.

But it is also true that one of the reasons why Kipling looked odd in his time was his acceptance of the institutions of Church and State. In fact most of the English people were of his way of thinking in this matter, but the rest of contemporary literature was proclaiming that these institutions were now held in contempt by all save a few financially interested reactionaries. He was, from the point of view of other writers, a dissenter from the current faith in his wholehearted acceptance of the English tradition, but he was an assenter from the point of view of the general public. He could have fairly claimed that everybody was out of step but our Jamie. Yet in his application of the English tradition he came to offend even the general public in his later years, by his inability to understand that for many of them the Labor and the Liberal parties were the new form taken by that tradition. It is a matter for wonder that a man who had such uneasy relations with his time won such colossal success, and even now he is not comfortable in his immortality. The books of his which establish his claim most firmly are those concerning children, who live in partial agreement and partial disagreement with the several worlds which exist in the period traversed between infancy and childhood. It would be strange to think of a future when children would not read *The Jungle Books* and *The Just-So Stories,* and when adults would not read *Kim,* in which a child acts as the central unifying intelligence in a confused scene, the need for which Henry James defined.

Neither of these writers, though their greatness abides no one's question, has any seminal quality. An author of another age who worked on the same material in the same style as either of them would be a copyist, for the two men were made by historical imbroglios, one in each hemisphere, hardly likely to recur for centuries. But their great contemporary, Joseph Conrad, writes of a situation which perpetually recurs. He was, though it was not then foreseen, an earnest of the things to come. He had the kind of wisdom that was to disconcert many of us when it reappeared among displaced persons; and he had come by it honestly. His father and mother, who were Poles of the landowning class, were displaced persons of their time, for they fled from Tsarist persecution to France, where both endured poverty and distress and died while their son was still a boy. He heard much of England and liked what he heard, and at seventeen he went to sea on an English merchant ship. He was a religious man and his life fostered his religion, and he strongly believed that the courtiers would be saved by the action of grace bestowed by God. The court was an instrument of grace, as it reconstituted itself wherever there was a group of men threatened by danger, which was the constant condition of sailors at sea. There time ran back to simplicity. It became necessary, in order to confront the storm, or fire, or the human enemy, that there should be one person chosen to command the others. Kingship was once more brought to birth. There was, in effect, an oath taken by which this selected person, the captain, swore to protect them, and another oath taken by the other persons involved, the crew, to give obedience in return for this protection. The safety of the ship and each human being on the ship depended on the keeping of these oaths; and it became more and more plain to Conrad that this was the type of all human situations, that in relations between human beings, and between states and citizens, nothing could go well if all persons did not take fidelity as their guiding principle.

This has some resemblance to what Kipling thought, but there is a fundamental difference. Kipling also was a religious man and he believed that a man could be saved by grace, which would be granted if he were loyal to some organization of high authority, such as the British Army or the Indian Civil Service. But he seems to think that grace is granted to the man because of that obedience. It is as if grace had been bestowed on the organization (secular though it be), as is conceived to be the case of the Churches. Conrad evidently thought that grace is granted to the man who can lend it to the organization by an effort of his will, which has been made innocent by the action of grace; and then the organization can reflect an atmosphere which is favorable to grace, though not identical with it. While Henry James believed that man kept the moral atmosphere in being by the constant exercise of refined discrimination, Kipling believed that man could keep it in being by the constant practice of obedience to the highest moral authorities; but Conrad regarded the moral universe as being constantly in danger of annulment by the weakness of man, and as constantly confirmed in being by cooperation between man and God. This belief gives *Lord Jim* its meaning and it pervades all his books.

He was in a sense nearer Shakespeare than any other modern novelist, because he was thinking of power in the same terms, and this has now made him seem one of the most modern of writers; for many of us have seen danger rebuild Shakespeare's court round us during the last forty years, as Conrad saw it rebuilt round him on board ship or in far tropical places. It is to be noted that Herman Wouk's *The Caine Mutiny*, which was a best-seller after the second World War, dealt with material which was common to Shakespeare and Conrad: with a question of keeping or breaking an oath taken to meet a danger. The treatment is more Shakespearean than Conradian, for Keefer belongs to Shakespeare's company of usurpers,

211

who may end a wrong but cannot themselves be right; but the author's sense of an operation of the spirit which is more creative and discriminating than mere obedience, though respectful to it, is exactly what Conrad meant by fidelity. But indeed this same situation, wherein the necessity for government is suddenly made visible in a confined and threatened area, is the better part of the material of most war novels, of widely differing degrees of merit though its significance is often obscure in the authors' own eyes and resented when it is perceived.

There were, of course, many works being written in the first fifty years of this century which did not concern themselves with the problem of power, the parallel between the public and the private life, the riddle as to whether either or both of these two lives can run to a good end: which take no part in the argument which, for the present purpose, has been taken as beginning with, or rather, so far as the English are concerned, as having its grandest early statement in, *Hamlet*. If nineteenth-century writers were below a certain merit, they simply followed the practice of spawning characters, which, once the exploration of character was limited to superficialities, became easy and was often entertaining, though quite often not entertaining at all. If later writers were above a certain level, they turned aside and engaged in a respectable research of their own. Instead of trying to find out where humanity was going, they tried to find out what humanity was. They refused to make any attempt to find a prose equivalent for the soliloquy, which should expose the essentials of a man or woman in pregnant but selective phrases. They wanted the whole of their men and women down on the page, and selection means exclusion. So they evolved the "stream of consciousness" method, they set about spinning "the interior monologue," which should give an account of the day-to-day, hour-to-hour, moment-to-moment impressions life made on their subjects. This was something which Fielding had not had in his mind. "One day this young couple accidentally met in the garden, at the end of the two walks which were both bounded by that canal in which Jones had formerly risked drowning to retrieve the little bird that Sophia had there lost." (*Tom Jones*, Bk. V, ch. 6.) And that was what he remembered: falling into the canal out of the tree where he had recaptured the little bird. The gardener may have had a little white dog, but Tom Jones saw no reason to recall it.

Trollope worked a little closer to his characters' impressions, but not much so; here is poor Plantagenet Palliser, standing on the portico of his hated grand house, which Lady Glencora has been pompifying to add to his glory as a prime minister:

> And now as he stood there he could already see that men were at work about the place, that ground had been moved here, and grass laid down there, and a new gravel road constructed in another place. Was it not possible that his friends should be entertained without all these changes in the gardens? Then he perceived the tents, and descending from the terrace and turning to the left towards the end of the house he came on a new conservatory. The exotics with which it was to be filled were at this moment being brought in on great barrows. (*The Prime Minister*, ch. 19)

There is still not a word about the gardener's little white dog. It is sometimes supposed that Henry James came so near to rendering the stream of consciousness that he could claim to have been the first explorer of its course, but though he describes a stream of something which is passing through his characters' minds, but it is very far from being the whole flow of their consciousness:

> It was quite for the Prince after this as if the view had further cleared; so that the half-hour during which he strolled on the terrace and smoked—the day being lovely—overflowed with the plenitude of its particular quality. Its general brightness was composed doubtless of many elements, but what shone out of it as if the whole place and time had been a great picture, from the hand of genius, presented to him as a prime ornament for his collection and all varnished and framed to hang up—what marked it especially for the highest appreciation was his extraordinarily unchallenged, his absolutely appointed and enhanced possession of it. Poor Fanny Assingham's challenge amounted to nothing: one of the things he thought of while he leaned on the old marble balustrade—so like others that he knew in still more nobly-terraced Italy—was that she was squared, all-conveniently even to herself, and that, rumbling toward London with this contentment, she had become an image irrelevant to the scene. (*The Golden Bowl*, Bk. III, ch. 9)

There is no chance at all for the gardener's little white dog to make itself seen across this broad river of comment by the self on itself, which is an artistic convention made by James to suit his hand, for few selves are capable of giving themselves such undivided attention. This is not because their egotism is weak, but because their faculty of attention is insufficiently strong. In fact the mind seesaws between broodings on its special situation and surrender to whatever sights or sounds or odors address it through the senses; and we get a deliberate effort to give a faithful representation of that see-saw when we come to Dorothy Richardson, who can fairly claim to be the originator of the method:

> The strange shock of the bedroom, the strange new thing springing out from it . . . the clear soft bright tones, the bright white light streaming through the clear muslin, the freshness of the walls . . . the flattened dumpy shapes of dark green bedroom crockery gleaming in a corner; the little green bowl standing in the middle of the white spread of the dressing table cover . . . wild violets with green leaves and tendrils put there by someone with each leaf and blossom standing separate . . . touching your heart; joy, looking from the speaking pale mauve little flowers to the curved rim of the green bowl and away to the green crockery in the corner; again and again the fresh shock of the violets . . . the little cold change in the room after the books, strange fresh findings and fascinating odd shapes and sizes, gave out their names . . . The White Boat—Praxiter—King Chance—Mrs. Prendergast's Palings . . . the promise of them in their tilted wooden case by the bedside table from every part of the room their unchanged names, the chill of the strange sentences inside—like a sort of code written for people who understood, written at something, clever raised voices in a cold world. In Mrs. Prendergast's Palings there were cockney conversations spelt as they were spoken. None of the books were about ordinary people . . . three men, seamen, alone, getting swamped in a boat in shallow water in sight of land . . . a man and a girl he had no right to be with wandering on the sand, the cold wash and sob

215

of the sea; her sudden cold sad tears; the warmth
of her shuddering body. Praxiter beginning without
telling you anything, about the thoughts of an irri-
tating contemptuous superior man, talking at the
expense of everybody. Nothing in any of them about
anything one knew or felt; casting you off . . .
giving a chill ache to the room. To sit . . . alone,
reading in the white light, amongst the fresh colours
—but not these books . . . to go downstairs was a
sacrifice: coming back there should be the lighting
of the copper candlestick, twisting beautifully up
from its stout stem. What made it different to ordinary candlesticks? What? It was like . . . a gesture.
(*The Tunnel*, ch. 6, sec. 4)

It is obvious that if the gardener's little white dog is not
on the page it is only because it was not in Miriam's
bedroom. But a lot of other things were. This passage
describes the state of being of an educated and gifted
woman, still young, who is friendless and poor and follows the occupation, far below her talents, of a dentist's
receptionist; she has written to an old school friend re-
viving their acquaintance, and her friend has answered
at once, telling her that she has married a well-known
writer, and giving her a warm invitation to stay with
them. When she arrives she is delighted at the welcome
they give her and by the comfort and charm of their
house, but at the same time she feels hostility to the world
of intellectuals to which they belong, suspecting it of
coldness and arrogance, and also fearing that she will
not measure up to its standards, while at the same time
she is honest enough to admire some of their achievements. The extreme skill of the presentation is to be admired: the tide flows, and changes channel as it flows,

and changes back again, "I see this, I like it; I see that, I do not like it; I see this, I like it." The presentation breaks down at one point, as writing is bound to break down if it tries too hard to do the work of painting: the reader is not clear about the promise given by Praxiter's books in their tilted wooden case. This is a pitfall which has engulfed many of Dorothy Richardson's imitators; but she herself failed in her later books for quite another reason. Miriam's interior monologue went deeper and deeper, and in the end Dorothy Richardson would not interrupt it to record such external facts as the going out and coming in of other characters, with the result that it is never certain who is speaking to whom. But even then the personality of Miriam is not breached; and the series is still worth reading for the sake of the solidity of Miriam and such minor characters as Alma and Eleanor Dear, as well as for its stud-farm interest as the progenitor of hundreds of later novels. It has a further interest in the realistic portraits it paints of English intellectuals at the beginning of the century in the circle that gathers round Alma and Hypo, and in the confirmatory material it furnishes regarding the educated and lonely and dispossessed city-dwellers which Gissing had taken as his subject.

Virginia Woolf can have been influenced but slightly by Dorothy Richardson, for they began writing about the same time; and indeed Virginia Woolf is recognizable as a child of Meredith, who cheerfully accepted her spiritual father's legacy of tropes, but rebelled against his love of well-made plots and chose to have no theme but character. Originally, and most notably in *Jacob's Room*, she concentrated on a patchwork of sensory impressions which gave clues to the preoccupations of her characters. But by the time she wrote *To the Lighthouse*

217

she had given a depth to the streams of consciousness she traced, by giving not only the sensory impressions of her characters, but the associations evoked by those impressions (Pt. I, sec. 17):

"Andrew," she said, "hold your plate lower, or I shall spill it." (The Boeuf en Daube was a perfect triumph.) Here, she felt, putting the spoon down, was the still space that lies about the heart of things, where one could move or rest; could wait now (they were all helped,) listening: could then, like a hawk which lapses suddenly from its high station, flaunt and sink on laughter easily, resting her whole weight upon what at the other end of the table her husband was saying about the square root of one thousand two hundred and fifty-three. That was the number, it seemed, on his watch.

What did it all mean? To this date she had no notion. A square root? What was that? Her sons knew. She leant on them; on cubes and square roots; that was what they were talking about now; on Voltaire and Madame de Staël; on the character of Napoleon; on the French system of land tenure; on Lord Rosebery; on Creevey's Memoirs; she let it uphold and sustain her, this admirable fabric of the masculine intelligence, which ran up and down, crossed this way and that, like iron girders spanning the swaying fabric, upholding the world, so that she could trust herself to it utterly, even shut her eyes, or flicker them for a moment, as a child staring up from its pillow winks at the myriad layers of the leaves of a tree. Then she woke up. It was still being fabricated. William Bankes was praising the Waverley Novels.

It is worth while turning back to Henry James and seeing how widely this method differs from his. If Adam and Maggie Verver had ever heard of Voltaire and Madame de Staël, we were not told of it. We are simply given what they felt under the harrow of an intense personal experience during a limited period of time. Mrs. Woolf gave us how her character lived, not necessarily under any acute strain, during a limited period of time, which seems unlimited, because the impressions she ascribes to her characters arouse associations which lead inward to their hidden natures and backward through time to their first formative years. Certainly Mrs. Woolf conveys much more of the selves of her characters than Henry James does, and though this does not mean that she tells more about the essential principle of each character than he does, it does mean that she by implication tells us more about the nature of the self. But her effort is sometimes impaired by a certain weakness which arises out of a trait which she freely confessed in conversation. Only the familiar gave up its secrets to her. She was, as *The Common Reader* shows, the most sensitive of critics; but, as she often said, she really did not know what to think of a contemporary work unless it bore an obvious relationship to some predecessor which she already understood. She often annoyed her friends, when they told her enthusiastically that some new book was really good, by telling them that she could not trouble to read it until they had told her what to look for in it. Once she was told what she ought to see in it, she could tell them with exquisite discrimination whether it was there or not, but she had to be given the clue. This is not an uncommon trait, though it is far from common to confess it, and it has a bearing on her novels. The best are those which deal with material familiar to her because she had lived with it. *To the Lighthouse, Mrs. Dalloway,* and *Between the Acts* were descriptions of people and events not only known but well known to her; and *Orlando,* the only successfully invented myth in English literature of our time, incarnates the development of the poetic genius in England, a subject with which she was deeply familiar. Where she dealt with material more remote, she became tame. *Jacob's Room* is gracefully written, but though Virginia Woolf knows her subject, the life of a young man about to lose it in the first World War, to be of great tragic importance, she is at such a distance from it that she makes no discoveries. The content of the book could be predicted by anybody who was informed of the subject and was acquainted with Virginia Woolf's work.

The Waves is open to the same objection. It is an ambitious book, her most ambitious effort, composed of a series of interior monologues delivered by a set of characters on their way from birth to death, and the intention is to show us the very flux of life. But the interior monologues turn out to be essays, not original in any way and not unlike those written by the Victorian writer Alice Meynell, and they are uncomfortable to read because they seem to be damming back some force which, had nature been allowed to take its course, would have flowed through them. This was perhaps merely a plot. It is right and proper for a novelist to take character as his starting point, and not a planned sequence of events; but characters, once created, enter into conflicts and alliances, and events follow, and the governing necessity forms them into a pattern. The most delicate novelist, loving plot no better than any lyric poet, could not create Mr. Plantagenet Palliser and Lady Glencora, the old Duke and Madame Goesler, Mr. Lopez and Mr. Sexty Parker, without finding a complicated plot on his hands, for the reason that these were people who dealt with complicated matters in the visible world. This failure of Virginia Woolf would hardly be worth noting, so much does her success outweigh it, were it not that the two writers who went further than she did in their exploration of the self made use of the plot.

D. H. Lawrence was to reject all modern technique, and after some straightforward writing, held to realism by its autobiographical character, he invented a new kind of novel which appeared to be realistic but was actually an exercise on symbolism. The characters in *The Rainbow* and *Women in Love* act and speak as real people would be unlikely to do, even if they possessed the attributes ascribed to the characters by their author and were enlaced in the same circumstances. Fielding's injunction that the novelist should always keep within the bounds of probability is disregarded, but for a purpose: these incredible actions and speeches declare the progress of the characters' inner lives with the clarity of poetry. In all his later exploitation of this new vehicle Lawrence never hesitated to display intricate plots. And he was not alone. James Joyce was to pursue quite a different path from Lawrence, and was to outdo every previous practitioner of the stream of consciousness technique by a procedure which demanded titanic genius. When he wrote *Ulysses,* he was able to choose the two protagonists who would best serve him as material for vivisection; his intelligence was mighty enough to grasp the totality of the Catholic Ireland which was their environment, it was refined enough to trace the network of association which ran from their sensory impressions inward to their obscurest infantile fantasy or outward to the furthest limit of their living or reading. This network thickens to a changing, heaving pulp of self, now solid, now translucent, now rigid, now fluid. The two selves, Bloom and Dedalus, are sometimes the same, sometimes a world apart; sometimes they are of today, sometimes they run back to the beginning of consciousness, to the threshold of the species. But from this pulp there emerges constantly the primeval intermingling of joy and fear, the myth, the legend: the plot.

But these two great writers, like their predecessors, were not concerned directly with the problem of power; they drew no analogy between the public and the private life. They were both (though Lawrence did not know it) prepolitical. They were both of them too busily engaged in finding out what the self had been before modern culture repressed and prettified it to follow any line of thought not concerned with those relationships which could be traced back to the primitive. If Lawrence's empty irritation with the modern world be contrasted with Shakespeare's firm grasp of history or Fielding's response to it, it is to be seen that he really cannot be considered as joining in this argument. His lack of feeling for developed society can be detected in his book on American literature, where nothing seems to him really important which is not on the pioneer level; when he describes the American individual as subjected to the pressure of environment, he thinks of the wildness of the virgin forest, the attack by enemies of another race, the inconveniences of having neighbors after living alone in the free lands. It would be absurd to try to gather from Lawrence's writings what it is like to live in a capitalist democracy, in either of the hemispheres; and it is as absurd to accuse him, as some have done, of sympathy with fascism on the basis of *The Plumed Serpent*. That book represents not support of Hitler but hostility to Rousseau. Lawrence too thought that man was born free and was everywhere in chains, but he considered this to be the source of all man's sorrows; and he was proposing a new sort of social contract in which the individual would not be forced to alienate his right to passionate being. A useful analogy can be traced, particularly by those who care to note how often artists get into trouble by projecting their inner conflicts into the visible world, between the accusations made against Lawrence and those made against the German poet Stefan George, who was even more patently innocent than Lawrence, since he lived to see Hitler and reject him. There is as little political matter in the works of James Joyce, though he knew the world about him better than Lawrence had done, being a man of greater intellectual stature. Yet he teaches the apt political lesson that there is a great part of humanity which can never be tamed by the statesman. But there we are back with *Hamlet* again, for it is part of the attraction of Hamlet that he cannot be tamed by the court; he proudly claims that there is a part of him which is outside its power.

2 *Loose Metaphysician and Strict Moralist*

The next important contribution to the argument about the court and the courtiers was to be made not in England but in France. In 1871, a year before Trollope died, eleven years before the birth of Virginia Woolf, a child named Marcel Proust was born in Paris. He entered the world in unpropitious circumstances. His father was a young doctor, son of a solid middle-class family, long settled in the Beauce, not far from Chartres; his mother was a beautiful Alsatian Jewess of stock remarkable for its intellectual gifts and its charm. They were married on September 1, 1870, the very day that the French Army surrendered to the Prussians at Sedan, and Marcel was born on July 10 of the following year. The intervening ten months had seen the horrors of the Siege of Paris and the Commune, and the Germans were still occupying France. This was perhaps the cause of Marcel Proust's congenital weakness of constitution; and the aftermath of the defeat certainly accounts for the sense of doom which darkens the pages of his great work. It is worth while turning to the Goncourt Journals for their picture of the despair which suffused the French mind for a good twenty years after the Franco-Prussian War, since it gives a picture of the atmosphere of despair and cynicism in which the child grew up.

Between 1913 and 1927 his great work, *A la recherche du temps perdu,* was published in seven separate parts. It cannot be appreciated in its full greatness unless certain precautions are taken, for this novel is almost as much swathed in misconception as *Hamlet.* It is thought of as an autobiographical novel about the passage of men and women through time, by an elderly neurasthenic, who did little work till the end of his life. In fact, his book consists only in part of his own experience and widely departs from it; and for a sick man he did a great deal of work in a life that was comparatively short. He pursued an exacting and successful course of studies, interrupted by his military service, through the Ecole des Sciences Politiques and the Sorbonne, until he was twenty-two, and between that time and his thirty-eighth year, in spite of constant attacks of respiratory disorders, he made himself known as a writer of literary articles and a translator of Ruskin. Between the ages of thirty-eight and fifty-one, although four years of this period were consumed by the first World War, he wrote what amounted to the equivalent of ten long novels. A man capable of such industry cannot be regarded as an ordinary neurotic, though he was eccentric; but a good part of his eccentricity may well be regarded as the struggles of a man who knew his time was running short and was torn between the necessity of leading a solitary life in order to finish his work, and keeping in contact with the society which was the subject of that work, though that society could hardly be persuaded to yield itself save on conditions hostile to work.

It is therefore absurd to consider *A la recherche du temps perdu* as the spastic obsessive pastime of a neurotic; it is much safer to take it as the carefully planned achievement of a man who, as an artist, enjoyed sound health. It is also a risk to take Proust too seriously as a metaphysician. In France philosophy has always been treated as a graceful and gracious entertainment, and it was not astonishing that Proust should present his work as a fusion of philosophy and fiction, just as (to take one example out of hundreds) Maurice Barrès presented

Le Jardin de Bérénice. Proust had been a pupil of Bergson at the Sorbonne, and in the first decade of this century Bergsonism was more than a philosophy, it was a fashion. It is not unnatural that he should have been thinking in Bergsonian terms, and though he denied that he was a true disciple, should gild some of his chapters with dissertations on time. This motive is introduced quite early in *Du côté de chez Swann* (Bk. I, p. 69):

One winter evening, when I came home, my mother, seeing that I was cold, asked me if I would have some tea, though usually I did not take it. At first I refused, and then, I do not know why, changed my mind. She sent for one of those plump, stubby little cakes known as "little madeleines," which seem to have been moulded in the grooved shell of a scallop, the pilgrim's emblem. And soon, depressed by a dull day and the prospect of a dreary tomorrow, I mechanically raised to my lips a spoonful of the tea, in which I had soaked a piece of the madeleine. But at the very instant that the mouthful of tea and cake touched my palate, I shuddered under the impact of an extraordinary sensation. An exquisite pleasure was stealing through me, which had no connection with anything else, that seemed to refer to no cause. It had at once made me feel that the vicissitudes of life were unimportant, its disasters innocuous, its brevity an illusion, in the same way that love acts, filling me with a precious essence; or rather that essence was not in me, it was I myself. I had ceased to feel commonplace, slighted, mortal. Where had it come from, this powerful delight? I felt it to be connected with the taste of the tea and the cake, but it infinitely transcended that, it was of a different order.

Where did it come from, what did it mean? How could I find out? I took a second mouthful, which told me nothing more than the first, a third which gave me rather less than the second. It is time to stop, the virtue of the brew seems to be lessening. Obviously the truth which I am seeking is not in the tea but in me. The tea has evoked in me, but does not understand, and can only go on repeating, with a gradual loss of force, this message which I cannot interpret and which I want at least to be able to call up again and find it at my disposition, later on, so that I can get to the bottom of it. I put down my cup and examine my own mind. It is for it to find the truth. But how? An abyss of doubt opens before me as my mind finds it has gone too far for its own understanding; when it, the explorer, is at the same time the dark country which it must explore, although its equipment will give it no help. To explore? Not just that: to create. It is face to face with something which does not yet exist, which it alone can endow with reality and bring into the light.

He then explains how by desperate efforts, by taking some more tea and concentrating on the mysterious sensation, breaking off the effort when it began to exhaust, and starting again, he at length is conscious of a memory stirring in the depths of his mind. His efforts to recover it are tremendous and are described in detail. "Who knows if it will ever rise again from its night? Ten times I had to begin again, leaning over the darkness." Ultimately he remembers that (Bk. I, p. 72):

The taste was that of the morsel of madeleine which on Sunday mornings at Combray (because on that

227

day I never went out before it was time to go to mass) my aunt Leonie used to give me when I went to bid her good morning in her bedroom, after having dipped it in her cup of tea or lime-flower infusion. The sight of the little madeleine had recalled nothing to me before I had tasted it, perhaps because I had seen them so often since, without eating them, on the pastrycooks' counters, perhaps because of those memories, for so long time put out of mind, nothing survived, all had disintegrated; the forms of things—even the little scallop-shell of cake, so richly sensual under the severe grooves of the familiar object of piety—had been annulled, or had been so long dormant that they had lost the power of expansion which would have permitted them to take their place again in my consciousness.

This is the keystone of the first book of the great series; and a rhapsody on the power of memory is the keystone of the last book also. In *Le Temps retrouvé (Time Regained)* the narrator, who has been forced to spend years of his life in clinics, has returned to Paris from a prolonged sojourn in one, full of a sense of despair. He feels that he will never be a writer, that perhaps he had no talent after all, and that perhaps literature itself is not of any real value, and he fears that he is losing his susceptibility to the beauty of nature. At his home he finds an invitation to an afternoon musical party, and because it is given by the Princess de Guermantes and much of his early life revolved round the Guermantes family, he goes to it. On walking into the courtyard of the Prince's great house in the Avenue du Bois, he is suddenly seized by a delightful sensation which he recognizes as just that same ecstasy which, long before, he had felt when the taste of the tea and madeleine crumbs had reached his palate. Time was at its work again; as indeed it is in the text. For Proust makes a chauffeur call out to the narrator because he nearly knocks him down in the courtyard, he makes other chauffeurs guffaw at him because he is momentarily overcome by his ecstasy; and in each case Proust uses the old-fashioned term "wattmen" (mistranslated in the standard English version as "linkmen"), a word which in fact Parisians used to apply to a chauffeur many years ago, and which they still apply to the drivers of tramways and electric trains, under the impression that this word is commonly used in America. But time was now carrying the narrator not only back into the years but across Europe, for he discovered that, as he had walked from one flagstone to one which had sunk to a lower level, he had been reminded of an occasion on which he had stepped on two unequal slabs in the Baptistery of St. Mark's, and so Venice was glittering around him. The sensation he felt was not only one of pleasure, it was one of liberation and solution. He felt that there was no reason why he should not be a writer, his doubts regarding the reality of literature were dispersed, and the thought of death became of no importance. Within the Prince's house, he found he had arrived while someone was in the middle of a performance, and he was therefore shown into a small library. There a servant, trying to make as little noise as possible, banged a spoon against a plate, and again the narrator is possessed by a delicious sensation and a feeling of reassurance, which on this occasion is connected with a scent of woodlands combined with the reek of smoke, and proves to have been evoked by a resemblance between the clatter of the spoon on the plate and the sound of the hammer used to test the

229

wheels of the train on the little Balbec line when it stopped in a station by a spinney. "Then," Proust says, rather nervously, "one might have said that the signs which were that day to raise me out of my discouragement and restore my faith in literature were of set purpose multiplying themselves" (*Le Temps retrouvé,* Bk. II, p. 10), for presently a butler brought him some orangeade and gave him a napkin, and when he wiped his mouth it reminded him of one he had used long ago when standing by the window of his room at a seaside resort, and again with ecstasy, he saw before him "the plumage of an ocean green and blue as the tail of a peacock" (p. 11).

The narrator then attempted to find out why these memories were so restorative, and came to the conclusion that it was because there is an element in the self which is terrified of time and mortality, and when it recognizes a sensation which it has felt in the past and is feeling in the present as it felt it in the past, it finds itself on an extratemporal plane and therefore ceases to fear death. He also noted that this element had never been active in him except when he had turned away from action and sensation to a state of rest. He went on to argue that these evocations of memory from the subconscious show that within him he had a source of rich experience, in its pristine intensity, not like the memories lying within range of the conscious mind, which is so ready to change them in order to make a story of the past redounding to the credit of the self. The unconscious, in fact, preserves the truth from the distorting and destructive force of time, and for this reason only memories evoked by involuntary association give the artist the reality he should use as his material. In addition to this forgetfulness which drives the memory down to the unconscious, absence can

230

preserve the truth. For on returning from an absence and seeing familiar places and persons changed by time, there is set up another sort of union between past and present, where the qualities of youth and beauty once observed in those who are now aging appear in those who are now young, thus achieving an absolute existence, while the identity of those who are aging persists in spite of their loss of these qualities, thus giving them an absolute existence.

The narrator resolves to write a book about the truth that is preserved within himself by his memory and presented to him by the passage of time, seizing the authentic memories by "going deeply down" into himself. But he realizes that he may die before he has completed the book, and his last sentence runs: "If only I were given enough time to finish my work, I would not fail to stamp it with the seal of that Time, the idea of which had stamped itself so deeply on my mind this day, and in it I would describe men, even if it were to make them seem monstrous beings, who occupied in Time a place far greater than that restricted area which is all they are given in space: a place, on the contrary, extended without limit, since they touch simultaneously, like giants immersed in a flood of years, all those epochs they have lived through, so far apart—between which so many days are interposed—in Time."

This sentence means nothing at all except that Proust intended to write a book which would show people living a long time and always finding their present affected by their memories of the past, and that Proust thought memory a wonderful thing, which indeed it is. The whole of this theory which links up time and creation and memory is nonsensical, insofar as it is not a platitude. It is very doubtful if Proust ever really meant more than what Fielding tried to convey when he advised writers not to be carried away by their "creative faculty" beyond the sphere of observation, that is, memories of past experience. The accounts of the magical moments evoked by the spoonful of tea and crumbs, the unequal flag stones, the clatter of the spoon, and the napkin, are founded on vague apprehensions of psychological truisms. In the infancy of the science it was taken as a fundamental law that the experience of an event B at about the same time as the experience of an event A creates a tendency for the subject to think of A when he has thought of B. If the narrator visited Aunt Leonie's bedroom and then was given a spoonful of tea and madeleine crumbs, the thought of Aunt Leonie's bedroom was likely to recur when the same mixture was tasted. But the sense of liberation the narrator ascribes to these magical moments seems to be derived, not wisely, from reports of the effects of the recovery of hidden memories under hypnotic and psychoanalytic treatment, which do indeed include exaltation; but there is a grave difference. In these cases the memories which have been recovered have been repressed because they were connected with painful material and have thus caused a block in the psychic life, and naturally there is a sensation of release and enhancement of power when the block is suddenly swept away. But the magical moments of Proust are no more than the recovery of agreeable association matter. The tea and the madeleine crumbs recall the narrator's childish days at Combray, the uneven flagstones recall Venice, the spoon recalls a railway man tapping a wheel during a pleasant journey, the napkins recall a seaside holiday. These four moments are connected with nothing disagreeable at all, and, indeed, so far as the narrator seems to know, with nothing

232

deeply personal. There is no reason why they should ever have been repressed, or why their release should exhilarate the narrator.

It is hard to accept the narrator's own explanation that there is an element in the self so idiotic that it believes death to be made more acceptable because a spoonful of tea and madeleine crumbs tasted the same at Combray in the late seventies as it did in the Rue de Courcelles thirty years later. It does not seem surprising that one should be more likely to fall into a reminiscent reverie when one is not concentrating on any action or line of thought. Nor is it possible that the narrator, or anybody else, could write a novel by engaging in the recovery of memories by the practice of free association; this would turn into a self-analysis, an exercise which has nothing to do with literature. It is also extremely doubtful whether such a process would furnish memories in the state of purity that the narrator supposed. Few psychologists would guarantee that a repressed memory might not become encrusted by fantasy. But such an attempt would not produce such a novel as *A la recherche du temps perdu*, which, in spite of indifference to accuracy in detail, is grounded on a symmetrical and intricate plan. As for time itself, Proust has really nothing to say about it that is an idea and not an image; and the picture of the guests at the afternoon party which closes the book is of the same genre as Thackeray's pictures of senile grandeur swept to its grave by a process which he did not call the irreversibility of time though he knew very well it could not be reversed.

Decidedly the little madeleine was not such a philosopher as has been pretended. But it was a very poetical cake. These accounts of such magical moments build up before us something to be compared to de Musset's *La*

Nuit de Décembre: the sad and aging man, dark with failure, in whose soul there is preserved the fragile and palpitating past, who hears the little bell on the door of the house at Combray ringing tin-tin-tin, through all the disastrous decades, all the sorrows and perversities, ringing and giving the child the signal that the visitor, living though long dead, has said goodbye and gone away, and that the child's mother, living though even longer dead and far more deeply mourned, is free to come upstairs to kiss him good night, though, in the remembered past, there was unhappiness, and she would not come to him. The theme is developed in convoluted prose, climbing like a creeper over page after page, yet it reminds us of the exquisitely concentrated lyric at the end of *Also Sprach Zarathustra:*

> Oh Mensch! Gieb Acht!
> Was spricht die tiefe Mitternacht?
> "Ich schlief, ich schlief—,
> "Aus tiefem Traum bin ich erwacht:—
> "Die Welt is tief,
> "Und tiefer als der Tag gedacht.
> "Tief ist ihr Weh—
> "Lust—tiefer noch als Herzeleid:
> "Weh spricht: Vergeh!
> "Doch alle Lust will Ewigkeit—,
> "—will tiefe, tiefe Ewigkeit!"

But Proust would not have it so. He treated his madeleine's intellectual pretensions very seriously. He suggested that not only was the narrator going to write his book by this use of memory, but that other great books had been written on this formula. Standing in meditation at the reception, the narrator involves Chateaubriand (*Le Temps retrouvé*, Bk. II, p. 82):

Was it not on sensations of the madeleine kind that the most beautiful part of "Les Mémoires d'Outre-Tombe" was built? 'Yesterday evening I went a walk by myself . . . I was distracted from my thoughts by the song of a thrush perched on the highest branch of a birch-tree. At once the magic sound conjured up before me my father's estate; I forgot the disasters of which I had lately been the witness and, suddenly carried back to the past, I saw once more the countryside where I had so often heard the song of the thrush.'

Proust goes on to another passage in Chateaubriand which cannot be gracefully translated, for it is about the scent of heliotrope, and when a great French romantic writer writes about a scent the English language is debarred from joining in the enterprise. The import of the passage is that the exiled Chateaubriand once found the fragrance of heliotrope in his nostrils, rising from a bean patch and not a garden, and borne to him not by a European breeze but by a wild wind of the New World, which was alien from the transplanted flower and the world of grace and beauty and cultivation to which it belonged, so that for him it was laden with a sense of sorrow and homesickness and hunger for lost joys. If this can be claimed as an example of the use of the narrator's madeleine technique, any example of reminiscence and association can be the subject of a like claim, and it follows that the technique must be of such a general nature, and must be allowed to differ so widely from the narrator's description of it, that it can hardly be called a particular technique at all.

Proust goes on to indicate Gérard de Nerval's *Sylvie* as a product of his method, which is not so patently

235

absurd, since that story deals with the intertwinement of past and present. But he goes on to a still greater absurdity (Bk. II, p. 83):

> And finally in Baudelaire, there are still more reminiscences, which are of a less fortuitous kind, and that to my mind clinches the argument. It is the poet himself who, with more power to select and in greater relaxation, finds spontaneously in, say, the scent of a woman's hair and her bosom the analogies which were to inspire him to such lines as *"l'azur du ciel immense et rond"* and *"un port rempli de flammes et de mats."* I was trying to think of other poems of Baudelaire which are built on a transposed sensation, to the end of establishing my artistic consanguinity with the noblest writers, and of giving me confidence that the work which I now felt no hesitation in beginning would be worth the energy I meant to dedicate to it, as I came to the foot of the staircase which led down to the library . . .

It is obvious that the evocation of past sensations by present ones could be carried out with much more exciting material than madeleines, and that Baudelaire would be likely to explore this possibility; but it is riding a hobby-horse too hard to suppose that he did so. Reference to the poems from which these lines are taken, *La Chevelure* and *Parfum exotique* is unconvincing. What happens when a writer sits down to create a work of art is, of course, profoundly mysterious. It is certain that the process must be based on the faculty of observation; the writer must look at the world and touch it and listen to it and taste, and take note of his own thoughts and feelings, all with such intensity that his impressions are worth storing. But to suggest that

236

the artistic process could consist simply of expert dis-
gorgement of those impressions is to do a disservice to
anybody who is trying to write, and a worse one to anybody who has written well. That disservice could never
be more gross than when Proust is its victim. Recently
there was a book published about him which was admirable in its scholarship and its piety, but which took
for granted that Proust had actually adopted the plan of
execution which he ascribes to the narrator; and this
seduced the author into explaining that *A la recherche du
temps perdu* contains some unpleasant characters, but
they have to be included in it because they had crossed
the path of the narrator, and he is describing time as he
knew it. But these characters are in fact the keystone
of a vast structure which would collapse without them;
not to see them as chosen by the author for a particular
purpose is to lose sight of the real purpose of his work
as he himself saw it.

To discover what that was one should turn to the
essay on Proust which was written by Paul Valéry, the
greatest critic this age has seen, perhaps the only first-
rate critic we have had among us. His essay begins, by
one of those curious pieces of panache which are so
common among the French masters and so difficult for
foreigners to understand, with a statement that he had
had the leisure to read only one volume of Proust's great
work; but his private conversation revealed that he must
have read at least half of it. Valéry deals thus with the
point which has distressed his latest monographist, the
unworthiness of some of Proust's characters ("Hom-
mage," *Variété, 1,* 157–65):

Proust was able to direct the powers of an interior life
which was singularly rich and exquisitely cultivated

237

to the interpretation of a small society which meant to be, and had to be, superficial. By reason of his treatment, the representation of a superficial society is a profound work of art.

Should he have expended such intelligence on this enterprise? Was it worth such devotion and such a sustained effort of attention? This is a question worthy of consideration.

What calls itself "the great world" is composed purely of symbolic figures. Nobody can play a part in it unless they represent an abstraction. It is necessary that all social forces should meet one another: that somewhere *money* should be talking to *beauty;* that *politics* should be on good terms with *elegance;* that *literature* and *birth* should come to an agreement and have tea together. As soon as a new force arises, not much time elapses before its representatives appear in society; and the course of history sums itself up clearly enough in the arrival, at regular intervals, of new social types who are bidden to the receptions and the hunting parties and the marriages and funerals of the governing class.

Since all these abstractions of which I speak have their hangers-on who are just what they are, there occur all sorts of incongruous complications such as could only be studied on this little stage. As a bank-note is a piece of paper as well as a bank-note, so a personage of the great world combines a token-value as a representative of a force with a human body and soul. This combination puts useful material in front of the subtle novelist.

It must be remembered that our greatest authors have nearly always written only about the court. They drew on the life of the city only for comedy, and on the country for fables. But the greatest art, the art of integrated forms and pure types of character, entities which permit the symmetrical, and as one might say the musical development of a quite isolated situation, is bound up with the existence of a society governed by convention, where a language is spoken that is adorned with veils and furnished with limits, where *to seem* controls *to be* and holds it nobly in a constraint which changes the whole of life into an exercise in the control of the mind.

The great world of today does not present such an orderly pattern as the Court used to do. It nevertheless deserves—and indeed because of this disorder and the interesting contradictions it represents—that the creator of Charlus and the Guermantes should find there the medium for his speculation and the bases for his arguments. But in the depths of his own nature Marcel Proust has found the metaphysic without which no world can exist.

There could hardly be a finer brief exposition of what Proust was trying to do. His book was not an account of the collision of an individual with time, and his subsequent attempts to remember the accident in spite of his concussion. The book appears, like the traditional works of art of the kind we have been considering, as a simultaneous evaluation of the beauty or repulsiveness of human beings, and the forces they incarnate, and the result of the interplay between these forces.

It must be noticed that under the surface Proust was a moralist of a severe type unusual among great writers. He wrote as broad farce as France has ever exported to our libraries; an English Proust would not have had a happy reception from his publishers had he presented

to them the famous account of the night the violinist
Morel spends in and about the seaside brothel, forever
seeking to achieve happiness with the Prince de Guermantes and forever frustrated by the Baron de Charlus.
Proust brought us near to the physical reality of sexual
perversion, and confronted us with what is still less
decorous, its intimate idiom. Nevertheless he was a
Puritan, to such a degree that he is capable of shocking
us much more deeply by his severity than by his sexu-
ality. All of us must be startled, and even repelled, by an
incident in *Swann's Way* to which he attached supreme
importance. It shows a Spartan belief in discipline and
the suppression of the natural man with which none
of the conventional moralists among novel writers, not
Conrad or Kipling or Henry James, not Trollope or
Thackeray, would have felt sympathy. The narrator,
when he was a little boy staying at his grandfather's
house at Combray, was one night sent to bed early because he looked tired, without his usual goodnight kiss
from his beloved mother. This is a great tragedy for him.
In anguish he goes up to his room, and when he has got
to bed he feels like a condemned prisoner in his cell.
He writes a note to his mother and asks the cook to
give it to her downstairs, but there is a guest for dinner,
and this is not a simple matter. The child lies in a sweat
of fear, hungering for the kiss and afraid that he will be
punished for sending the note, which would be considered by his family as a shameful act (*Du côté de chez
Swann,* Bk. I, p. 53):

> In the system of upbringing which my parents were
> applying to me, faults were not graded in the same
> order as in other systems, and they had taught me to
> rank above all others (doubtless because these were

240

the very ones to which I would have been most liable) those faults which I now see had in common their origin in a nervous impulse. But at that time nobody used that term, nobody spoke of this origin in a way which might have suggested to me that I had an excuse for giving way to these faults, or even that I could not help it.

When the clatter of the gate tells the miserable child that the guest has gone, he gets up and waits for his mother to appear. Presently he hears her coming upstairs and goes out into the passage (p. 56):

My heart was beating so violently that I could hardly move, but at least it was no longer beating because of anxiety, but because of excitement and joy. I saw in the well of the staircase the light thrown by my mother's candle. Then I saw her, and rushed towards her. For an instant she stared at me in astonishment, not understanding what was going on. Then she looked angry. She did not say a single word; and indeed for far less than what I had done that night I had been punished by being sent to coventry.

But just then the child's father came out of his dressing room, and the mother, afraid that the father would be exasperated by the scene, said in a voice choked with rage, "Run away and don't let your father see you standing about like an idiot." But it happened that the father, though he was a strict man, always lacking in geniality and often inclined to issue arbitrary prohibitions, happened to feel a flash of tenderness for the child's evident distress, and bade the mother have a bed made up in the child's room and stay with him for the night.

Instead of being pleased, the child felt wretched. As soon as he was left alone with his mother he burst into

241

tears, and a sense of tragedy possessed him. He had been suffering, that was true, but the door had been opened on greater suffering (p. 59):

> Mamma spent that night in my room; when I had just committed a sin so grave that I had expected to be sent away from home, my parents treated me far more kindly than they had ever done when I had been specially good. . . . And thus for the first time, my hysteria was not treated as a fault for which I ought to be punished, but as a misfortune beyond my control, which had been officially recognised as such, as a nervous condition for which I was not responsible; hence I was relieved because I needed no longer to mix shame with my tears, I could weep without sin. . . . I ought to have been happy; but I was not. It seemed to me my mother had just made a first concession to me, which must have been painful to her, which was the first abandonment on her part of the ideal she had conceived for me, and that for the first time, brave as she was, she was owning herself beaten.

The child feels no gratitude to his father for this sudden flash of compassion, but rather blames him. He regards it as just another manifestation to his father's arbitrary nature, this taking a positive instead of the usual negative form. It seems to him a proof that his mother and grandmother loved him more than his father did, that they would have preferred him to go on suffering his nervous distress because "they wanted me to learn to conquer it, in order to lessen my nervous instability and build up my will." They would, in fact, have liked him "to turn from his wickedness and live." Though the child only vaguely apprehends their case, he agrees with what he can understand of it with an alarming intensity. He realizes that a moral catastrophe has occurred which has turned him back from the path to salvation.

What is truly remarkable is that Proust accepted this as the proper point of view, and the whole book leads up to a restatement of it in the closing passage of the book. There the narrator names his father's clemency as the cause of all his misfortunes (*Le Temps retrouvé,* Bk. II, p. 258):

> It was from that evening, when my mother had resigned her power, together with the slow death of my grandmother, that the decline of my will had set in, that my health had been ruined. Everything had been decided in that moment when, not being able to bear to wait till next morning to kiss my mother, I had taken my resolution and jumped out of bed . . .

It even appears that it was one of the chief achievements he hoped for from the practice of his technique of memory that he might live through this moment; and (from what is said earlier in the book) it is certain that he succeeded, and prized his success (*Du côté de chez Swann,* Bk. I, p. 58):

> Recently I have begun to be able, if I listen attentively, to hear the sobs which I had the strength to stifle in front of my father, and which broke out only when I was again alone with my mother. In reality they have never stopped. It is only because life is now growing silent about me that I hear them afresh, like convent bells which one might believe were not rung nowadays, because during the day

they are drowned by the city hub-bub, but which may be heard clearly enough in the stillness of the evening.

This is an extraordinary judgment and highly anachronistic. It is strange to find it in a book written in the second decade of this century. According to *Jean Santeuil* (the rough draft of this novel) the child was only seven years old. By that time most people were sufficiently instructed to know that when a child suffered from chronic hysteria it was probably the result of some environmental strain acting on a constitutional peculiarity which might be weakness or merely a quite desirable sensitivity; and they would also know that it could rarely be cured by punishment, and that a single act of not excessive indulgence would be unlikely to produce lifelong neurasthenia. Certainly the narrator's mother and grandmother are represented later as quite idiotic in their encouragement of his valetudinarianism: it is impossible to understand why, at Balbec, the grandmother should (as is related in the section of *Within a Budding Grove* called "The Intermittences of the Heart") have been in the habit of kneeling on the floor and taking off his shoes for him, since by his own account he must at that period often have dressed and undressed without her assistance. That the narrator should afterward have felt horror at his acceptance of such coddling would be explicable, but that he should pass a final judgment of such extreme comminatory force on the act by which his father designed to dry his tears takes us back to the days when Mr. and Mrs. Wesley, to restrain the workings of the original sin in their infant children, taught them to "cry quietly."

244

We are, in fact, on theological territory. The theology is tinged with heresy, for the episode confronts us with the redemptory female, who could save the individual, who would save him, were it not for the arbitrary intervention of the father, who has (it is specifically stated) no fixed principles. Surely we are in the presence of something like Manichaeanism, with the creator Ormuzd pouring into existence a disorderly universe compounded of good and evil in a state of inextricable confusion and (a feminized) Ahriman the redeemer, who with the co-operation of the human race uses a divine power of extricating the inextricable and preserving good while expelling evil from the universe. There is indeed a tendency to exploit the Manichaean dichotomy all through *A la recherche du temps perdu;* people are always splitting into pairs, one a vessel of honor, the other a vessel of dishonor. But there is also an orthodox aspect of the scene. The child has fallen away from grace, and he can be saved only by the infusion of righteousness (in the form of the element which by its vigilance over memory places time within eternity) and by appointment to a vocation (in the form of his self-dedication to his book). It should be noted that there is a significant ambiguity in the title of this book, for the word *perdu* has connotations hardly present in our word "lost," except in the expression "a lost soul." There is a suggestion of waste and ruin and despair: the great hall in French law courts where litigants wait their turn is called *la salle des pas perdus,* a dress which has been irretrievably spoiled is *perdue.* There is also a suggestion of recklessness, even of dementia: *à corps perdu* describes a movement made without restraint, *crier comme un perdu* means to shout like a madman. This is a book about

245

an attempt to reverse spiritual time, to turn back when far on the path to damnation and to seek salvation. Though it gives a pessimistic account of life on earth, it is a work of optimism, for it holds that though the human will is corrupt it can be purified.

3 *The Dissolution of the Court*

Two of the three qualities which make *A la recherche du temps perdu* a great work were prescribed for the novelist by Fielding: first, "that power, or rather those powers, of the mind which are capable of penetrating in all things within our reach and knowledge, and of distinguishing their essential differences," and second, "the sort of knowledge beyond the power of learning to bestow, and this is to be had by conversation." The third was the serious attitude to life which Fielding did not prescribe because he himself was so full of it that he took it for granted. The book is also given a three-dimensional solidity, a corporeal splendor, by a technical device which would have been quite beyond Fielding's comprehension and was beyond the reach of any of Proust's contemporaries, even those who were most anxious to catch the whole of time in their net. In threefold industry, Proust built up his world by setting down with the closest fidelity every essential impression which stamped itself on the narrator's sense, and every essential idea which passed through his mind as the result of the impact, and by showing how this impression and this idea dove-tailed into the context of reality as he saw it at that time, and finally by suggesting how the pattern thus established appeared to him at the moment of writing it down at the end of his days. It is not irrelevant to regard this as a matter of industry, for indeed the book is a triumph of character in the Arnoldian sense, and this is congruous with its purpose of writing a raffish, modernistic, godless, but relentlessly moral *Pilgrim's Progress*.

It is the story of two people who are perhaps one.

The two people are the narrator, the son of a Catholic family belonging to the well-to-do middle class, and Charles Swann, an old friend of his parents, a wealthy and elegant and cultured Jew. Proust was himself half Catholic and half Jewish, and was brought up as a practicing Catholic. It is not unnatural, since Proust's great love was given to his Jewish mother, that Swann is represented as gifted and strong and self-possessed and much sought after. The narrator himself is sickly and inhibited, incapable of using his gifts because of his neurasthenia, and socially successful only because he is biddable and amiable. The narrator spends his holidays with his parents at his grandfather's home at Combray, a small town near Paris, and when they go for long walks they have a choice of two routes: one skirts the park attached to Swann's country house, the other follows the river to Guermantes, where the family bearing that historic name has its splendid château. Both walks are very beautiful. The special glory of "Swann's Way" is the hedge of pink hawthorn, the special glory of the "Guermantes Way" is the path through meadows where the ruins of an old castle are half buried under buttercups, beside the dark green river which flows by under a mantle of water lilies. There are two such routes which run through the social landscape inhabited by such people as Swann and the narrator, who are not fixed in any group by any hereditary duty, by the ownership of great estates or the management of a business, but who live on invested capital. They can go where they please and choose what friends please them, in a world where there is a hierarchy based on personal distinction, or in the other world where there is a hierarchy of families who in the past have established their value to the state and who carry on a stately tradition. In fact these two worlds mix, for those who are brilliant enough to please both, just as on the geographical plane "Swann's Way" and the "Guermantes' Way" lead to the same destination.

The social relations of these two men are important to them because they are unfortunate in their more intimate lives. Both are heterosexual, and each finds that his greatest love is simply a waste of spirit and expense of shame. Swann, who could have married any woman in France, gives the heart of his heart, the emotional gift which cannot be given twice, to a courtesan named Odette de Crécy, who is the essence of natural beauty as seen by those who are not pantheist. She delights the eye, but is empty of significance. Whensoever a man or woman credits her with a manifestation of intelligence or sentiment, it is an error, due to the hypnosis exercised by her loveliness, which also is an error. For she is not in fact very lovely; she only creates an illusion of loveliness, by her bearing and her dress, by her shrewd calculation of what means are necessary to provoke desire, which, since desire is linked in many people with the poetic faculties, often evokes far more than her shrewdness had foreseen or could understand. When she appeared in the Allée des Acacias in the Bois de Boulogne, with violets at her bosom or in her hair, veils floating about her, her slim hands raising a lilac parasol while her lilac train trailed behind her, she was "dressed as the mob imagines queens to dress" (*Du côté de chez Swann*, 2, 290); and in her own house, in wintertime, she made herself a fantasia of the season, sitting in her overheated drawing room as fresh as spring in her teagown of crêpe-de-chine, "white as the first snows," or her pleated robe of silk muslin, "which seemed nothing more than a shower of white or rosy petals" (*A l'ombre*, Bk. I, pp. 232–4); surrounded by huge chrysanthemums, which repeated in a more lasting form the colors of the sunset then vanishing from the skies outside. But though she talked continually, she talked of nothing, and though she loved continually she could not love. A permanent affair was to her only as the condition which made the possibility of unfaithfulness more serious and more exciting. But her beauty was undying, and when she was old and Swann was dead, and she had married again and been widowed again, she became the mistress of the old Duke of Guermantes, in some senile simulacrum of love, and produced another senile simulacrum of unfaithfulness. True, she also looked after him, but "without charm, without grandeur. She was as mediocre when she played that part as she had been in all the others. Not that life had not given her some wonderful parts, but she had not been able to play them" (*Le Temps retrouvé,* Bk. II, p. 222). She was, indeed, another version of Hamlet's mother. Like Gertrude, she was a crowned bore on an illumined stage; and when Proust describes how she deceived Swann with the greatly inferior de Forcheville he convinces us of what Shakespeare failed to prove in the Portrait Scene, that such lack of taste is an act of aggression against the superior man's universe. Since Odette did not surrender herself to Swann, who could lift her to his own level, he had to pursue her down to the lower level on which she had established herself with de Forcheville, and his life was planned on a petty scale quite inappropriate to his natural grandeur.

The narrator's principal love affair was as disastrous. It is to be regretted that the significance of this part of the book has been obscured by the disposition of many people to suppose that because Proust himself was homosexual, Albertine must be the portrait of a man disguised as a woman, and even of a particular and identifiable

250

man. The reasons for this belief are insubstantial. It is true that Proust remarked to Gide that one can tell all in a novel provided that one does not use the word *je;* but if Proust had wanted to write about a homosexual love affair, he could easily have invented another character like Swann to whom he could have ascribed it. As most of the characters in the great work prove to be homosexual in the long run, it is preposterous to imagine that Proust suffered from any inhibitions regarding the portrayal of this kind of love. It is also recalled by those who wish to regard *La Prisonnière* and *La Fugitive* as transvestite exercises that even as the narrator kept Albertine a prisoner in his mother's flat, so Marcel Proust imprisoned in his flat in the Boulevard Haussmann young Agostinelli, who was his chauffeur and became his secretary, and died a curious death just before the first World War, flying at a school for aviators in the South of France, at which he had enrolled himself under the name of Marcel Swann. But this does not take us so far as might be supposed, for Agostinelli was living in Proust's flat with his mistress, who passed as his wife and to whom he was devoted. It has also been pointed out that it would have been unlikely that the narrator's parents would have let him, their son, take into the flat during their absence an unchaperoned girl, and live alone with her for months, and that therefore he must have been an unchaperoned young man; but the narrator's parents would certainly have objected as strongly to the presence of a young man, for they were no fools about such matters.

It appears probable that Proust is simply following out his symmetrical and intricate plan doing what he appears to be doing: writing an account of a second type of heterosexual love which shall balance the account of

Swann's infatuation with Odette. He certainly had not lived this story himself, but a friend had done so. A man whom he had known for many years and who made him his confidant had gone from Paris to live in London and there had met a beautiful young woman of good family who had left her impoverished country home in order to earn her living. They fell in love, and, unknown to all her friends, she shared his house in London. The man had a cruel nature and enjoyed tormenting her by affected jealousy, and the girl, deeply in love with him and anxious to marry him, endured this maltreatment for a long time. The phrase that the narrator used to Albertine, "I know that I could be of use to you intellectually," was one that the friend of Proust often used to and about the English young girl; and the pleasure the narrator felt when Albertine spoke her fantasy about ice cream was such a pleasure as Proust's friend often reported to him when the girl had shown herself witty and imaginative. This story was being unfolded to Proust when he added the section on Albertine to the book; and it fulfills a function. Swann, the strong and generous man, is destroyed by his love for an unworthy woman; the narrator, weakly and mean, destroys the relatively inoffensive girl whom he loved. Our attention is forced back to *Hamlet*. The very reason for the continued dominance of the play over our minds is that it presents us with the archetypes of character, the primal pattern of behavior, which succeeding artists have dealt with again and again because they must write of what they know, and this is what there is to be known.

It may seem surprising if any resemblance is found between Ophelia and Albertine, whose only stable attribute (for in different parts of the book she has eyes of different colors and at one point even develops a different Christian name) is a certain robustness. But Albertine shared with Ophelia the characteristics which derive from the dependence of the female. It was so important for her to marry that her pride was impaired; she was as much lamed as if her foot had been injured. She had to submit to the narrator's inquisition about her Lesbian practices as Ophelia had to listen to Hamlet when he talked of country matters; she could not free herself from the narrator until another possibility of marriage appeared, and it is proof of her miserable position that that saving vision had to appear not to her but to her guardian before it could free her. Albertine died by an accident, as Ophelia did: an accident which is hard to recognize as such, because it came when this condition of dependence had become so humiliating that it would seem inevitable that even the most painful and drastic kind of escape would be welcome. And she is killed twice over, just as Ophelia is: Ophelia drowns in the brook and then is drowned in Hamlet's coarse indecorum in the graveyard scene, and Albertine breaks her neck in a riding accident and then is reconsigned to death when the narrator, some time later, receives a telegram in Venice which appears to come from Albertine. It comes from another woman whose signature he has misread; but for a time he thinks her alive, and he feels no joy, no desire to welcome her back to life, because he had never loved her, she had never been real to him. As he puts it, "I should have been incapable of resuscitating Albertine, because I was incapable of resuscitating myself, of resuscitating the self of those days."

It is to be asked whether we have grounds for believing that Proust thought the narrator a bad man, as there are for believing that Shakespeare thought Hamlet a bad man: whether there is any equivalent in *A la recherche du temps perdu* to the murder of unshriven men. Surely an affirmative answer is to be found in the episode of the narrator's dispatch of the headwaiter of the Balbec Hotel down to the district by the Loire where Albertine had lived, so that he could find out whether she had engaged in Lesbian practices there, which errand he fulfilled by sleeping with a laundress and getting her to give him her confidences about the dead girl. The narrator knew better than to do this, for he concurred in his family's disposition to take Madame de Sévigné as their pattern of what a civilized human being should be, and though that lady might have recorded such squalid behavior it would have been with derision, as part of the misbehavior which degraded the court.

Proust is therefore of the opinion, like Shakespeare, that "but to the girdle do the gods inherit." But this loathing of sex is more comprehensive than Shakespeare's, for Shakespeare was plainly willing to give homosexual love the benefit of the doubt and to assume that there could be men lovers who would be less terrible than Antony and Cleopatra (Sonnet 144):

> Two loves I have of comfort and despair;
> Which like two spirits do suggest me still:
> The better angel is a man right fair,
> The worser spirit a woman colour'd ill.

Proust has looked into the matter and makes it quite clear that Monsieur de Charlus cannot be justly described as the better angel or as a man right fair. The tremendous scene in *Du côté de Guermantes,* where Monsieur de Charlus first reveals himself as homosexual to the narrator makes revelation also of a hectoring sadist, anxious to destroy the self-respect of the desired person,

254

preparing, while he begs for a passionate surrender, to reward it by betrayal. This was what Proust sincerely believed about homosexuality. He saw it as cruel within its own field and, for some reason never made quite clear, as spreading a stain outside that field, as breaking up the civilizing achievement of good fortune and debasing its practitioners till they forget the morals and manners of their station and sink to a lower level. If there were any man who could be a homosexual lover without demoralization, it would be the brilliant and amiable Robert de Saint-Loup, with his exquisite breeding, his well-taught manners, and the kindliness which comes of being universally admired. But at the end he is heard talking with one of his aunt's footmen in a way that shocks the other: "Do you mean to say that you don't know how to get a chap fired when you don't like him? It's not hard. You need only hide the things that he has to take in, then, when they get in a fluster and ring for him, he can't find what's wanted. After that's happened four or five times, they're bound to sack him." There is in *Du côté de chez Swann* a description of a scene between two Lesbians, whom the narrator watches through their uncurtained window at night, seeing the one woman, as part of their orgiastic ritual, spit on the photograph of the father of the other woman, who has just died of grief at her scandalous ways; and it appears that Proust is going to explain the mechanism by which homosexuality exercises this disintegrating influence. But the explanation is confused, and it contains nothing which would not apply equally to heterosexuality, though Proust thought of this as much less dangerous than homosexuality, though that was not safe.

The explanation is, moreover, too simple, and indeed one must recognize a variation in Proust's powers of analysis. These were superb in the intellectual and aesthetic field. From his description of what he felt the first time he saw the great actress Berma, it is possible to understand how it was that Virginia Woolf did not know what to think of contemporary work until her friends explained to her its relationship to the literature which she already knew and understood, and that her taste, having received this clue, was flawless. To give another example, there is *La Prisonnière* a passage in which the narrator tells Albertine that "the great writers only write one work" (Bk. II, pp. 235–43), of which their many works are each a part; that all Hardy's books show the same stoney, geometric landscape on which people form stoney geometric relationships, and all Dostoevsky's women are the same although each is unique, and all his vast and gloomy houses too; and in three pages the paradox is proved reasonable that a great writer must show the most exquisite recognition of differences and a compelling unity of vision. But Proust's moral analyses are often of a startling baldness. He writes of the Lesbian daughter that she perhaps suffered the evil practice of her companion because she identified pleasure with evil and not being evil did not really understand what she was doing but merely passed into a transient relation with its forms, as one might visit a foreign country where a langauge is spoken which one does not understand (*Du côté de chez Swann,* Bk. I, p. 237):

> Perhaps she would not have thought of wickedness as a state so rare, so extraordinary, so exotic, which it was such a change to visit, had she been able to recognize in herself (as she was able to do in other people) the power to cause suffering and to remain unmoved by it: that indifference which,

256

whatever other names be given to it, is the terrible
and enduring form taken by cruelty.

This does not really go deep enough. To be callous and
unaware that one is causing suffering need not necessarily put into one's head the notion of practicing bizarre
kinds of cruelty. We cannot really believe in this explanation of the picture of homosexuality he presents,
any more than we can really believe that because the
narrator's father was weak and made his mother relax
her severity toward her little boy, he grew up a neurasthenic.

This rejection of both forms of sexual life as degrading gives social life a new importance. It was still
possible for the narrator to imagine friends meeting together, and without partaking of the poison of the flesh,
manifesting the integrity, the intelligence, the compassion, the fidelity which he knew to exist, because they had
been visible in the lives of his grandmother and his
mother. But the bourgeoisie could not give him this cultivated and civilized society. That class can throw up men
of genius, and the narrator knew a great musician, a great
painter, a great doctor. But the musician had no social
life; he was isolated by his fatherly concern for the
Lesbian daughter, whom, after his death, the narrator
had watched through the uncurtained window, consenting while her companion spat on her father's photograph.
The painter and the doctor were content to frequent a
dreary social circle presided over by the vulgar, postur-
ing, grimacing, mindless, heartless Madame Verdurin.
Therefore it became the narrator's hope that he might find
the dreamed-of blossoming of thought and manners in the
salons and ballrooms of the great families of France.
Their personal beauty, their charm of manner and the

257

splendor of their houses persuaded him that perhaps they had made a life which was the moral equivalent of the visible beauty of the medieval and Renaissance France so often recalled by their historic names.

The young man is disappointed. These aristocrats are as petty and vulgar as the bourgeoisie, but because they have been encouraged by the admiring world to develop a spectacular quality their pettiness becomes microscopic and their vulgarity huge and obtrusive. They are proud of their blood, which links them to the legendary dead, but they are capable of mean unkindness to their servants. They practice exclusion as a sport, refusing to know people for no other reason than that these people want to know them and they can inflict pain by such refusals. They have no intellectual virtue. The famous "Guermantes wit" is simply the same ill-natured chatter that falls from Madame Verdurin's lips. But there is also a certain ominous quality about them not to be accounted for by their bright unrepentant stupidity; and it is presented for us in the famous scene which shows the Duke and Duchess of Guermantes confronted with a tragic development in the life of Swann. He was an old friend of theirs; having been admitted to their lives as a tame intellectual, he has refined their relationship by his own intelligence and sensitiveness till it has become a friendship of which they would otherwise have been incapable. He comes to see them one evening, and sits talking to them while they wait for their carriage, which is to take them to a dinner party. The Duchess presses Swann to accompany her and her husband on a tour to Italy ten months later, when the spring has come, and Swann refuses. In the midst of chatter about snobbish trifles ("Let's go down to the hall, then we'll know anyway how we descended from your study, though we'll never know

258

how we're descended from the counts of Brabant." "But I've told you a hundred times how the title came into the house of Hesse") the Duchess keeps harking back to her invitation, and finally Swann's reticence, though not his stoicism, breaks down, and he tells her that by the time she and the Duke start on their trip the disease from which he is suffering will have killed him.

The existence of the Duke and Duchess can be justified only on the assumption that it has enabled them to spend their lives in mastering the art of living, so that no occasion will ever find them at a loss. But they do not know what to say (*Du côté de Guermantes,* Bk. II, pp. 250-1):

> "What's that you say?" exclaimed the Duchess, stoping for a moment on her way to the carriage, and raising her beautiful blue eyes, which were full of sorrow but also full of uncertainty. Placed for the first time in her life between two duties as different as getting into her carriage to go out to dinner and showing sympathy with a man who was going to die, she could not think of anything in the social code which indicated the right precedent to follow, and not knowing which duty to take more seriously she thought it well to pretend to disbelieve that the second alternative was there for her to consider, so that she followed the first, which at the moment demanded less effort, and felt that the best way of resolving the conflict was to deny that it existed. "You are joking," she said to Swann. "That would be a joke in the very best taste," he replied ironically. "I don't know why I am telling you this, I have not spoken to you about my illness before. But as you asked me, and as I have now got to the stage when I

259

may die any day. . . . But whatever happens I must not make you late for your dinner-party," he added, because he knew that for other people their social obligations took precedence over the death of a friend, and he was putting himself in their place, because of his good manners.

This passage leaves us with a horrified conviction that the Guermantes really lived in a state of barbarous confusion about their environment which made them think it impossible to be late for a dinner party given by a host of social importance equal to their own, though possible to turn their backs on an old friend who has just told them that he is under sentence of death. But, as it turns out, even that interpretation does them too much credit. The Duke grumbles that dinner is at eight, and that it is now ten to eight (ibid., p. 251):

Now Madame de Guermantes made a definite move towards the carriage, and once more bade Swann farewell. "You know, we'll talk of this again. I don't believe a word of what you've told me, but we must talk it over together. They must have given you a horrible fright, come to luncheon, any day you please" (for Madame de Guermantes everything resolved itself into a luncheon-party). "You must let me know your day and your time," and, picking up her red skirt, she set her foot on the step of the carriage. She was about to seat herself when the Duke's eye fell on her foot and he roared in a voice of thunder, "Oriane, what have you done, you appalling person! You've kept on your black shoes! With a red dress! Run upstairs and change your shoes, or better still," he said to the footman, "get her Grace's maid to bring down a pair of red shoes at once."

"But, my dear," gently replied the Duchess, who was annoyed at seeing that Swann, who was leaving with me and had hung back to let the carriage go first, was within earshot, "we really are late." "No, we have all the time in the world. It's only ten to, we won't need ten minutes to get to the Parc Monceau. And what are you making a fuss about, if we didn't turn up till half-past eight they'd possess their souls in patience, and in any case you simply can't go out in a red dress and black shoes. Anyway, we shan't be the last, be sure of that, the Sassenages will be there, you know that they never appear before twenty to nine." The Duchess went up to her room.

The situation is far worse than it had seemed. These barbarians were not moved by an insensate loyalty to the tribe, which made them deem the obligation to attend a tribal gathering as outweighing any appeal made by charity or friendship. No shadow of concern for the convenience of their fellow tribesman had crossed their minds from first to last. They had been moved simply by a desire to appear before the tribe in the trappings that would claim and confirm their exalted position in the tribal hierarchy. They were beautiful and happy and completely heartless monsters. The scene is a masterpiece. Yet it is vitiated by a serious flaw. The incident as far as it concerns the shoes could never have happened as it is described. Madame de Guermantes would certainly have been dressed by her maid, who would indeed have been guilty of culpable negligence had she let her mistress go out without putting on evening shoes, and Madame de Guermantes was, as we are told more than once, extremely unkind to her servants. Yet neither she nor her husband utter one word of censure on the maid. But indeed the incident could never have happened at all, for an elegant woman would have changed her shoes and her stockings in the evening as a matter of routine.

It should be noted that Proust, great artist though he be, is not the polished craftsman he is often represented. He is given to defying reality as a writer of realistic novels has no right to do. We may forgive constant juggling with his characters' ages, for there we have only another example of the arbitrary time scheme which has been found necessary in the construction of so many serious works of art, though indeed things grow most confusing in the last volume, *Le Temps retrouvé*, when the narrator, who cannot be much over forty, is represented as an aging man, while his cook, Françoise, who was old enough to have a son-in-law when she looked after the narrator in his childhood, is still in practice and is physically alert. But it is not so easy to forgive Proust for making Albertine and the narrator share a Paris apartment in conditions not credible in France simply because he would not take the trouble to adapt a story which was credible enough of people living in totally different circumstances in London. Sometimes this indifference went further still, and not only diminishes the reader's power to suspend his own disbelief but actually impairs the value of what he is asked to believe, as when Proust weakened the effect of this very scene about the Duchess' slippers by embedding it in an incident which makes the point in a more diffuse and less plausible form. For earlier that evening four elderly ladies of noble birth, all relatives of the Duke, had called on him to warn him that his cousin, the Marquis d'Osmond, is about to die, and the Duke refuses to hear what they have to say, obstinately answering them as if they had brought good news of the invalid; and before he goes out to dinner he forbids his footman to go his usual errand to the Marquis' house to ask for news of his progress. For the Duke wants to fulfil his evening program, which consists of a dinner party, a reception given by his cousin the Prince de Guermantes, and a fancy dress ball, at which he has an exciting assignation with a new mistress, and he would have to stay at home if his cousin had died. But he is unlucky; when he and his wife return to their house from the reception for the purpose of putting on their fancy dresses, in the middle of the night, two of the elderly ladies are waiting at his door to tell him that his cousin is dead. To this the Duke replies that this must be an exaggeration, and rushes on to assume the costume of Louis the Eleventh.

This second demonstration that the Guermantes were heartless even in the presence of death not only weakens the impact of the first, it is also not in character. Surely the strength of such people lies in the very fact that they give themselves away very rarely, and they would be most unlikely to do so several times in one night: their tribe owes its ascendancy in great part to its practice of wearing benevolent masks so continually that its enemies are often deceived and lay down their arms. But Proust will not leave the incident alone, and brings it into his picture of the other social world, the circle of the Verdurins. When they are giving the disastrous musical party at which Monsieur de Charlus wishes to display the gifts of his beloved Morel, the violinist, it happens that Saniette, the butt of the circle, tactlessly blurts out to his host that the great friend of the family, Princess Sherbatoff, has just died, and Monsieur Verdurin snarls at him, "Oh, you always exaggerate"; and Proust draws the reader's attention to this parallel with the Guermantes family. It is true that here he makes a fine point: the Duke is too well-bred to be rude to the elderly ladies even when he is distressing them by violating what they consider a fundamental decency, and frees his words from any accusation against them by saying: *"Mais non, on exagère, on exagère!" (Sodom et Gomorrhe,* Bk. I, p. 124), whereas the ill-bred Verdurin charges the wretched Saniette directly by saying: "Vous, vous *exagérez toujours" (La Prisonnière,* Bk. II, p. 35). But this hardly justifies Proust in imposing on his readers the strain of supposing that just before a particularly conspicuous reception given in each of the two opposed worlds a close associate of the host should die, and that both the Duke of Guermantes and Monsieur Verdurin should then be inspired to utter words in which there sounds an echo of one of Mark Twain's most famous jokes. Many other complaints can be registered against Proust. Is his dialogue not quite often a ferocious caricature? We wonder if the Duke would really have said, when he was minimizing the condition of his cousin (*Du côté de Guermantes,* Bk. II, p. 245):

Ah, these invalids, people do a lot of little things for them they don't do for us. Today at luncheon a blackguard of a cook sent up a leg of mutton with bearnaise sauce, which was simply perfect, I must admit that, but just for that reason I ate so much that I can still feel it in my inside. But that doesn't make people come round and ask how I am, as they do to good old Amanien. We do too much of that sort of thing. It wears him out, we ought to give him a chance to breathe. They're killing him, poor chap, making all this fuss round him.

Surely Dickens never drew the outlines thicker. At the end of the first part of *Du côté de Guermantes,* the grandmother, struck suddenly by her last illness, goes to a public lavatory in the Champs-Elysées and overhears the horrid chatter of the woman attendant, bragging of her wealthy customers, and boasting of how she refuses the poor the use of the *cabinets,* and proving the truth of what she said by turning away an ill-dressed woman. The grandmother says, "Could anything have been more like the Guermantes, or the Verdurins and their 'little circle'?" (ibid., Bk. I, pp. 278-9). But surely this is too recognizably a cliché dear to the French tradition? Is it not a pity, too, that Proust, notably in *A l'ombre des jeunes filles en fleurs,* tries to make literature do the work of painting? And is not that business of the little phrase in the Vinteuil sonata preposterously, and not helpfully, overwritten? Proust had a sense of fun about music. It is worth while getting hold of *Le Pauvre Fou* of Tagliafico, to learn just what Proust was telling us about Odette when he made her leave instructions in her will that it was to be played at her funeral. But his serious discussions of the subject are surely not valuable. When Swann repeatedly recovered the phrase in the Vinteuil sonata which had captivated him, he was fortunate in that he went through the reverse of the experience recorded in the Victorian lyric, "A Lost Chord," which describes how a musician, "seated one day at the organ, weary and ill at ease," accidentally struck one chord of music, "Like the sound of a great Amen," but was unable to find it again, and in the end came to the conclusion "It may be that only in Heaven I shall hear that grand Amen"; and doubtless an analysis of such a success should interest us all. But Proust seems to think that he is telling us something about music itself in passages such as these (*Du côté,* Bk. I, p. 300):

An impression of this order, lasting an instant, is, so to speak *sine materia*. Without doubt the notes we hear at such a time tend, according to their pitch and their volume, to form visual images and appear to cover surfaces of different dimensions, to trace arabesques, and to give us sensations of breadth and delicacy, stability and caprice. But the notes die away before these sensations are sufficiently developed to resist submersion under those which are aroused by notes which follow or even sound simultaneously. And this confusion would continue to smother under its fluidity and mass the themes which would now and then emerge, hardly discernible, to be overwhelmed again and to disappear, recognised only by the particular pleasure which they give, impossible to describe, to recall, to define, ineffable, were it not that our memory, like a workman who toils at the laying of firm foundations in the midst of the waves, fashions for us facsimiles of those fugitive phrases, and enables us to compare them with those which follow them and to differentiate between them. So, hardly had the delicious sensation which Swann had experienced died away, when his memory provided a transcript forthwith, summary and provisional, but one on which he could set his eyes while the playing continued, to such purpose that when the same impression suddenly came back, it was no longer impossible to grasp it.

Does this mean anything at all except that the sounds in music succeed each other very quickly, but it is possible all the same to remember them through clarifying confused first impressions by repetition?—and did anybody not know that before?

Because there are signs of a reaction against Proust, based on the assumption that he is in fact the mnemonic gymnast and pincushion of sensuous impressions which many of his admirers represent him to be, it is as well to admit his real faults, and to recognize that they are of no importance compared to his genius. He was able to achieve greater majesty and greater depth than any other writer of his time because of his two outstanding qualities. His craftsmanship enabled him to employ his peculiar threefold technical device of giving a man's immediate impression, the conditions of his external and internal life which make up the context of which that impression was a part, and the relationship of this particular experience to his whole life, the great experience which is the sum of all such minor experiences. He had also the power of creating consistent characters; and here we may go back to Fielding. A character must not "act in direct contradiction to the dictates of his nature," he said. "Should the best parts of the story of M. Antoninus be ascribed to Nero, or should the worst incidents of Nero's life be imputed to Antoninus, what would be more shocking to belief than either instance?" This is to make the supreme claim for the artist: that he can come near to recognizing the uniqueness of each spirit with which God is fully acquainted. Proust was able to go far in this imitation of a divine faculty, because his intelligence and industry and humor enabled him to become a great gossip in the same sense that Chaucer was; but he noticed that of the observed comedians some were damned and some were saved, and therefore what they enacted was really a tragedy. So great was his excitement at this spectacle, which was not what it first appeared, that he wrote prose as if he had hypnotized himself, as poets intoxicate themselves with verse, and indeed his

267

prose did not always remain what the French consider prose; and in his impatience he was able to burst the chains which usually bind the prose writer and to devise incidents (such as the duel in which Monsieur de Charlus engaged himself) which stripped men nearly as naked as the soliloquy.

Proust often described with emotion the exterior of churches, though (and perhaps it is a sign of a strong sense of guilt) he hardly ever ventures inside one. He translated Ruskin's "The Bible of Amiens," and in *A l'ombre des jeunes filles en fleurs* he ascribes to the artist Elstir a very Ruskinian speech, in which he recommends the carved porch of the church at Balbec with more reference to its religious inspiration than to its aesthetic features. *A la recherche du temps perdu* may be compared to this form of art, which was so dear to Proust: to a medieval church encrusted with sculptures representing men and women of the archetypes which were at the beginning and persist through the ages, identified as they are in the Testaments, but seen as the sculptors recognized them in their own generation. In the last part of the series, *Le Temps retrouvé*, the narrator is on his way to the reception given by the Prince de Guermantes at his new house in the Avenue du Bois, and sees Monsieur de Charlus driving by with his pander turned nursemaid, "his eyes staring, his bowed figure propped up rather than seated, as if he were a child who had been told to be good and sit straight. But under his straw hat was a shock of wild hair, quite white, and on his chin just such a white beard as snow gives the statues of rivers in public gardens" (Bk. I, p. 227). He was, indeed, turning to stone; and so were the people at the reception, which is so oddly colorless for a Proust party, though full of indications of character and events. It is as if they were all

taking their place in the representation of the Last Judgment which so often fills the place of honor in such an
ecclesiastical exhibition, the tympanum over the church
door.

Nearly all the souls are damned. We have long known
the fate of the Guermantes, though there is an odd suggestion that Monsieur de Charlus' damnation was not so
simple as appears. Proust makes it plain, with a harshness
rarely shown by any heterosexual writer, that he really
believes Charlus to have been destroyed by his tastes;
for the narrator describes how, although Charlus began
by despising the homosexuals who did not bear themselves with as much virile dignity as heterosexuals, he too
ended by squeaking and wriggling. But Proust also let it
be understood that in some mysterious way Charlus was
morally superior to his kinsmen, though they were free
from such vices, or not so obviously a prey to them. It
is as if the familiar field had been invaded by another
religion, sinister and not occidental in its origins, just as
at Balbec, Chinese dragons had wound themselves round
one of the capitals, and Charlus had endured this deg-
radation for the sake of others, like a Manichaean priest
giving his life to scatological rites in order that his con-
gregation might be pure. But even if he performed a
redemptory service he is nevertheless damned, with all
his kind, and so are the Verdurins and their smaller
breed; and it is indicated, more briefly, since parricide is
a terrible crime, that the *haute bourgeoisie* is damned
too. For it was the narrator's father who, because he
lacked principle and was an opportunist like all his tribe,
committed the uncalled-for act of pampering which
vitiated his son's will.

Not even the obscure are spared. Proust held as poor
an opinion of the mob as Shakespeare. Jupien, Aimé,

269

Françoise are as deeply damned as their masters; and he is careful to prove that his is just enough by providing in the earlier part of *Le Temps retrouvé* an instance which showed Françoise on the same level of insensibility (though she enacted it less dramatically) as the Duke and Duchess and Monsieur Verdurin when it comes to confronting another's doom. After an air-raid the narrator comes back to his house and finds Françoise and the butler coming up out of the cellar, and they tell him that during his absence Saint-Loup, on leave from the trenches, has called to see him. Both the servants speak of the caller very coldly (Bk. I, p. 201):

> Certainly all the efforts that the butler's son and Françoise's nephew had made to keep out of the army, Saint-Loup had made in reverse, and with success, in order to get into the greatest danger possible. But Françoise and the butler could never believe that, for they judged him according to themselves. They were convinced that the rich were always taken care of. Besides, had they really known the truth about his heroism, it would have left them unmoved. He did not call the Germans "boches," he praised the courage of the German troops, he did not account for failure to win an early victory by saying there had been treason. But that was what they wanted to hear, that was what they regarded as the sign of courage.

Saint-Loup goes back to the front and is killed. Françoise and the butler, we may plead, were merely ignorant. Yes, say Shakespeare and Proust, but how horrible ignorance is; and a harsh sentence echoes in our ears, "Ignorance of the law is no defense."

Very few souls are saved, and the means of salvation available are few. Proust, again like Shakespeare, sets down beauty on the credit page of his ledger as society's only real asset. The narrator is to be saved from his futility and fears, ostensibly by his invention of a mnemonic technique but actually by immersion in the ancient artistic process. He is going to take his grateful apprehension of the beauty of this earth and his shamefaced resentment against its hideousness, and will reconcile them in a shapely and luminous work of art, which can make life stand still and let the reader examine it at his leisure. The narrator's grandmother and mother also are saved, because their capacity for love is as spontaneous as the flowering of a hawthorn hedge, or any other delightful operation of inanimate nature, and at the same time is refined by their knowledge of the best which man has achieved by self-cultivation. Their devotion to the works of Madame de Sévigné showed them to belong to that army of readers who match in greatness the great writers whose works they study, who respond to their most original thought and make it current, who make their prescriptions real by practicing them. Swann, too, is saved by his loyalty to beauty, his readiness to discern it and appreciate it and evangelize it. But there is another reason for his exemption from the common doom. Swann belongs to the order of characters who are esteemed by the writers who create them because they do not rebel against society; they realize themselves to be living in time and not in eternity, they are capable of compromise; yet they preserve intact a moral sense which comes into action when evil threatens to vanquish good and they abandon compromise.

The catastrophe which led Swann to reveal his nature was the Dreyfus case, which was of supreme importance to Proust. Those who regard his work as an unusually successful exercise of memory should realize how much political material he excised from his early recollections in order to give prominence to the Dreyfus case. His family and their friends must have been moved to frequent discussions by the scandals in which President Grévy was involved and the threat of dictatorship in the rise of General Boulanger, but these events are the subject only of vague allusion. The Dreyfus case meant much more to Proust than any sexual matter, just as the murder of Hamlet's father meant more to Hamlet than any wantoning with Ophelia. It struck all the enlightened of Proust's time as a terrible crime, for it is always terrible when an innocent man is persecuted and deprived of his freedom and honor, and both Jews and Gentiles must feel it specially terrible when he is thus persecuted, not because of what he is or what he does, but because of a racial label, since this is to abandon the faculty of perception by which we live. Proust, half-Jew, half-Gentile, at one and the same time felt the pain of martyrdom and the guilt of the martyr-maker, and his distress was increased because of the political organization of his time. The court, which so many writers have conceived as an entity in its own right, benevolently assisting the courtiers to check the corruption of their individual wills, was no help to Proust or to his characters. It had become an amorphous institution which gathered the whole people, courtiers and mob alike, under a billowing and insubstantial marquee.

Proust succeeded, where many modern writers have failed, in conveying exactly what it feels like to live under a capitalist democracy. He is not a reactionary, he knows we cannot turn back the clock, he knows a modern state could be governed in no other way. But he admits that it represents grave difficulties which were not raised by the medieval monarchy. When an injustice was committed at the court of Elsinore, the blame could be justly laid upon the king. But when a crime was committed in nineteenth-century France, the blame could not be laid on the king, because there was none; it could not be laid on the president of the Republic, for he was a figurehead; it could not be laid on the legislative assemblies, the Civil Service, or the Army, for these were not distinguished from the whole people, as a king was, once he was elected and crowned and anointed. These institutions existed by favor of the people, and they were staffed by the people. Hamlet could have avenged his father's murder by killing Claudius, but no vengeance was available to a Dreyfusard unless he was willing to kill himself and all other Frenchmen of electoral age. The guilt of the Dreyfus case stained everyone, but the crime could have been prevented by no one. Proust gives several illustrations of the idiocy of the anti-Semitism which was the cause of the crime: he shows his grandfather humming tunes such as "O, God of Our Father's" from Halévy's *La Juive*, not the words but only the music (although that was recognizable enough), if any of the schoolfellows the narrator brought home was a Jew. He records how the fatuous Duc de Guermantes, in a discussion about territorial titles, hesitated to mention that both the king of Spain and the Austrian emperor claimed to be king of Jerusalem, because Swann was present and he thought it indelicate to utter the word Jerusalem in front of a Jew. The élite should be able to control such idiots and their idiocy. But no machinery exists for this purpose nor could be set up without danger of mischief. So inherently mischievous was it, indeed, that when it was set up in the next generation it served the interests of anti-Semitism and depraved it further.

Nobody could extirpate anti-Semitism, and nobody could stop the Dreyfus case, except by a process which was so slow and was operated by such a multiplication of delegated powers that no man could boast to himself that he had been aware of guilt and had been strong enough to cleanse himself. At the party given by the Prince and the Princess de Guermantes, Swann is deeply moved when he is taken aside by his host, who tells him that he and his wife, formerly anti-Dreyfusards like all their friends, have suffered such a change of heart through study of the case that each, without the knowledge of the other, has had masses said for the benefit of the intention of Dreyfus and his family. This is sheer ecstasy for Swann. The conversation gives him the joy of learning that people whom he admired as beautiful and well-bred are also capable of making sacrifices for a principle, and that the Prince de Guermantes feels deep pleasure in bearing witness to the truth. But the state of Dreyfus remains unchanged. There should be scribbled as a note on the margin of *A la recherche du temps perdu*: so cumbrous was the machinery of the state that though Dreyfus was freed and his status restored to him, the verdict of the courts was never technically reversed. In the first volume of *Le Temps retrouvé* Proust describes how there was never any real, restorative climax to the case, no final vindication of Dreyfus' innocence, no general sense that individuals had been able to force the state which was their other self to seek forgiveness for its sins. He explains that there had come a time when, to get into the government, one had to be Dreyfusard, or at least not anti-Dreyfusard, and thereupon the waters of opportunism closed forever over the great conflict. At least the moral problem of Hamlet's life remained before him in a visible form, and he was aware whether he had discharged his duty or repudiated it. Now it was not so.

There was an unhappy conjunction of stars in the skies over Proust's head. In the tympanum which he covered with his vision of the Last Judgment, there was a vacant space, which in the porch of Balbec would have been filled by the vision of God. The Proustian world contains no hint of any belief that the bizarre quality of life may be due to man's involvement in a divine plan the purpose of which has not been explained to him. Those who had rejected this belief felt that they were making a happier world, since a God who puts man to such pain by involving him in this plan and does not reveal what his pain is buying must be callous, and man must feel exhilarated by learning that his destiny is not decreed by such a God, and it is for himself to control it as he wills. But at this very same hour it became obvious that men's affairs had become uncontrollable. Proust, like Trollope, complains of congestion. The problem of organizing the vast populations of the modern world could only be solved by the use of machinery so complicated that no ordinary man, unless he be one of a small number of statesmen and bureaucrats in positions of administrative importance, can have any sense that there is a connection between his individual will and the actions of the state.

This was the condition which Rousseau foretold when he declared that the social contract could not work satisfactorily except in a small state: he pointed out that "liberty diminishes the larger the state becomes," because the more fractional the share of authority exercised by the individual, the less he can exercise his will. Thus he is enslaved not by oppression but by imposed impotence.

There is no more acute observation in Rousseau's pages, and none which has been more disregarded. Nor is it, indeed, possible, except in the most limited sense, to base any practical action on it. It is true that the foolish should have been discouraged from saying, "It's all the fault of the small nations," as they did when the climate of the thirties was disturbed by threats of a war which, in the event, was not waged by Denmark and Esthonia. But the danger of the great state, however vividly realized, cannot be averted. If a large number of people inhabiting a large tract of land agree to act as a unit, it is usually a decision taken for the sake of safety, under the threat of hostile external forces. This threat is not going to be annulled because the citizens of the state suffer from a sense of frustration. Proust's France had been assembled by historical necessity, and it could not be partitioned, nor could it revert to simpler political forms. It had to remain vast and powerful, with its machinery operated by Polonius, reborn under the name of Monsieur de Norpois, while its inhabitants grew more and more sick with a sense of helplessness.

The essence of Proust's complaint lies in his portraits of the Guermantes, who sit golden with beauty and good breeding under inherited tapestries across which sprawl gods and goddesses engaged in amours with mortals, from whom they themselves might be descended, so much more magnificent are they than the common run of mortality. They charm, they amuse, they deeply disappoint. They have the air of being able to exercise power, but they prove perpetually that they can do nothing of the sort and only raise troubling moral problems in those who take power seriously. With the exception of the Prince and Princess de Guermantes they are anti-Dreyfusards; but it would be almost as foolish to blame them for this as it would be to penalize race horses for political nescience, and in any case their opinions had really very little influence on the course taken by events, for they were so idle and light-minded that they had no contact with the anti-Semite conspirators in the army and the ministries, who, whatever else they might be, were industrious. Since Dreyfus was not a penny the worse off because the Guermantes believed him guilty, and since they gave such agreeable parties, which indeed bore some relationship to the traditional culture of their family and were therefore linked to an indisputable good, was it necessary for the well-intentioned to shun them just because they were anti-Dreyfusard, or to insist, in the rare instances when they were Dreyfusard, that they make public profession of their faith? The Guermantes had no real power, but they had all that could be imagined of social prestige, and it was a great, and surely unnecessary, sacrifice not to warm one's hands at their splendid hearth.

It is with hatred that Proust records this instance of how man may be tempted to moral compromise at the very moment when he has been shocked into realization that the moral law is absolute. This intensity of emotion is part and parcel of Proust's ethical preoccupation; but we are reminded of de Tocqueville's theory that a class arouses real hatred when it loses power, but continues to enjoy the privileges which were conceded to it when it enjoyed that power. Proust is feeling something very like the irritation that is felt when an anointed king rules so ill that he has to be deprived of his throne, but goes on insisting on his kingly state, like Shakespeare's Richard the Second. Even when the setting is comedy instead of tragedy it exasperates. How near to this classic area Proust had strayed is to be seen when, at the reception given by the Prince and Princess de Guermantes at the end of the book, he suddenly, and with great emotion, produced the usurper figure. For the gentle, vague, Germanic Princess de Guermantes, of the earlier volumes, who had masses said for the intention of Dreyfus and his family, has died, and the Prince de Guermantes has taken as his second wife the detestably vulgar but very wealthy Madame Verdurin. This is a complicated variety of usurper, for Madame Verdurin has usurped the place not of a queen but of a dethroned queen. But the whole situation has become extremely complicated and nostalgic. The Guermantes are reproached by the descendants of those they used to govern because they handled the old machinery of government so ineptly that there was no concealing it was obsolete, and cruel change had to occur; and they are reproached also because, having learned many things from the centuries during which they wielded power, they had not learned enough to make them able to control the new machinery also. Indeed, their position was well described in these words:

> They were given the choice of becoming kings or the king's messengers. As is the way with children, they all wanted to be messengers. That is why there are only messengers racing through the world, and since there are no kings, calling out to each other the messages that have now become meaningless. They would willingly put an end to this miserable existence, but they cannot because they are bound by an oath of loyalty.

This saying is apposite to the work of Proust, but it was written by another writer, who also lived in a world where power was diffused, where there was no longer a king, but who believed in God and therefore came to another conclusion about the condition of man: Franz Kafka.

278

4 The Twentieth-Century Bureaucrat

We are constrained to study Kafka for the same reason which constrains us to study Proust in connection with a theme that first attracts the attention of most of us when we read *Hamlet*. Proust and Kafka are not English writers but most English readers read Proust and Kafka, and literature is a reciprocal process. But it is an uncomfortable inclusion, for it is almost impossible to study Kafka as a great writer should be studied. His production is too incoherent. He was for most of his life ill and often in pain; he died at the age of forty-one in 1924, which meant that he had lived through a hideous historical crisis; he was terrified by intimation that another and more hideous crisis was to come; he was exposed to a disintegrating intellectual climate. Hence his writings are in themselves disorderly, most of them mere sketches and beginnings, and he handled them with the carelessness of a sick man; and even the major works are so feverishly taken up and set aside that the actual sequence of chapters in one of his two masterpieces, *The Trial*, is uncertain. When he died he took no measures for the preservation of his writings, but on the contrary ordered their destruction, and it is only to the disobedience of his friend Max Brod that we owe our knowledge of them. Of the papers he left, many were seized by the Nazis, long after his death, and are lost. It is therefore necessary, in considering his work, to abandon sometimes the simple duty of the reader to attend to what he wrote, and take it that that is what he meant, and instead to guess at his meaning, often by reference to his personal life.

The ground should be cleared by recognition that a great deal of what Kafka wrote is not worth studying. There are a number of short stories and unfinished stories which have been treated by his admirers as holy writ with little or no justification. *The Judgment* is an absurd *avant garde* story of a kind that was being published all over the world in the Little Reviews at that time, about a young man with a friend in Russia and a bedridden father, who makes incoherent and disparaging remarks about the friend in Russia, with the result that the young man runs out of the house and throws himself into a river, remarking that he loved both his parents. One of his interpreters finds a special significance in the fact that when he passed the servant on the stairs in this flight, he was running downstairs, while she was running upstairs. There is another absurd *avant garde* story called *The Metamorphosis* about a man who was changed into a monstrous louse, which is greatly admired by the faithful but has no merits except its discovery of a striking symbol for an inferiority complex. Kafka was well acquainted with the theory of psychoanalysis, as was the circle of young intellectuals which surrounded him, and a number of his stories, such as *The Dog, The Giant Mole*, and *The Burrow*, are more or less mechanical attempts to make a literary formula out of the symbolic system which Freud had detected in dreams. These, and a number of fragments which amount to little more than the opening paragraphs of abandoned stories, please by their masterly handling of language, particularly by their presentation of visual images. We may here remember Proust's address to Albertine on the consistent universe which is the private property of every great writer: just as Hardy always shows us the same stoney and angular Wessex, so Kafka always shows us the same solid, three-dimensional,

280

sharply defined, yet ambiguous landscape that is Czecho-slovakia, and perhaps somewhere else as well. But much that Kafka wrote has little interest. Kafka's title to im-mortality lies in his two long works, *The Trial* and *The Castle*, his short story *A Penal Settlement,* many short passages which (though they are sometimes embedded in short stories) present a thought or impression complete in itself, and a number of aphorisms. His novel *America* and some other short stories are entertaining, but they are not of great moment.

Both *The Trial* and *The Castle* present us with a chain of mysterious events which are never explained in ra-tional terms. *The Trial* describes the last days of a bank clerk who was suddenly visited by some warders and told that he was charged with a crime, never defined, by a court of which he has never heard, which has no recognized courtroom, and of which people seem to have only a sort of folkloric knowledge. "K." more and more clearly realizes that by all standards of human justice, he is the victim of injustice, and that the court's dealings with him are clumsy, inefficient, and cruel, above all in its refusal to give him the least hint of the charge that is being made against him. Yet the whole pattern of events makes him feel more and more that he is indeed guilty, and that there is a way of looking at this injustice which would reveal it as absolute justice. In the end he is exe-cuted for his crime, without the pretense of a fair trial. *The Castle* is the story of a land surveyor, who is also called by the initial of Kafka's own surname, who arrives in a village to take up a position to which he believes he has been appointed by an authority housed in a great castle which overlooks the village. But he cannot himself get in touch with the castle, for any attempts he makes to communicate with it are rebuffed; and all that happens is that various officials send down messages suggesting that the appointment has not really been made, and that anyway there is no need for the services of any land surveyor in the neighborhood. The wretched man drags on his days, surrounded by hostile or at least derisive villagers, his hopes occasionally stimulated by messages from the castle which suggest that perhaps he was appointed after all, perhaps his services would be valuable, and had the book ever been finished we were to see him die in this state of uncertainty, which is the more bewildered because he comes toward the end to feel that perhaps the castle has reason for its attitude.

It is important to understand that these fantastic stories are not fantasies. They have a realistic basis, and they strain belief only because Kafka was looking at an institution about which he knew more than most people and about which he had a completely objective but ardent feeling, so that he set down the best and the worst about it with an intensity usually associated with prejudice. For these books are on one level about bureaucracy, as *Hamlet* is on one level about the affairs of the royal family of Elsinore, though on a deeper level they are, like *Hamlet*, about the soul of man and his prospects of salvation and damnation. Kafka knew a very great deal about bureaucracy. He was brought up under the highly bureaucratic political system of the Habsburg Empire, and he lived his mature life under the democratized bureaucracy of Czechoslovakia. It is to be noted that the bureaucracy of Europe is an impressive institution, particularly in Eastern Europe. It is said that the civil service in that area enjoys a special prestige because the fathers of that service were the scribes who acted as intermediaries between the kings and princes of the aboriginal peoples in their dealings with the barbarian invaders. The civil service had also, in more recent ages, a special value to the population, for when a peasant or artisan family produced an intellectual, he could go into the priesthood, or take up a profession, or, if he wanted to avoid the limitations of the ecclesiastical life and the insecurity of professional life, become a civil servant. This became an even more useful social resource when Maria Theresa opened the civil service to her Jewish subjects. The consumer also was in favor of the institution, for it operated efficiently enough in spite of the many jests at its *Schlamperei,* and it covered a large territory with a network of social services which did in fact protect the interests of most of the population, and met nearly all eventualities. The inhabitant of the Habsburg Empire had great reason to feel gratitude to its bureaucracy. But that it was reasonable to feel such gratitude provoked a conflict of a complicated nature in any man placed as Kafka was.

He was a Jew living in the Czech division of the Empire, then called Bohemia. The Czechs did not wish to be part of the Empire, which was dominated by Austrian Germans and Magyars, whereas they were Slavs, with all the Slav passion for independence. Therefore they resented the Habsburg law and bureaucracy, even when these worked well; but the German inhabitants rejoiced in them. The Jews ranged themselves with the Germans, because the Habsburgs had treated the Jews well on the whole, and also because they were suspicious of the Czechs, precisely because they were anti-German, and because they were Slavs and kin to the great Slav power Russia, which was then the most anti-Semitic power in existence. The Jews' relation to Russia was not only hostile but shamefaced. Russia was the promoter of pogroms and the maintainer of ghettos, and it had succeeded in oppressing its Jews till they had become nightmare figures which the Western Jews did not like to recognize as brethren, since, isolated and terrorized, shut up with their religion in a state of tension which revived all their primitive fantasies, they had become at once barbaric and pedantic. Inevitably the Jews of Prague were driven over to the side of the Germans. But the Germans were often anti-Semitic.

Kafka was acutely conscious of this dilemma. He related to Gustav Janouch, a Gentile who was for a brief period his Eckerman, how the Prague Jewish poet Oskar Baum had as a little boy attended the German primary school where there were frequent fights between the German and Czech pupils. During one of these, little Baum was hit over the head with a pencil-box by a Czech child, so hard that he sustained a detached retina and ultimately lost his sight. Kafka said: "The Jew Oskar Baum lost his sight as a German, although in fact he never was one, and no Germans would have accepted him as one. Perhaps Oskar is merely a melancholy symbol of the so-called German Jews of Prague" (*Conversations with Kafka*, p. 67). There was therefore the paradox that Jews, by the mere fact of acting as loyal Austrian citizens and upholding the Habsburg law, might cause outbreaks of lawlessness; and it must be remembered that this was not a merely local predicament, for the heart of the Empire had been profoundly influenced at that time by the demagogics of its famous burgomaster Karl Lueger, who was an apostle of anti-Semitism. The Habsburg law that the Jews respected was therefore hostile to the Jewish law, to which they paid more than respect. To many people this would have meant that they had to choose which of the two laws they would uphold and which they would repudiate or consider of secondary

284

importance. But Kafka was not a rebel. It was part of his doctrine that the time had come to conform. However much that the Habsburg law and the Jewish law might conflict, he meant to uphold them both. The reconciliation of opposites, of making consistency out of inconsistencies, was, therefore, a familiar idea to him.

When he grew up he became a member of the staff of the Workmen's Accident Assurance Association, and, irritable though he was, and artist though he was, he did not rebel even at the actual routine of bureaucracy. He lamented that it left him so little time for his own writing, but he bowed to the social importance of his work; and in time he came to write the following letter to a woman he loved, who had begged him to tell a lie and get leave of absence to spend some time with her (*Letters to Milena*, pp. 127-8):

> I can't come because I can't tell a lie to the office. I can lie to the office, but only for two reasons, out of fear (it's actually an office privilege, it belongs to it, there I tell lies unprepared, by heart, inspired) or out of dire necessity (for instance, supposing it were 'Elsa ill,' Elsa, Elsa—not you, Milena, you don't fall ill, that would be direct necessity, of this I won't even talk) thus out of necessity I could lie at once, then no telegram would be needed. Necessity can get by in the office. In this case I leave either with or without permission. But in all cases where, among the reasons that I would have for lying, happiness the necessity for happiness, is the main reason, there I cannot lie, can do it as little as I can lift two Kg. dumb-bells. If I came to the Director with the Elsa-telegram, it would certainly drop out of my hand, and if it fell I would certainly

step on it, on the lie, and having done that, I would certainly run away from the Director without having asked for anything. You must realize, Milena, that the office is not just any old stupid institution (though it is this too, and superabundantly, but that is not the point, as a matter of fact, it is more fantastic than stupid) but it has been my life up to now, I cannot tear myself away from it, though perhaps this wouldn't be so bad, but up to now it has been my life, I can treat it shabbily, work less than anyone else (which I do), botch the work (which I do), can in spite of it make myself important (which I do) can calmly accept as due to me the most considerate treatment imaginable in an office—but lie, in order to travel suddenly as a free man, being after all only an employed official, to a place where "nothing else" but my natural heartbeat drives me— well, in this way I cannot lie. But one thing I wanted to tell you even before I received your letter—that right away this week I'll try to get my passport renewed or otherwise made valid so that I can come at once if it has to be.

. . . Perhaps it's more difficult for me to tell lies in the office than for someone (and most officials are like this) who is convinced he is unfairly treated, that he works beyond his capacity—if only I had this conviction it would almost mean an express train to Vienna—someone who considers the office to be a stupidly run machine—which he would run much better—a machine in which, owing to the management's stupidity, he is employed in the wrong place —according to his abilities he should be an upper-upper-wheel and here he has to work as an upper-under-wheel and so on, but to me the office—and so was elementary school, grammar school, university, family, everything—to me the office is a living person who looks at me wherever I am with his innocent eyes, a person with whom I'm connected in some way unknown to myself, although he's stranger to me than the people whom at this moment I hear crossing the Ring in their automobiles. He is strange to me to the point of absurdity, but just this requires consideration, I make hardly any effort to conceal my being a stranger, but when does such innocence recognise this—in a word: I cannot lie.

This is, of course, a modern version of "I could not love thee, Dear, so much Loved I not honor more." But it is more than that. Here was a man who was feeling for the bureaucratic system in which he lived something like the emotion which Shakespeare felt for the monarchy; and like Shakespeare he was clear-eyed for all his loyalty, and he knew the worst about the object of his loyalty. A storm of blood and misery has raged over Eastern Europe since his time; but these two letters have survived.

To Herr Dr. Franz Kafka, clerk in Prague V, Mikulasska tr 36. You are required to answer the communication from this office, dated 25th September 1922, Rp 38/21, within eight days. In the event of your failure to do so the matter will be referred to District Finance Headquarters, Prague, and you will become liable to payment of a fine.

To the Revenue Department, Zizhov, Prague. Your enquiry of the—has already been answered by me, not verbally, because I am seriously ill, but on a

287

postcard and immediately. The card was certainly delivered, for some time later I received from your Department an enquiry as to what I was referring to on that card, there being no record at your office of any summons dated 25th September 1922 Rp 38/21. In order to avoid complicating this matter, as completely unimportant to the Revenue Department as to myself, I did not answer this second enquiry, incidentally wishing to save postage; if the original letter of the—, was no longer on your files, I was quite justified in letting it go at that. But since the matter has now been revived by your communication of the 3rd November and I am now, in spite of having long ago answered in a correct manner, even being threatened with a fine, I should like to inform you again that since Paul Hermann's entry into the firm of First Prague Asbestos Works no further investments have been made by the partners and that the firm ceased to exist in March 1917. I hope that this time my answer will reach the department concerned.*

We see here the confusion of the overcomplex modern state of which Proust complained: but Proust saw it from the consumer's point of view. Kafka saw it as a producer. The product was more innocent than it had been in the past. The State did not cut off people's heads any more; it might send a sick man to hospital but it might suddenly and by error cut off an old man's pension and let him starve. It is therefore possible for Kafka to see the bureaucracy of which he was a part as beneficent, comic, absolutely necessary and murderously cruel. (This is,

* *Wedding Preparations.* The first letter is in the Notes, p. 445; the second is in "Paralipomena," pp. 428–9.

of course, what Shakespeare thought about the monarchy.) That vision of the bureaucracy undoubtedly inspires both *The Trial* and *The Castle,* which must be read as being satires on the subject. But there are three reasons for considering them as having another and more important significance.

The first reason is objective: both books contain material impossible to relate to bureaucratic affairs. The most devoted civil servant would admit that the atmosphere of Whitehall or the Pentagon does not accord with the solemnity of the cathedral chapter in *The Trial;* and indeed the execution scene at the end of the book does not correspond with any part of normal office routine. Nor is there anything in any known bureaucratic system which exactly corresponds with the strange collection of women found in the village in *The Castle.* Frieda and Olga and Amalia and Pepi might conceivably be members of a typists' pool, but the two landladies of the inns resist classification. The second reason is also objective: Kafka was deeply concerned with religion, and it would be odd if he wrote two books in which he dealt with ideas so closely associated with religious thought as guilt and punishment and redemption, and kept his mind exclusively on bureaucracy. The third reason is subjective: many persons who read these books find that they awaken associations of a philosophical and religious nature. But this might be a protective device put up by posterity against a masterpiece, like the misreading of *Hamlet.*

Both books can be interpreted as religious allegories. It is possible to regard K. in *The Trial* as not only a bank clerk who gets involved with a piece of state machinery which he does not understand, but a soul laboring under the conviction of having sinned against God. His rational self asks what sin it is that he has committed, because he has kept the laws of man faithfully, and longs to seek God and ask him how He dares find him, or any other man, guilty of sin when he created the sinner and gave him the opportunity to sin. It is also possible to regard K. in *The Castle* not simply as a land surveyor who cannot do his work because the authority which employs him has got into a muddle, but as a soul who is anxious to serve God but who cannot find out what it is that God wills him to do, nor even how to conceive God. In both books K. wants to look upon the face of God and fails; and there is here a correspondence with the lot of modern man, who when he looks at the social power which shapes his material destiny, looks not at a king but at a faceless democracy. But it is not to be taken for granted that Kafka justifies the ways of God to man, that he accepts either the spiritual or social world. The end of *The Trial* describes how K. is taken from his home by his two executioners, in a state of consent to his own death. He knows that in some sense he is not innocent. The executioners take him to a place outside the town where there is an abandoned quarry with a house standing beside it, they lay him down on the ground, they take out a long butcher's knife. As he is stabbed the casements of a window in the top story of the house fly open, someone leans over the sill and stretches out his arms. There is a sense of someone watching who is on his side; and the executioners have folded up K.'s clothes "as if they were likely to be used again at some time, though perhaps not immediately." There is thus a promise of resurrection, but the last words of the book are bitter beyond any sweetening. "'Like a dog!' he said; it was as if the shame of it must outlive him." Could eternity ever wipe out the humiliation of time? Could man ever be at peace with a God who had forced him to endure life?

290

The Castle contains a like admission of man's guilt followed by a counterattack on God. When the land surveyor arrives in the village to take up the post to which the Castle has appointed him, the Castle takes up an equivocal position, sometimes denying this and sometimes admitting it, and doing nothing whatsoever to protect him from the villagers' hostility. It is to be noted that Kafka suggests sometimes that K. has in fact been appointed and sometimes that he is an able but un-scrupulous man who wants this appointment and hopes he may get it by pretending he has got it. Thus he is shown as both the king and the usurper; and as the spiritual parallels of the king and the usurper are differ-ent phases of the same man, this is apparent nonsense and real sense. The king is man at any given moment; the usurper is that same man when, discontented with his state, he performs an act of will, and changes himself. But in the end K. admits that the castle was in any case right. He says to Pepi the chambermaid (p. 378):

> It is as if we had both striven too intensely, too noisily, too childishly, with too little experience, to get something that for instance with Frieda's calm and Frieda's matter-of-factness can be got easily and without much ado. We have tried to get it by crying, by scratching, by tugging—just as a child tugs at the tablecloth, gaining nothing, but only bringing all the splendid things down on the floor and putting them out of its reach for ever.

He means, surely that they had lacked what Keats called "Negative capability, that is, when a man is capable of being in uncertainties, mysteries, doubts, without any irritable reaching after fact and reason." To that degree K. is shown to be at fault. Yet the village women in *The*

Castle make an accusation against God. All of them are involved in love affairs with the officials in the castle, principally with the very important Herr Klamm, who seems to be the permanent under-secretary; and so much is this approved that one woman, Amalia, is universally scorned because, on receiving a brutally indecent summons from an official who had seen her at a festival, she tore it up and closed her window on the messenger. To understand this curious situation, it must be realized that Kafka had a great distaste for sex, even greater than Shakespeare's. "Love," he once remarked, "always appears hand in hand with filth," and he was therefore forced to regard women as involved in evil, although he recognized that the material world could not survive without sex and women. Here we may look back at *Hamlet* and remember that Hamlet thought Fortinbras as a king was murderous but was necessary because he was a good king. Women were seen by Kafka as Shakespeare saw soldier-kings, so he had to face the fact that God had committed Himself to a scheme for the human race which involved imperfection, and of a peculiarly gross kind. Kafka was willing to admit that God must be right, and that explains the episode of Amalia. She is considered a sinner for refusing the indecent summons of the official because she was thereby refusing to cooperate with the Divine Will on the grounds that it did not conform with human standards of decorum. Frieda, on the other hand, who has been Klamm's mistress, enjoys the peace of acceptance, which for Kafka was a paradox. But it is not certain that Kafka ever found a way of reconciling himself to the strange decree of God that such impurity should be necessary. This may be why he left the book unfinished.

Kafka was not with Shakespeare in the permanent

argument which we have traced. He was not with Fielding; it is almost comic to think of him in conjunction with that serene Pelagian. He was not with any of their successors whom we have discussed. He thought of the will of man as corrupt with a corruption even fouler than Shakespeare ever ascribed to it; and he thought a little better of the court than Shakespeare did, for though it reeked of corrupting humanity it was also part of a divine plan which oriented it, corruption and all, toward salvation. But this was not of final consequence, for God would redeem the soul of man and gather it to Him in eternity, and the court would pass away, as all things which belong to time. This is a not unusual religious opinion, and it illustrates the curious dislocation of modern thought that many people find it astonishing that a major imaginative writer should have been inspired by it, and can hardly believe that that is what Kafka meant. It is also true that Kafka makes his point obscurely, because of a conscious decision he made regarding method. He rebelled against the spawning of characters which was choking the brooks of fiction with fish not worth the taking; and he would have liked to write a novel so far as possible without the use of character, concentrating on the development of a theme. Janouch says that he asked Kafka if the characters of Rosman and the Stoker, in the story named *The Stoker,* which was afterward incorporated in *America,* were drawn from life, and Kafka answered impatiently, "I was not describing people, I was telling a story, these characters are only images, symbols." Obviously he handled this method successfully; the distress of K. in both volumes is clearly etched on a not too cluttered background. But it was not without its perils. It made his critical judgments absurd; he thought Balzac a poor author, for no other reason than that he created many characters, and would have liked Dickens better (though he liked him well enough to write *America* in imitation of him) had he created fewer characters. But there are grounds for suspecting that this was not a purely aesthetic decision; it seems to have been in part the result of a personal defect.

Kafka seems to have lacked the power to perceive and appreciate character. This is not to say he was unsociable or uninterested in his kind. From an early age he was an object of veneration to a number of his contemporaries and his juniors, and he gave them and the people he met through his work genuine guidance and help. But his benevolence was impersonal; it flowed out to people in whose idiosyncracies he was not interested. This is exactly the sort of kindness which is to be expected in a born bureaucrat. But in his closer relationship he might even be called insensitive. When he was well on in his thirties, he wrote a letter to his father, many pages long, and gave it to his mother in order that she should pass it on to his father, though happily she had the good sense to withhold it. It is an extremely cruel document, which shows a smattering of psychoanalytic knowledge, and is an early example of the painful truth that Freud gave sadists a new weapon by enabling them to disguise themselves as hurt children. It is also significant that Kafka was engaged to two girls, and constantly writes about his engagements and their dissolution in terms which give absolutely no clue to the girls' personalities or even to their appearances.

There is an even more striking example of his failure to register the facts of others' being in his love affair with a Czech girl named Milena Yeshenka, a young writer. She kept his letters and gave them up after his death for publication, and they are love letters of a certain austere beauty and undoubted sincerity. He has one playful sentence which convinces: "Today I saw a map of Vienna, for an instant it seemed to me incomprehensible that they built such a big city when all you need is just one room." He writes to her as if she were a beautiful and gifted person, but shows no sign that she was a person of any remarkable moral worth. Indeed, when he turns from her he seems to feel that he is turning from levity to seriousness. Yet she was, as the future was to prove, a very great woman. We have a detailed picture of her end in a book written by Margarete Buber-Neumann, who was a prisoner in the Nazi concentration camp of Ravensbrück, to which Milena was sent for her anti-Nazi activities. Milena, who was by then a middle-aged woman and crippled by arthritis, worked in the medical post, and she saved many lives by deliberately falsifying the reports, by such tricks as representing a sputum test as negative when it was positive, in order to save a patient from instant consignment to the gas chamber. Each time she did this she risked her own life, as she did when she smuggled rations to prisoners who were on starvation diet in the punishment cells. She also kept her mind intact, and wrestled for the sanity of those not so fortunate, and preserved her grace and humor until she died, after great suffering, in 1944. It is almost as disconcerting to discover that the Milena of the Kafka letters is the Milena of Ravensbrück as it would be to find that the Dark Lady of the Sonnets was a saint and martyr of the order of Joan of Arc.

It can hardly be doubted that Kafka's renunciation of the novelist's power to create character sprang from a defective perception of character, but for all that it might not affect him disadvantageously as an artist. There is the diagrammatic clarity of the theme of *The Trial,* the almost as impressive emphases of *The Castle*. Yet there is cause for regretting this defect and this decision. The exact point at which many of his fragments break off is of some significance. To take one example (*Wedding Preparations*, p. 276): Kafka's room opens and a green dragon slides round the door and Kafka asks him to come in, and the dragon smiles and says, half in embarrassment, half in slyness, "Drawn here by your longing, I have pushed myself here over quite a distance, and I have scraped my underparts quite raw, but I am glad to do it, gladly do I come, gladly do I offer myself to you—" the fragment ends. There is a shop full of people doing incomprehensible things; at the back of the shop there is a door, which opens and everybody is surprised —the fragment ends. A woman sitting with her husband at the opera is importuned by a stranger who lies along the velvet balustrade in front of them, and she hands her husband a little mother-of-pearl knife—the fragment ends. All these fantasies break down at the same point, when the motive behind some action must be explained; and motive can only completely be explained by reference to the character which conceives it. This may account for the large number of unfinished works which Kafka left; it may even account for his failure to finish *The Castle*. As he came to the end of the book, he was attempting to prove the necessity that human beings should accept the impure conditions of this life, by contrasting Frieda, who had bowed her neck to the yoke of matter and, in the words of Keats, "was capable of being in uncertainties, mysteries, and doubts," with Amalia, who sulked at them, and Pepi, who was full of "irritable reaching after fact and reason." But Kafka's exposition fails by reason of his failure to give Frieda, the most important figure of the three, any recognizable character.

We learn from K. that she struck him as serene and disciplined but nothing she says or does makes that impression on the reader. She simply seems more voluble than Amalia, and her volubility is cast in a style not too easily distinguishable from Pepi's despised crotchetings. It does not matter that Kafka hurries on to the landlady of the Herrenhof, the lady of many dark dresses, who is perhaps the angel of death; the failure to convince us of the different effects of obedience and resistance to the demands of the castle lies like a barricade across the book. The refusal to create character has here seriously interfered with the development of the theme.

That so much of his work was unfinished seems part of his excellence to the kind of mind which likes to play with literature but does not wish to commit himself to what may be the harsh pain of listening to what literature has to say. When Hannah Godwin wrote to her brother William recommending Miss Gay as a possible bride, she included among her attractive attributes that she had "about as much religion as my William likes." There is also such a thing as about as much literature as my William likes; and it is possible to find that in Kafka's work, to ignore everything in it except the satire of Swift (who in fact influenced him) and the grotesquerie of Hieronymus Bosch and an enigmatic pictorial beauty which recalls certain of Rembrandt's work, notably *The Polish Rider*. But Kafka also presents the real and insoluble problems of man's nature so truly and so cruelly that he is one of the few authors who can keep pace with the cruelty of history. His work even seems to show a certain foreknowledge of the fate which was to befall his world through the establishment of the totalitarian governments. Many passages might be read as prophetic visions of the occupation of his country, of the deporta-

297

tions, of the concentration camps. Though the unjustified arrests, the irregular trials, the murderous executions are symbols chosen to illustrate his themes, they also come oddly close (even to the details of the uniforms worn by some of the more sinister officials) to the forms in which destiny was to destroy his world with a completeness which recalls some of his own ravaged landscapes; for his three sisters were all to be murdered by the Nazis, and so were many of his friends, while others died in exile, some by suicide. But there is no need to look to clairvoyance for an explanation. Kafka had lived through the first World War and the starvation and uncertainty that followed the collapse of the Habsburg Empire, and if Czechoslovakia enjoyed a favored position, there was the threat of what might happen in Germany, which nearly happened even then, in the early twenties, since the Hitler Putsch and the unrest of the Ruhr had the germ of the pestilence in them; and there were enough manifestations in his own Prague to make him know that if the pestilence were to spread, his fellow countrymen would not be immune. In one of his letters to Milena he describes how he looked out of the window and saw a Jew-baiting riot (*Letters to Milena*, p. 213): "mounted police, *gendarmerie* ready for a bayonet charge, a screaming crowd dispersing, and up here in the window the loathsome disgrace of living all the time under protection." Since it was his fellow countrymen who were to fall sick, it was not impossible for him to guess what visions they would see in their fever, what acts of violence they would commit in their delirium. His greatness lies not in magic but in his exceptional courage, which enabled him to explore the most dangerous areas of the mind, where familiar objects display an unfamiliar significance which leaves nothing sure.

298

He is at his bravest in *In a Penal Settlement*. Here he shows us how punishment, an age-old and accepted feature of all civilizations, can be extended to include the most bloody tortures, which no man should inflict on another. When we read the description of the officer proudly explaining the operation of the lethal machine to the explorer, within earshot of the man who is condemned to die in its embrace, we are aware that a human being could behave like that, human ideas are of a nature which would permit it; and history was to prove that this was so not very many years after Kafka wrote this story. But as we contemplate the disturbing identification of punishment and obscene ritual cruelty of a sort that civilized humanity would like to disown, we are confronted with a still more disturbing identification between such obscene cruelty and a sacred self-dedicated sacrifice; for the officer takes the place of the condemned man and himself lies down in the lethal machine. This action is apparently regarded by Kafka as a truly sacred sacrifice, for when the officer gives himself to the lethal machine it breaks itself as it kills him, and can do no harm to the condemned man or to any other. But at the same time there is no mysticism about the sacrifice. The officer does not rise again, but lies, with a spike through his forehead, as dead as any other slaughtered animal, nor does his death start a procession of events which might lead to a reign of mercy in the penal settlement. All we know that promises a counteraction to the cruelty is that the other officials of the settlement and their ladies feel vaguely humanitarian impulses which made them refuse to attend the execution of the condemned man. But we are given to understand that these officials and their ladies were poor things, who could think of nothing better to do for the condemned man than give him some fine handkerchiefs, whereas the officer who was inhumane and admired the lethal machine actually saved the life of the condemned man by taking his place in the machine, though he did it for no humane reason, but to vindicate the authority of the machine and its originator, which had been impugned by the explorer.

He died, indeed, a strangely legalistic death, for he was inspired by the injunction "Be just!" which was contained in the script that gave instructions regarding the use of the machine; and when the explorer questioned that in giving the machine the condemned man to kill, justice was being done, then the officer was correcting the situation by offering himself as a substitute victim, for to Kafka (as to Kierkegaard) it is self-evident to every thinking man that he is guilty before God. The whole story indeed recalls Kierkegaard, for it is relevant to his belief that the Incarnation and the Atonement are realized to be facts by the thinking man, but cannot be reconciled with any kindly or logical system of thought. The truth that has to be embraced by the man who desires to be saved is cruel, unreasonable, and incomprehensible. But among Kafka's own aphorisms there is one which is also highly relevant. "The German word *Sein* has two meanings; it means to exist, and it means to belong to Him" (*Wedding Preparations*, "Reflections on Sin, Suffering, Hope, and the True Way," No. 46). This aphorism in its turn has two meanings. It may mean, "The world is full of many things, and some of them are beautiful, and all of them will at the end of time be revealed to be so, since they belong to God." It may also mean, "The world is full of many things and some of them are foul and shameful, yet they are all the work of God, and therefore our conception of beauty, and all our thought is a delusion due to our imperfection."

But the force of this aphorism is weakened by our uncertainty as to what Kafka saw when he wrote the word "Him," as the story *In a Penal Settlement* is weakened by our uncertainty about the character of the officer who gave himself to the lethal machine. After all, the point of the Crucifixion lies in who it was that gave himself to be crucified. We are back again at Kafka's indifference to character; and we have again to consider the effect of man's social environment on his view of the inner life. A man who lived under a monarchy belonged to a more or less rigid caste system, which restricted his knowledge of the effects of government, but made him able to visualize the head of the government easily enough. It also made him able to think of God as the center of the universe as easily as he could think of the king standing at the center of the state. But a man who is part of the bureaucratic democracy has a far greater chance of learning the effects of government on different classes of human being, yet he has no model before his eyes to give him the idea of a single source of power. Kafka, who was so specially interested in the bureaucratic system, gives us half the religious story. We see in his pages what it is to be set down in the desert by God and picked up by Him and set down at another point in aridity, or raised to some unmapped peak of salvation; but we receive no intimation of God Himself.

This is not to say that Kafka had no intimation of God; God is the context of his work. But the temporal mode of his being hampered him in expressing what he knew. Included in the volume entitled *A Country Doctor* he has represented the difficulty under which the artist labors when he seeks to tell his revelation (*In a Penal Settlement,* p. 155):

> The Emperor—so the story goes, has sent a message to you, the lone individual, the meanest of his subjects, the shadow that has fled before the Imperial sun until it is microscopic in the remotest distance, just to you has the Emperor sent a message from his death-bed. He made the messenger kneel by his bed and whispered the message into his ear; he felt it to be so important that he made the man repeat it into his own ear. With a nod of the head he confirmed that the repetition was accurate. And then, before the whole retinue gathered to witness his death—all the walls blocking the view had been broken down and on the wide high curve of the open stairway stood the notables of the Empire in a circle—before them all he empowered the messenger to go. The messenger set off at once; a robust, an indefatigable man; thrusting out now one arm, now the other, he forces his way through the crowd; where he finds obstacles he points to the sign of the sun on his breast; he gets through easily too, as no one else could. Yet the throng is so numerous; there is no end to their dwelling-places. If he only had a free field before him, how he would run, and soon enough you would hear the glorious tattoo of his fists on your door. But instead of that, how vain are his efforts; he is still forcing his way through the chambers of the innermost palace; he will never get to the end of them; and even if he did, he would be no better off; he would have to fight his way down the stairs; and even if he did that, he would be no better off; he would still have to get through

302

the courtyards; and after the courtyards, the second outer palace enclosing the first; and more stairways and more courtyards; and still another palace; and so on for thousands of years; and did he finally dash through the outermost gate—but that will never, never happen—he would still have the capital city before him, the centre of the world, overflowing with the dregs of humanity. No one can force a way through that, least of all with a message from a dead man. But you might receive that message as you sit by your window and drowse, while evening falls.

This is an event which one can imagine as meat for a number of writers. Shakespeare might have seen it as what happened at the deathbed of an English king; one noble would have forced his way through the crowd, his passage made possible by the magic of his belief that the dead king had been truly anointed and had been faithful to his coronation oath. Fielding would have trusted Tom Jones and Amelia to perform the errand by virtue of the magic of good sense and sound instincts. In later hands the accounts of the messengers might have been too circumstantial for deep interest, until we came to Proust, who might hold us by writing the passage as an account of the last hours of a president at Rambouillet: some festivity was being given by a Guermantes in the district, and all the roads were blocked by his guests' cars, while Monsieur de Norpois' friends in the ministries and in the press were monopolizing all the telephone lines, but the lone integrity of Swann saw that the message was delivered. It was, however, Kafka who wrote the passage, and according to him the messenger never started. Yet what he had to deliver was of the greatest importance, for it came from the lips of the emperor before he died, from God at some time when he was not veiling Himself from the gaze of humanity, when he was willing to communicate with him otherwise than by the operations of an incomprehensible law, when he was not hiding Himself in the castle. Nevertheless the message could not be delivered, because of the courtiers who blocked the staircase, the lesser officials who thronged the courtyards, the rabble in the streets of the capital city. These have many names. They are the circumstances of family life, the terrifying father, the embarrassing sister; the disabling sicknesses; the love which one is not strong enough to achieve and which is therefore a painful distraction, the interruptions of history, the wars, the inflationary crises, the jew-baiting in the streets. They may be purely internal and not really discreditable; a man may be so intellectually vigorous that he cannot let the message remain as it was given by the emperor, he must seize it as it goes by him and improve it by debate, injecting into it ideas that are perhaps really brilliant, though not those conveyed by the words which actually passed the emperor's lips. It may also happen that the intervention is more remote; that the world will do to the message what it has done to *Hamlet*, and will dislike its meaning so much that it will pretend that it means something else.

But Kafka tells us that what happens to the messenger does not really matter, because the message will be delivered in any case, "as you sit by your window and drowse, when evening falls." There are two things which he might mean by this. He might mean that the artistic process is so sure, though unpredictable, that in spite of all forms of external and internal pressure it will discover the truth and convey it, and there is a hint that Keats' "negative capability" is the means of resisting such pressures. But it might also mean that if the artist should fail to discover the truth and convey it to his readers, they might themselves receive it by direct mystical experience. The first meaning emphasizes the dependence of society on the artist and his special gift; and the second lays stress on the deeper solidarity of the artist and society. The experiences which the artist celebrates are not peculiar to him, they are common to all human beings; his only peculiarity lies in his power to analyze these experiences and synthesize the findings of his analyses. That being so, it is not surprising that the artist should deviate from his straight aesthetic course and occupy himself with the interests which preoccupy the society of which he is a member. He still has his particular grace, to which William Blake referred when he wrote: "If Homer's merit was only in these Historical combinations and rival sentiment he would be no better than Clarissa." Nevertheless it is a tendency of creative literature, when it rises above a certain level, to involve itself with statecraft and with religion: to exist and to belong to Him.

THE *Dwight Harrington Terry* FOUNDATION
LECTURES ON *Religion in the Light of*
Science and Philosophy

This volume is based upon the thirty-first series of lectures delivered at Yale University on the Foundation established by the late Dwight H. Terry of Bridgeport, Connecticut, through his gift of $100,000 as an endowment fund for the delivery and subsequent publication of "Lectures on Religion in the Light of Science and Philosophy."

The deed of gift declares that "the object of this Foundation is not the promotion of scientific investigation and discovery, but rather the assimilation and interpretation of that which has been or shall be hereafter discovered, and its application to human welfare, especially by the building of the truths of science and philosophy into the structure of a broadened and purified religion. The founder believes that such a religion will greatly stimulate intelligent effort for the improvement of human conditions and the advancement of the race in strength and excellence of character. To this end it is desired that lectures or a series of lectures be given by men eminent in their respective departments, on ethics, the history of civilization and religion, biblical research, all sciences and branches of knowledge which have an important bearing on the subject, all the great laws of nature, especially of evolution . . . also such interpretations of literature and sociology as are in accord with the spirit of this Foundation, to the end that the Christian spirit may be nurtured in the fullest light of the world's knowledge and that mankind may be helped to attain its highest possible welfare and happiness upon this earth . . .

"The lectures shall be subject to no philosophical and religious test and no one who is an earnest seeker after truth shall be excluded because his views seem radical or destructive of existing beliefs. The founder realizes that the liberalism of one generation is often conservatism in the next, and that many an apostle of true liberty has suffered martyrdom at the hands of the orthodox. He therefore lays special emphasis on complete freedom of utterance, and would welcome expressions of conviction from sincere thinkers of differing standpoints even when these may run counter to the generally accepted views of the day. The founder stipulates only that the managers of the fund shall be satisfied that the lecturers are well qualified for their work and are in harmony with the cardinal principles of the Foundation, which are loyalty to the truth, lead where it will, and devotion to human welfare."

Volumes Published by the Yale University Press on the Dwight Harrington Terry Foundation

Concerning Evolution. *By J. Arthur Thomson.*

*Evolution in Science and Religion. *By Robert Andrews Millikan.*

The Self: Its Body and Freedom. *By William Ernest Hocking.*

Fate and Freedom. *By Henry Norris Russell.*

Science and Personality. *By William Brown.*

Nature: Cosmic, Human, and Divine. *By James Young Simpson.*

Belief Unbound: A Promethean Religion for the Modern World. *By Wm. Pepperell Montague.*

The Open World: Three Lectures on the Metaphysical Implications of Science. *By Hermann Weyl.*

The Universe and Life. *By H. S. Jennings.*

*A Common Faith. *By John Dewey.*

The Freedom of Man. *By Arthur H. Compton.*

Order and Life. *By Joseph Needham.*

The Structure of Religious Experience. *By John MacMurray.*

The Brain and Its Environment. *By Sir Joseph Barcroft.*

*Psychology and Religion. *By Carl Gustav Jung.*

*Medicine and Human Welfare. *By Henry E. Sigerist.*

Anthropology and Religion. *By Peter Henry Buck.*

The Furtherance of Medical Research. *By Alan Gregg.*

Religion, Science, and Society in the Modern World. *By Alexander D. Lindsay.*

*Education at the Crossroads. *By Jacques Maritain.*

Ourselves Unborn. *By George W. Corner.*

Conversations with an Unrepentant Liberal. *By Julius Seelye Bixler.*

On Understanding Science. *By James B. Conant.*

*The Divine Relativity. *By Charles Hartshorne.*

*The Meaning of Evolution. *By George Gaylord Simpson.*

*Psychoanalysis and Religion. *By Erich Fromm.*
*The Courage to Be. *By Paul Tillich.*
*Aeronautics at the Mid-century. *By Jerome C. Hunsaker.*
*Becoming. *By Gordon W. Allport.*
*Use and Abuse of History. *By Pieter Geyl.*

* In print

308

Index

315